"John Hansen has presented in 'Song of the Waterwheel' an outstanding example of love, faith and commitment. The interactions of families will be strengthened in their relationships. This book is a 'must read' for anyone who has experienced the loss of a loved one."

Pastor David Friend
North Scottsdale Christian
Scottsdale, AZ

"In reading Song of the Waterwheel' you will meet a variety of personalities and be invited into their life's journey. Each of them, through their story, addresses the deepest need in all our lives: to give and receive unconditional love."

Joseph Tosini
CEO of Ark Sciences
New York, NY

SONG
of the
WATERWHEEL

The true story of a love and
marriage that beat the odds

JOHN HANSEN

WESTBOW
P R E S S
A DIVISION OF THOMAS NELSON

WestBow Press books may be ordered through booksellers or by contacting:

WestBow Press
A Division of Thomas Nelson
1663 Liberty Drive
Bloomington, IN 47403
www.westbowpress.com
1-(866) 928-1240

ISBN: 978-1-4497-3022-2 (sc)
ISBN: 978-1-4497-3023-9 (hc)

Library of Congress Control Number: 2011919332

Printed in the United States of America

WestBow Press rev. date: 09/12/2012

DEDICATION

This book is dedicated in loving memory of my beloved, Kristene Kinssies Hansen, whom God gave to me for a time, who loved me like no one else ever did, and through whom He taught me what true love is, and what it can do in the lives of all people everywhere.

FORWARD

This is a true story written for the benefit of couples and single people looking for lasting love.

If your marriage is in trouble and you wonder if there is any hope, or if you are single and need to know if the one you are spending time with is right for you, or if you are divorced or widowed and you wonder, after looking over an endless parade of disappointing candidates, if you should even hope for another shot at true love, this book was written for you. If you are burned-out looking for the 'right one' among an endless parade of disappointing candidates, this book was written with you in mind.

In a time of national recovery and renewal from the unprecedented cultural disillusionment and anguish of the 1970's era in America, John and Kristene, both new Christians, fell in love at first sight and married quickly. Their fiery passion had others saying they wed too quickly and doubting their union was anything more than a flash in the pan—doomed to flame out quickly. But John and Kristene proved them wrong. Their story is a true account of *personal* recovery and renewal; of defying the naysayers and beating the odds stacked against marital success through the transforming power of unconditional love and actually living the rules and principles of the Bible. The result was a love adventure of the rarest order, a marriage that was durable to the end—better than Hollywood fiction, that was an inspiration to many people who knew them. The intensity and depth of John and Kristene's love for each other not only survived hard times, but was made stronger by the troubles and trials they went through together. Song of the Waterwheel is the story of their success, and the pathway they found to achieve unending love.

ACKNOWLEDGEMENTS

The writing of this book would not have been possible without the help of Kay Kinssies, widow of Ron Kinssies; Kay was helpful to me in recollecting family chronology and the chain of events of much that is recorded in this story. Of great help also was Kristene's cousin, Helen Scott, perhaps the closest female relative Kristene ever had. Helen was exceptionally useful in helping me understand more the extent to which Kristene's early childhood was abusive, both mentally and physically. Along the way I was helped consistently by my sister, Cynthia Davis, and my dearest friend and confidante, Bob O'Leary, whose beloved wife of 51 years, Joan, passed away as this book was about to go to print. Both Cynthia and Bob unselfishly gave of their time as sounding boards and informal editors of my work. Special thanks also to my friend Ann Reiff, a nurse practitioner and a devout follower of Christ, for her valuable assistance in helping me understand the medical terminology in Kristene's medical reports and help me correctly decode them into comprehensible layman language. Finally, I give special thanks and highest honors to Kristene's uncle, Leo Swiergula, himself a widower. Without knowing it, Leo's personal example of manly humility, unconditional love and selfless devotion to his beloved wife Kate, (an invalid who was the dearest of Kristene's aunts) influenced my devotion to Kristene, more than anyone I have known.

Place me like a seal over your heart,
like a seal on your arm;
for love is as strong as death.
Its jealousy as unyielding as the grave.
It burns like blazing fire, like a mighty flame.
Many waters cannot quench love;
rivers cannot wash it away.
If one were to give all the wealth of his house for love,
it would be utterly scorned.

Song of Solomon 8:6,7

CHAPTER ONE

The most beautiful woman on the planet, whom God entrusted to me for many seasons, is gone now. Her passing created a terrible void in me, and I live with the knowledge that I will never get over the loss of her. My expectation and my hope always was that we would pass into the next life together, or close to the same time, at least, with me going first, after a full lifetime. When she departed this life prematurely, I barely survived the grief that came afterward.

Including a brief courtship, we savored twenty eight joyous years that I never thought would end. The story of our life together is one of God making something beautiful and worthy out of nothing. We were two unlikely people with unstable pasts; poor marriage risks both, yet God fused us together into a fiery, romantic union that burned joyously hot and clean down to her last breath.

Kristene was so beautiful; other women both admired and envied her. She was my life, my desire, and my occupation from the moment we met, and our marriage never lost its honeymoon glow. Women were my weakness before I met her; but after I met her, none of them counted. Our passion and devotion for each other was greater even than that of Solomon and the Shulammite woman. Through our marriage adventure, the God we know and trust as Creator of Heaven and earth, revealed Himself as the Author of marriage and romance, of new beginnings and second chances, for Whom nothing is impossible.

I write to reinforce marriage as God intended it by sharing with you that what God did for us when we took up His ways, He will do for you, no matter how impossible things may seem. As for me, I still cannot believe Kristene is gone; I never will. Never. Our life together was a foretaste of Heaven.

We became Christians as adults, before we met, and the Lord used those years to prepare us for each other. I was a bigger project for God to get turned around than Kristene was. For one thing, I had no grasp of Christian fundamentals because I wasn't raised in a Christian home, and for another, as a young man I was tough, brash and full of myself, with a heavy-handed approach to life. I would have to come to the end of myself before God could work with me.

The values and priorities of the family I would be born into was influenced by the economic lessons of the Great Depression of the 1930's, threadbare times when paying work and cash were scarce and many lost their jobs and their homes through no fault of their own. Growing up in that time, my parents saw that those who were debt free, whose homes were paid for, and had cash reserves, survived the Depression best. Ray and Shirley grew up a block away from each other in the working class small town of Kirkland, across Lake Washington from Seattle. They worked a variety of part time jobs through their high school years after class and on weekends to help their families stay above water. They married after the war and worked shoulder-to-shoulder to build, from scratch, in just a few years, a showcase home on seven acres, and a new car dealership downtown, the building and land of which they owned outright, without borrowing.

They were an attractive young couple. My mother was tall, fair and slim with raven black hair, of English-Irish descent, a coloration some call 'Black Irish.' She was well-meaning, and sincere, but self-deceived, and manipulative, a lifetime adherent of Christian Science.

My father's marriage to her was his second or third trip to the altar, only he knew for sure. He was a handsome, masculine man with no religious background or values, the second son of Norwegian immigrants, a wartime Marine Corps veteran, a gifted businessman who had the Midas touch when it came to making money. A brawling alcoholic he was, a former bare-knuckle prizefighter, a womanizer who cheated on my mother and frequently mocked religion and religious people. "The church would fall down if I walked in," he loved to say, bragging about his badness.

The years Dad was at home with us were a living nightmare. Decades later we all still bear the emotional scars from his drunken rampages at night, waking up to smashed dishes and broken furniture, remembering our mother's cries for help, me fleeing the house in my pajamas, flashlight in hand, to hide in the bushes with Champ, my collie dog until he either left or the police came and got him. Our only shield from his abuse was our mother's considerable bravery and fortitude, and our refuge was the home of our maternal grandparents, Ray and Gladys 'Mom' Gardner.

I spent weekends with them, watching westerns and baseball on black-and-white television with Granpap, listening to old time radio programs and reading many books of classic American literature in their bookcase. Mom Gardner taught me the old ways of chivalrous manners toward women: to rise when they enter or leave a room, to walk between a woman and the street, to use 'sir' and 'ma'am' when in conversation with adults.

My refuge during the week was a horse my parents gave me when I was nine. When I wasn't in school I was on Rocket; in horse shows for which I trained many hours with others in equestrian skills, and riding alone the many miles of wooded trails near our house. My next horse was Tex, a calm-tempered Quarterhorse who was a better companion for me, and I spent many hours with him making day camps in the woods and swimming on his back across deep forest ponds. I came to identify with the ways of the cowboy genre during those early years.

I loved my dad, as abused children will, but I didn't want to be like him. I detested his cruel treatment of women, his own children, and weaker people; it infused in me a protective instinct toward women, children, the infirm and the elderly, and animals too, a hair-trigger quickness to start a fight in their defense, a trait that often got me into trouble.

Mom always tried to make the best of our situation, but the havoc was too much. And I wasn't much help to her: as the eldest of four I was a rebellious, trouble-prone youth, and a poor student. Even when our father wasn't there, our home was a dysfunctional environment devoid of warmth, laughter, music or doing fun things together as a family. As children of an era of economic collapse that was followed by war, our parents' priorities in life tilted heavily toward achieving material success through hard work. Kids and family were just what one did, sort of a by-product to them, a mark of social achievement. Neither of them spent one-on-one time with us or passed on skills or knowledge that would prepare us for adulthood. What was worse, both parents were in the habit of betraying our confidences and making one of us the 'bad guy' to the other siblings. The result was that the four of us kids were all social loners who were dead to trust and loyalty.

My parents' fifteen year marriage finally ended in divorce in 1961, after a long and bitter struggle in and out of court. My mother raised the four of us herself and never remarried. My father continued on the path of serial marriages and affairs.

Years later I would appreciate that God was working behind the scenes all that time, using our troubled circumstances to plant the seeds that would eventually bring us to Him, one at a time. He started with me. I had never heard the Gospel until my parents had to send me to a parochial school for eighth and ninth grades because the public school kicked me out after seventh grade for low grades, smoking and gambling on campus, and skipping class. By my second year there, all four of us were in that school, hearing the Gospel every day. After ninth grade I was barred from returning, this time for fighting. But the seed was planted.

It wasn't until my teenage years when I started going to my friends' homes after school that I noticed that their homes were not like mine: they had less materially, but they were harmonious, the parents married once and stayed together, with happy children after them. I saw and envied the warmth and loving laughter that prevailed, and this became what I desired most for my own life, to find the 'right' mate, settle down and build a family. Thus it was desire to establish a stable home and family that motivated me onto a quest for the one meant to be with me, and that, as much as the hormonal drive of youth, led me through many relationships with girls.

Because of my father's bad example and my grandmother's good influence, I never used women for what I could get from them. I was never a 'ladies' man' or what some call a 'player' and I scorned men who were. I just had a natural liking and appreciation for women, and women liked me. This trait led to many romantic involvements, which in turn were the cause of nearly all of my personal and social conflicts.

The Good Book says God hates divorce, yet it was through marital failure that I turned to Christianity. I had two divorces to my credit (or discredit, depending on your point of view) before I met Kristene. My first time at bat was when I was twenty five. I had been home from military service and on the police force for two years when I met

Norma, a real looker with naturally platinum blonde hair, a girl who had a striking resemblance to Marilyn Monroe. It was 1972, a time of national angst and disillusionment when the Viet Nam War was winding down to become the first war America had ever lost, and a new sort of spiritual darkness, manifested by rejection of traditional moral values, civil unrest, contempt for the country and the military, dabbling in Eastern religions and the occult, riots and demonstrations in the streets, free sex and drugs as its mantra, flooded the land. The Lord raises a standard when the enemy comes in like a flood, the Bible says.

The standard the Lord raised to counter the tide of evil besetting the land was one no one even dreamed of: He poured out His Spirit upon multitudes of the nation's youth, many of them long-haired hippies and counterculture types, some were convicts, others former Satanists. It became known as the Jesus Movement, and its adherents were derisively called 'Jesus freaks.' They received national attention in the news media as thousands repented of their sins, former values and lifestyles, and confessed Christ as Savior. Most retained their counterculture style and demeanor, publicly undergoing water baptism in lakes, rivers and swimming pools, even receiving the baptism of the Holy Spirit with the evidence of speaking in other languages. They took Christianity back to its First Century roots, stripping it of layers of man-made rituals and conventions accumulated over the centuries.

Rebuffed as unwashed and untrained by old mainline denominations, the fiery new movement swept the nation. Many found homes in Pentecostal churches and others founded new churches; it revitalized and redefined American Christianity. But Norma and I were barely aware of it; we were on a different track then.

The truth of it was that Norma and I weren't really in love; we were just two wild kids who were physically attracted to each other, who married in a time when many of our peers were marrying and having babies; we wed out of boredom and group-think mentality, not love. Because our intent was that our marriage would last, we bought a brand-new little three bedroom rambler on a standard postage stamp size lot close to the police station, and became friends with our neighbors when we moved in. But, two years exactly was all it lasted.

Norma was unfaithful to me from the very start, and eventually she left me for another man and filed for divorce, leaving me the house. I should have known better than to marry her: she had been raised by her mother, who had been married many times, making Norma a statistically poor marriage risk. It wasn't entirely Norma's fault; it takes two. But rather than take responsibility for my share of the failures and face my need to change, I self righteously nursed my wounds, blaming it all on poor Norma. Self pity and not taking responsibility for my actions set the stage for my next marriage to fail before I even met the hapless girl.

Because divorce was the norm in my family, I was just as bad a marriage risk as Norma. In spite of my best intentions to achieve domestic stability during my first marriage, divorce was the end result. I couldn't figure it out; divorce happened so inevitably that it seemed like a generational curse was following me. Instead of dealing with the pain of my first marital failure and allowing time for the dust to settle, I plunged briefly into multiple affairs with married women, single women, one-night stands; women young and old passed through my life in a blur. I was 'scoring' well with the ladies, but I was miserable inside. My life was without purpose or substance, but I wouldn't admit it to anyone, not even to myself. That would be admitting failure.

About seven months later I was still on the rebound, still unstable, but fed up with making the rounds with different women, when, on the spur-of-the-moment, I impulsively eloped to Idaho with a lovely young brunette named Shelly, a girl I barely knew. She came from a large, loving, working class family that did a lot of things together.

Her parents married at a young age and stayed together despite many troubles and differences. I was drawn to the warmth and the stability of her family and wanted to be part of it. We set up housekeeping in the same house Norma and I shared. After two years we had a baby girl we named Sara.

For all my sincere desire and efforts, I had remarried too soon. The anger and embarrassment of my first divorce was not dealt with and it writhed within me like a coiled snake, fouling everything I did. To my shame and in spite of myself, I mistreated Shelly; in return for loving me she got only harsh treatment and marital betrayal. We mutually separated after four and a half years with the understanding that I would file for divorce. Shelly left the house to me and moved back with her family, taking Sara with her. At first I was glad it was over. On my second weekend of bachelorhood I left for Idaho to hunt deer with a buddy who was also a cop there.

That six hour drive to Lewiston was the turning point in my life. It allowed me ample time for self-assessment, to face the futility of my life as it was. I recognized that I was caught in a cycle of dysfunction and divorce that seemed to have a life of its own; a second divorce would set me back even more than the first because now I had a daughter who would be impacted by her home being broken just as I had been. I no longer saw myself as the 'good guy' I thought I was by the time I got to my buddy's home.

"He got called out on a case while he was waiting for you. Don't know how long he'll be gone. The kids and I are all in bed. You can sleep on the couch until he gets back," his wife told me.

By this time I was done with living by my own rules and wanted change. I was ready to surrender my life, my free will, everything to God. My heart was in it when I knelt in front of the couch, repented of my sins, and asked Christ into my life. My prayer went something like this:

"Lord, I confess that I am a sinner. I know You are the Son of God and that You willingly died on the Cross to pay the price for my sins. I ask You now: please forgive me. I'm sorry and I repent of all of them. Please forgive me and come into my life. I want to be a new man; I want the Holy Spirit in my life. Thank You"

At the end of my simple prayer a strong sense of renewal filled me; I felt clean inside, as if the clock had been turned back, and I knew God had taken me up on my request. I was a changed man. By repenting first I had let go of any notions of personal virtues and that allowed God to impart His life to me, life that hadn't been there before. I couldn't articulate what had happened; but I knew I was a new man.

It was almost sunrise when my buddy returned from his callout. We headed out for the mountains in his truck, stayed in his cabin and had a successful hunt. On our last night we joined some friends of his at their deer camp in the woods. With the rest I drank a large quantity of beer by a large crackling campfire as we sang country songs to guitar accompaniment and swapped lies, but strangely I couldn't feel a thing; even after more than ten beers I felt as if I had been drinking water. Something inside me was different.

I headed home right after we split up the venison. I felt an urgent need to see Shelly. My attitude about my marriage changed overnight; our marriage would work now, I was sure. To Shelly I planned to acknowledge my mistakes and ask her for another chance to make it work. I knew I would need a miracle.

I prayed all the way back and saw Shelly before going home. I stated my case, hoping and asking for reconciliation, but she would have none of it. Not one to give up easily, I went to work on proving my new self to her, and waiting in hopes of another chance.

Thomas Watson, the Puritan writer of long ago, said "repentance is the vomiting of the soul." That's how it was with me. I realized that in spite of myself I was too much like my father: I was harsh and selfish and was already on the same path of serial marriages that he had been on. I was horrified by the realization that I was dragging my daughter down the same path of pain that my parents did to me and my siblings. I utterly turned away from what I had been, throwing myself on God's mercy to change me into a new man. I instinctively understood that no one comes to God on their own terms; the first step of a new life must be repentance, *before* the decision to confess Christ. I abhorred my past actions and the harm I had done to others. I sought out those I had wronged and asked their forgiveness. I had no unrealistic expectations that the past could be undone; I was out to right the wrongs I had done the best I could; after that it was out of my hands. I expected that many would doubt or even mock me for my efforts, and I wasn't disappointed.

It was the fall of 1978 when I came to Christ, at age thirty one. The Jesus Movement of the late 60's and early 70's had matured into a revival that was followed by what could be called the Third Great Awakening in America. It was a time of a major move of the Holy Spirit that was unprecedented in my lifetime. Catholics especially were being drawn in and Pentecostal and charismatic churches were overflowing with new converts. I was one of the non-Catholics who received salvation and later the baptism in the Holy Spirit. I was a cop with eight years' seniority then; and so on fire for God that my fellow officers were turned off by me, many of them displaying their true character by mocking me behind my back and then avoiding me completely.

The timing of my rebirth was maladroit in one sense, because the fall of '78 was also the time that cult leader Jim Jones lead his flock of about 900 souls to the largest mass suicide in American history in the country of Ghana. The tragedy dominated national headlines for weeks and partly because of it, Shelly and most of my friends reasonably looked askance on my conversion. My friends began avoiding me; my parents and my three siblings wished they could, but one can't pick one's relatives, as the saying goes; they had to put up with me.

Biblical Christianity was a completely new thing for me. It had taken seventeen years for the seed planted at the parochial school to germinate, but now it had. Because I am an intense man by nature, the first few weeks of my Christian walk were a bit wild. I was determined to follow through on the Christian life because I knew I had finally locked onto the truth at last. I wasn't about to let go. To really live the faith was my desire, but for all my zeal I lacked even basic knowledge of the faith. Of a truth, I was a fiery spiritual ignoramus. Like a Roman Candle on the Fourth of July that spins out of control after it's launched, I turned off just about everybody I knew or thought I might like to know. The problem was I didn't know any other really serious Christians, or even how to pray; nor did I understand the difference between Old and New Testaments. When I picked up the Bible, I didn't even know where to start, but read it I did.

After floundering and alienating nearly everybody for the first few weeks, I finally had the presence of mind to ask God to lead me to the church He wanted me to be in. The very next day I was invited by a friend to attend church at Neighborhood Church, the Assemblies of God church in Bellevue.

I was hesitant to accept at first because my perception of the Assemblies of God people was that they were overly spiritual, unworldly and useless, impractical people who were usually old and poor, their women were fat and ugly with hairy legs and armpits, no makeup, gingham dresses and coke-bottom bottle glasses. Their men I thought to be timid, frail, uneducated, pacifistic pasty-faced wimps with thin, slicked-down hair. Assemblies of God people, I believed, were the down-and-out, disconnected segment of society, worthy of scorn; their humble roots were in early tent meetings with sawdust over dirt floors. But I also perceived that more than anyone else, they were zealous about God; they practiced industrial-strength Christianity. My father used to mockingly call them 'holy-rollers' and my maternal grandmother told me she refused an invitation to join them back when she was a young mother, why I never knew. I had been to mainline denominational churches since accepting Christ, and was turned off by the tepid stuffiness of both the clergy and the congregation. But, being a risk-taker by nature, (a trait I inherited from my father), I accepted my friend's invitation: "OK God," I said in my heart, "as long as it's really You that is leading me here, I am ready: here I come.'

The service had already started and worship music could be heard as we walked up the front steps to the lobby. When an usher opened the door for us, for the first time in my life I saw and felt the Holy Spirit in the sanctuary. Never had I experienced such a charged, reverential atmosphere. The impact of it overwhelmed me as we entered. The whole place was packed, with only a few folding chairs in the very back of the overflow section still available. I was completely stunned at how good looking, well dressed and groomed everyone was; the men were virile and manly; and the women? To my surprise they were downright attractive, regardless of age. The people were much younger than I expected, too, and I immediately felt like I was one of them. *Hah! I sure was wrong about this one,* I thought, inwardly smiling at myself.

An usher led us to the very back where we sat on two metal folding chairs, the only seating left in the whole place, as if they were reserved just for us. As the music played and hymns were sung, people everywhere were raising their hands in adoration and worship, some stood and swayed with the music, others sat, but some paced the aisles praying, and some actually left their seats and knelt with heads bowed in the aisles. Such liberty in worship was something I had never seen before, and in watching it my heart was overtaken; my meltdown began. I resisted it as long as I could, but I was engulfed by the great, great love of God, in Whose Presence I really sat; tears of deepest gratitude and humility flowed so that my body shook with silent weeping.

I was worried that my show of emotions might be offending those around me. To my surprise no one stared irritably at me at all; instead, a couple of the men stood behind me and laid their hands on my shoulders and prayed for me. Pastor Jack Rozell preached a sermon, of which I heard not a word save for exclamations of "amen!" "that's right!" and "preach it" that came from the congregation. At the end of the service I was a new man on the inside; I had met Christ there, I was home where I belonged, and I felt clean and new. I had no doubts that I would fit in and I cared not who didn't like it. I had been wrong about the Assemblies of God, they whose heritage was old-time meetings in canvas tents with sawdust floors, and freedom to worship in your own personal style, no matter how expressive. Great depth did I perceive in them; from that very moment I wanted to be counted as one of them, and willing was I thereafter to be mocked for it.

It was the elderly couples there that really caught my attention when we were meeting people in the lobby after the service. I could see that these marriages were long and happy ones, that was obvious, but what impressed me most was the peace in their eyes. It seemed I could see into eternity in them, and I was sold. *This is it! I found it! This is what's right! This is what I want. They have what I have been looking for. I will do what it takes to establish my life to become like these people!* I commented mentally.

One of the men who had stood behind me praying during the service, whom I later came to know as Bud Smith, came up to me.

"While I was praying for you during the service, God showed me the wonderful things He plans to do in your life," Bud told me, shaking his head in amazement. "It will be far more than even what you are asking Him for now."

Stunned to think that God still speaks to men in this modern day and age, I asked Bud what it was God had shown him.

"I am not to say, except that God wants you to follow Him no matter what, and He will show you. He says that your life will be rich beyond your imagination and hopes, if you trust and obey Him, no matter what. If you do, it will unfold for you over time."

I went home that day in a daze, pleasantly bewildered by the gentle power of it all. At the conclusion of a Sunday evening service three weeks later I received the baptism in the Holy Spirit when Bob Calvert and a missionary evangelist named Denny Strand laid hands on me and prayed for me to be able to pray in the Spirit. It was another step in my new life of change from the inside out.

The chance to regain my family I hoped for never came, the emotional damage had gone too far; Shelly was too bitter to give me any more chances. She filed for divorce when I wouldn't, and though I strove mightily to demonstrate that the change in me was real, (at which I sometimes failed) the change of heart in Shelly I hoped and prayed for never came. It was a dark day for me when the divorce was finalized. For weeks afterward there was a cold knot of despair in the pit of my stomach, but I didn't give up on God. I had seen the light, as it were, and I would not be dissuaded from pursuing Him and the Christian way of life. I reasoned that I had nowhere to go but up.

For about a year I held out hope for another chance with Shelly. In my heart I never felt reconciliation would occur; I couldn't blame her for being bitter, or for not believing me either. As an awkward new convert the changes in me would not be outwardly discernible for some time, so Shelly and others would perceive my 'religious talk' as just so much hypocrisy, or insanity, or maybe both. Even so, I clung to hopes of a possible turnaround later. I wanted my family back. But when Shelly moved in with a man she would later marry, I let it go.

A rather monkish lifestyle initially followed my Christian conversion that my friends and relatives thought odd and some mocked me for. "What the h--- has come over him?" others were saying about me, for my life was monkish in the sense that I sequestered myself: I only left home to work, shop for groceries, go to church and do things with Sara. The rest of my time I spent at home alone, praying, listening to Christian teaching tapes and immersing myself in the Bible. As my knowledge grew, I prayed constantly for God to turn my life around. I wanted true change. I was frustrated by the pattern of mediocrity, bad decisions and failure that plagued my life in the past, despite my best efforts.

I became quite the desirable bachelor after my second divorce, and eligible women were drawn to me. There were three sides to my image. Besides a big four-wheel-drive, heavy-duty pickup with deep lug mud-and-snow tires, heavy-duty suspension and a winch on the front bumper (it was a beast of a truck) that I used for cutting and hauling firewood, camping, hunting deer and elk in the mountains and deep woods, I had a jaunty little Toyota sports sedan with a stick shift that I fondly called my 'little red buggy.' The truck gave me a rugged, flannel shirt-and-logging boots-and-jeans, rifle-in-the-rack image (that was the real me), and my car presented a sporty, sophisticated, well-dressed side. I knew how to dress for the occasion, too: my going to church and dating wardrobe consisted of two sport jackets, navy blue and camel, four pairs of slacks and brown and black dress shoes. And then, I had an exciting, charismatic job as a uniformed police officer, physically I was well-groomed, tall, lean and fit; I had my own private digs, a small three bedroom house that was my roost, my cave that I shared with my daughter on visitation weekends.

My quest for the right woman was still in play, of course, and women were still my weakness, even after my Christian conversion, for I was still an intense and romantic man: that is how I am wired. I was still drawn to the female gender: the form, sounds, scent, subtle complexities and romanticism of womankind. My understanding of women wasn't the best, but I grasped that women are by nature more intricately wired than men, and thus I was hopelessly intrigued, captivated and confounded by the mysterious female gender. Years later in my life, the mystery of woman is still one I ponder often, how after many centuries each side still shakes their heads in bewilderment at the other, yet ever yearning for each other, and I came to the conclusion that when God created men and women, and male-female chemistry, He did it with a wink and a twinkle in His eye.

Being a proper father to Sara and avoiding repeating earlier mistakes depended on my growing and becoming mature in the faith, and God pointed me in the right direction. For months I was tutored at home every Tuesday night by Mike Jones, a young man from the church who had just returned with his wife from a year of missionary work in the Philippine Islands. Mike gave me reading and written assignments in the Book of First Corinthians and personal teaching, from which was poured the foundation of my grasp of the basic tenets of Christianity. I also took home study courses that I bought at Christian bookstores and I devoured books by Christian writers such as Dr. Paul Cho, Watchman Nee, C.S. Lewis, and others. I read a lot and left the television off.

Mike counseled me to not grieve the Holy Spirit by listening to the lyrics of secular music, especially rock music. He introduced me instead to contemporary Christian music, a rather new phenomenon, an outgrowth of the Jesus Movement of a decade ago, and I enjoyed the music of early artists Nancy Honeytree, Phil Keaggy and a group called The Second Chapter of Acts that he loaned me.

My weekends with Sara were the highlight of my life in those times. We developed our own little traditions when we were together: Friday and Saturday nights we would make hot cocoa, read Bible stories, recite Bible verses and pray together while oat groats, the hard grain in the oat husk, were soaking overnight, for our favorite breakfast in the morning. Saturdays we fixed meals together, went to children's movie matinees, visited my mother who was then raising my niece Mary, four years older than Sara, went trout fishing and visited church families. Sundays we dressed up in our best for morning worship service at Neighborhood Church, where Jack Rozell was pastor. Sara would always sit with me quietly through the service, after which we usually had lunch with another church family at their home or a restaurant. I would have Sara with me for a week during summer vacation, a time when I took her camping out on the coast, with a tent and a borrowed canoe. I always brought along a volume of stories by O. Henry, a short story author known for his surprise endings. These I would read aloud in camp, stopping just before the ending of each tale to see if we could predict how it would end.

Certain Christian teachings seemed severe and especially difficult at first to accept. One was that being a serious Christian severely limited the women I could consider as marriage or dating material, because the New Testament teaches that Christian believers are not to be 'unequally yoked' with unbelievers. This seemed narrow-minded at first, but I understood the practicality of it when I briefly dated a very attractive non-Christian girl only to discover an unbridgeable lack of common beliefs and values. After this breakup I dated only Christian women.

Another difficult teaching was that if we don't forgive those who hurt and misuse us, God won't forgive us either. I was struggling with feelings of anger toward Shelly at the time, fueled by self pity. This is still a work in progress.

Next there was the matter of the tithe. Teachings about giving and tithing seemed to suddenly pop out at me everywhere I turned:

in my reading, conversations, and listening to Christian radio, God was speaking to me. "You can never out-give God," a radio preacher pronounced. "'Give and it shall be given unto thee,' thus saith the Lord," announced an old woman on television with a microphone in her hand. Figuratively I clapped my hands over my ears. 'It's my money. I earned it,' I reasoned.

The more I clung to this stand, the more it seemed there was a hole in my pocket; my account often was in the red before the next payday, I had nothing in savings, and something expensive always broke down, requiring repair or replacement just as I was about to get paid, gobbling up my disposable income. I read Malachi 3:10, the only place in the Bible in which the Lord invites us to test Him. I took up the challenge: though I couldn't afford it and it made no sense, I gave my last fifty dollars to the church, wondering how I would buy enough gas now to get to work until payday. The next day, an elderly woman I had helped in the past just handed me a one-hundred dollar bill.

"What's this for?" I asked.

"Don't know – I came into some extra income and the thought just came to me that you might need it," she said with a shrug. And similar instances followed every time I tithed.

One would think I would be an unswerving giver after this. But no, for years after that I was merely an intermittent giver; usually giving God merely tips. But God was patient: every time I gave, He more than met my needs, often in unexpected ways. The net result over time was that tithing right off the top when I received income reformed my thinking so that I began putting God first in everything. But even then, tithing was so against my grain that it wasn't until years later that I eventually gave to the Lord's work willingly and consistently, out of choice, not compulsion.

Then there was my enslavement to tobacco: I had been a pack-a-day smoker since I was fifteen; hopelessly hooked. Winston was my brand.

I sometimes smoked a pipe, too, and had a small collection of pipes, as Granpap had. As a Christian I recognized that my body is the temple of the Holy Spirit: I felt terrible about smoking and wanted to be rid of it but the monkey on my back was too strong. For a year I guiltily sucked on those little white cancer sticks while I studied my Bible at home in a perpetual cloud of smoke. It bothered me so much that I called Bob Calvert, the other man who prayed for me that first day at Neighborhood Church.

"Don't worry about it right now," Bob told me, "your smoking is like a spiritual scrape on the knee, when you have a broken leg to be treated first. God is working on your more serious needs now. The urge to smoke will leave you in His time."

Sure enough, after a year, my tobacco addiction ran its course, never to return. I opened a fresh pack one day when suddenly I knew this pack would be my last. Halfway through it, all desire for tobacco left me; I could hardly believe it. God had freed me when nothing else could, but it was in accordance with His timing. And because it was God that delivered me from my addiction, not my own effort, there were no withdrawal struggles, no urgings to smoke again to 'gradually withdraw' that I had to resist; it was a clean, 'cold turkey' break, as if I had never smoked in my life. The effects of smoking began to reverse themselves almost immediately: I could taste food again, I felt better, I had more energy; I even smelled better to other people!

Prayer for my family to come to Christ began immediately after my conversion. I was burdened for where they would spend eternity. I knew I lacked credibility with them; that was a given, for they all knew the old me and thought I had gone over the deep end. My sister Kathy, two years my junior, was the first in my family to take my conversion seriously. She had married right after high school and moved to Colorado where her husband was stationed in the Army as a way of leaving home to escape the turmoil. Since then she only returned to visit. Kathy attended church with me on her first visit since my Christian conversion to see what all the hype was about and was awestruck by the Presence of the Holy Spirit and power of the worship. Such was her spiritual hunger that she attended more services on her own until it was time to leave, and thus more seed was planted in my immediate family that would bear fruit in later times. About ten years later the next member in my family to come to Christ would be my other sister, Cindy.

Changes in me continued to unfold. A newfound compassion for the suffering people I met as a police officer responding to calls of domestic violence, runaway juveniles, drug overdoses, homicide and suicide had me witnessing to people and going out of my way to get them help from and through the local church. That was now my response to the vast majority of the hurting people I encountered on these calls, most of whom were un-churched and unaware that the church was even there. *There's all this desperate need right here, so where are the Christians*, I often wondered. 'Sitting in pews' was my mental answer to my own question. I was also bothered by the fact that there were Christian officers I had been working with for years who had never bothered to share Christ with me when they saw I needed to hear it.

After my second year in the faith it was time to road-test my maturity and my commitment. Enough time had been spent sitting, being merely a hearer of sermons and teachings and then going home. I wanted to please God, to reciprocate, to demonstrate my gratitude for what He had done for me in such a short time, which was a lot by now. Reaching out to the lost on my own time was the surest way I could think of. I wanted to, but how I knew not. I prayed for an open door to minister; then I went to see Pastor Rozell.

"There's a group of men forming a street witnessing team right now. They'll be going on Monday nights. I think it would be good for you to put what you have learned to the test. It'll surely accelerate your growth. But where they're going it will be rough," Pastor Jack cautioned me.

The timing was perfect: my schedule for the next three months was for Mondays off until my next shift rotation which would be in January. I was nervous about going the first time, but I am not an armchair type: I wanted to get into some action. I was quickly accepted onto the street ministry team of five men from my church. Every week we met at the church and prayed together as we carpooled to the rough parts of downtown Seattle, the waterfront, where we shared our faith with Skid Row denizens: the homeless, hookers, pimps, boy male prostitutes, and human predators of all persuasions. We were mocked and reviled by some, (as we expected), and a few times found ourselves in personally dangerous situations in dark alleys, surrounded by hostile thugs, but we were never harmed. We led many to Christ and helped them connect with certain downtown missions; and we planted the seed of the Gospel in the lives of others.

Very often we were confronted with challenging questions that I was unprepared to answer, such as 'how could a loving God condemn anyone to an eternity of suffering in hell?' or "Churches are full of hypocrites, why should I go?" to which I learned to reply "Well, there's always have room for one more." What was amazing was how many street people told us that they felt they were okay with God in their present lifestyles. No conscience at all. "God loves me no matter what I do" and "I'm a Christian too. I was baptized in the church when I was a year old" were common responses we often heard. Rarely did we hear anyone say they were aware that what they were doing was wrong and they needed to repent as a first step to freedom. The more experienced men on our team were able to ask penetrating questions, give solid answers to tough questions, deal with hostility and draw men out to the point of repentance. I learned a lot just by being there.

Street ministry was over for me in three months, at the next shift rotation, but it was life-changing: strong, soldier-like friendships were formed with the men I paced the mean streets with that I treasured, and thereafter I sought to associate with men in the church who were proactive and bold about their witness. It rooted me deeply in Christianity; I identified myself with Christ and fellow Christians more and less with the world. My worldview was changing; I had begun to see the world as a passing thing and myself as one passing through this temporary life to another that was permanent and far superior. The experience of practical application helped me connect the dots, as it were, and deepened and strengthened my roots in the faith; it took my focus off myself, I became burdened and prayed regularly for the unsaved relatives and friends, and I became sensitive to the hurting.

My Christian walk made me a better cop, too. I became more stable and more mature. No longer was I regarded as the department's loose cannon. I recognized that my authority, symbolized by my badge and gun, belonged to the community and was *on loan* to me; when I left police service it would be *loaned* to someone else. It wasn't about me. The quality of my work, especially in arrests and use of force incidents, improved dramatically, and because I won the trust of my superiors over time, I was sent to instructor schools to train officers on the use of various non-lethal weapons.

The Friday of my graduation from the instructor school of the new side-handle 24-inch baton, was a case in point. My weekend visit with Sara had to be canceled for some reason and instead of staying at home that evening, I decided to work my 8 to 4 nightshift, though it would mean a long day for me. An hour into my shift, dispatch called me:

"Radio to Unit 304."

"304 go ahead," I replied.

"Respond Code Three to a fight-in-progress involving two combatants in a fistfight at Nick's Lounge, corner of NE 24th and 140th. Unit 307 will respond as backup."

"304 enroute."

Both units arrived in about a minute's time. A jeering, shouting, half-drunk crowd of about twenty adults, animated by alcohol and blood-lust, surrounded and cheered on two bloody men appearing to be in their early 30's, who were slugging each other toe-to-toe amid overturned tables and chairs when I and the other officer crossed the threshold into the bar.

"OK, boys - police! Break it up!"

I forced my way through the crowd to the fighters. I had to shoulder several almost to the floor to break through the crowd to the center of the action. One man was succumbing to the steady rain of blows from the other. His face was bleeding and his eyes were swollen almost shut; he would have fallen to the floor but the table behind him propped him up. He held his hands up weakly in a defensive stance, occasionally striking back at his opponent, but he was clearly fading under the withering blows of the other man, his and arms shirt covered with his own blood. His opponent was in better shape and a better fighter whose fast, bloody fists were a skilled, pummeling windmill; every punch hitting its mark.

"Stop! You're under arrest."

He ignored me and continued beating the other man, who was fading fast. I drew my new baton to the ready with my right hand, its point protruding past my fist as I stepped between them. When the aggressor turned his fist-windmill toward me, I blocked his first punch with my left arm, and struck him once, a strike that stopped his other fist from reaching me when I rammed the tip of the baton deep into his solar plexus.

"Urggh! Please don't hit me anymore, officer," the fighter gasped as he instantly doubled over and collapsed, holding his stomach with both hands and falling backwards between overturned chairs in a crash. The crowd behind me both cheered and screamed.

"Yah, get 'im! He started it!" "Hey pig, ya gonna hit the other guy now?" "Cool, man, thanks for saving our friend!" were some of the comments I heard as I cuffed the one and the medics tended to the other.

It was over in a single blow that I delivered with mature, controlled effectiveness. Gone were the days when I would have enjoyed making this a drawn-out battle. Instead I took immediate control, administered the appropriate amount of force and defused the situation. Word of the effectiveness of the new baton got around the department, and nearly every patrol officer was eager to be my student. The story of the fight was told many times in my classes, it gave me credibility as an instructor, and to my surprise I found that I enjoyed teaching.

My social life had been heating up too. After nearly three years of singlehood I was informally engaged to a beautiful, blonde Christian girl of petite dimensions named Lynne. It was the same old cycle of one-girl-after-another I was on before I became a Christian. Just weeks before I became involved with Lynne there was Michelle, another devout yet sensual and attractive young Christian woman of American Indian descent whom I also thought was 'the one' and who was heartbroken when I broke up with her. And there were, of course, other 'right ones' that preceded Michelle. As I said: even as a Christian, women were my weakness as I remained on the lookout for The Right One.

I had been dating Lynne for two months, and on this particular day I was on my way to see her again to discuss further our wedding plans. Weak winter sunlight bathed the tree-lined road as I drove to Lynne's apartment. Down deep, in my inner man, I was never quite at peace with the thought of marrying Lynne, but I didn't know why. As I neared Lynne's apartment complex, out of the blue the Holy Spirit told me with absolute clarity to end the relationship as soon as I arrived. That I had heard from God was unmistakable. This was no gentle leading; I was being *told* to end it, right now.

'OK Lord, but give me the words to say,' I replied inwardly.

The Lord's directive was not a surprise. Several times I resolved to break it off with her, but time and again Lynne's attractiveness, quiet spirit and obvious longing for me melted my resolve. When I looked into her big blue eyes I was helpless. Aware that I was too weak toward women for my own good, (as always) and that I had struck out twice already, I was wary about making another trip to the altar and got cold feet every time I got close. But in my weakness I had not been cautious enough. When Lynne greeted me at her door I asked if we could sit for a minute.

"Sure, Johnny" Lynne smiled (she always called me Johnny). As soon as I sat on the couch my mind began racing to catch up with what I heard myself saying.

"Well, uh…I…uh…I, you see I have been thinking that we are just not right for each other, and we should stop seeing each other," I stammered, looking down at the floor. Lynne sat next to me in stunned silence.

"Does this mean marriage is off?"

"Yes, it does."

"Then, Johnny, I'll ask you to leave now, and you will forgive me if I don't see you out" she said sadly, looking down, her voice almost a whisper.

I left quickly, without another word, gently closing the door behind me. I was surprised when a sense of relief flooded me immediately. I knew I had done the right thing, even though I didn't understand what the Lord was up to: Lynne was a head-to-toe knockout, fashion model material. I went directly home. I had been single for almost three years now and though lonely for female companionship, not just any woman would do; she had to be the *'right one'*, the soul mate, the true life partner meant to be mine, inseparably one with me. Now I was exasperated with my situation, and glad it was over with Lynne. I knelt at the foot of my bed to pray, and concluded as I did that it was better not to date anymore; it was futile and frustrating, time-consuming and expensive.

"Lord, I am done. I have had it," I prayed, "You know I want to be married and build a family, but whether or not that happens I am leaving up to You. If You want me to be married again, You do the choosing. If You want me to be single for the rest of my life, I am okay with that. If You want me to remain in Patrol for the rest of my career, so be it – I accept." An amazing calm came over me when I finished this simple prayer.

Months passed. It was a strangely calm time, a time of easy-goingness and serenity. I felt snug and satisfied to be where I was in life. Significant change for me was in the air, just around the corner, in fact, but the slightest inkling of it I had naught. I happily busied myself with work, church life, roaming the mountains in my truck with my rifle and a fishing rod and working on projects at home. I saw as much of Sara as possible, prayed and read my Bible constantly.

For the first time, I was truly content with being alone and single. I let go of the notion of finding the right woman to settle down with; I only wanted what God wanted for me. I delighted myself in the things of God, and the peace and contentment that followed were amazing. I enjoyed being able to come and go as I wanted, with or without my buddies, without having to check in with anyone. I could date when I wanted, and I did on occasion, but with no more wondering if the girl I was dating was right for me: I just assumed that I would know if she was.

Whether it was the mountains or the deserts of Eastern Washington or fishing on the coast, it was the bachelor's life for me. Another boon was that it no longer bothered me to come home to an empty house or wake up alone; I was content. And I enjoyed my work more than ever before, too. Police work was more than a job to me; it was my calling, a lifestyle of action, danger and adventure in which the same thing never happens twice.

The following spring I was one of twelve patrol officers who tested for the one position in the detective division that became available. I was on my days off as I climbed into the bed of my big Dodge Power Wagon in the driveway and began power sanding the roof to prepare for a new paint job when I was suddenly flooded with the knowledge that God had given me that position in detectives. The revelation was so strong that I shut off the sander, removed my goggles and stood in the truck bed, my face and body covered with dust and paint chips, absorbing the message. The house phone rang as I pondered. I leaped out of the truck bed and raced through the front door into the kitchen to answer it on the third ring.

"Hello?"

"John, this is Major Davis, calling to congratulate you."

"For what, Major?"

"You have been chosen to be the new detective. The review board's decision was unanimous. You start first thing next week. Report to me Monday at 8 AM."

Excited but still not believing what I had just heard, I hung up the phone, put my tools away and went to J.C. Penney's where I updated my wardrobe with two new sport jackets and two pairs of slacks that were on sale. At this time I was a uniformed patrol officer with ten years' seniority with the police department. With the Lord's help I built a solid reputation among my peers and my superiors. I had become a respected instructor to my fellow officers, I had made or assisted in about a thousand full custody arrests; not a few were at gunpoint. I broke up fights, overcame resistance to arrest, was suspended for excessive force, sustained injuries, recaptured escaped prisoners, caught burglars and car prowlers and drug dealers and sex offenders in the act, engaged in high-speed vehicle pursuits and outran and captured fleeing criminals on foot during those years. It had been a season of action, change and adventure, and God had blessed me in all that I did.

The major's call signaled that the former season was over; change beyond anything I could imagine was at hand.

CHAPTER TWO

Every day of the first week of my detective career was all action, like a TV cop show. On my first day, right after a first-of-the-morning meeting with Major Davis and being shown my desk, complete with typewriter, phone, and a stack of cases, I went out on a dead body call at an athletic club with a senior detective. An athletic-looking young man in gym clothes lay dead on the elevated indoor running track; around him were debris from the medics' attempts to revive him. I took photos of the body and the scene and interviewed witnesses. The victim was twenty-five, a fitness instructor at the club. He was single. Witnesses told me he was doing cool-down laps when he suddenly grabbed his chest with both hands and fell forward, apparently dead before he hit the floor. I helped the investigator from the medical examiner's office lift the body onto a gurney and wheel it to his van.

"We'll be going to the autopsy in the morning," my partner told me.

7 AM Tuesday. King County Medical Examiner's Office.

I looked around the room. We were in the company of fifteen corpses, by my count. I had handled dead bodies in the military and in the patrol division, but this many in one room was a shock. Our victim was there, his extremities stiff with rigor mortis. Young and athletic, lean and free of injuries, he seemed out of place among the dead. His roommate told us he complained of chest pains two weeks earlier while on a hike but didn't see a doctor.

Every one of them had lived long enough to reach adulthood, to have built a personal history, but the life that had animated them was gone, our victim among them on stainless steel gurneys, each totally naked, most stiffened with rigor mortis and having bluish extremities, with only a name tag attached to the big toe and the body weight written on the side of the abdomen in black felt marker ink. The smell, a mixture of industrial disinfectant and decaying flesh, was nauseating. I watched the procedure for first time of many times to come. The body cavity is sliced open with scalpel and pruning shears are used to cut through the sternum to remove and examine the vital organs, then the brain is removed by peeling the scalp over the face and opening the top of the skull with a power saw. This young man's heart tissue was gray from disease; it looked like rotting meat. The pathologist in charge showed me signs indicating he had ignored warning symptoms until it was too late: plaque buildup clogged his arteries and scars were in and around the heart muscle. It was sobering to see, a reminder that death can come at any time.

We went to Chace's Pancake Corral after the autopsy, a popular mom-and-pop diner south of the Bellevue downtown core. Chace's has been around so many years it's become sort of an offhand test of Bellevue citizenship: if you say you're from Bellevue and you don't know about Chace's, you're either a newcomer or a liar. I ordered ham and eggs but could only eat a few bites when it arrived; the eggs on my plate reminded me of the foam rubber- looking yellowish fat that coated and clogged nearly everything inside every one of the opened body cavities I saw that morning. The thought stuck in my mind that my own insides were like that and made me feel queasy. Later that afternoon I went with senior detectives and uniformed officers on a search warrant at an apartment on the east side of the city for evidence of a recent armed robbery.

The next day I assisted detectives at the search of a house and the arrest of a fugitive who was hiding there. I was guarding the back when the fugitive we were searching for came through the door at a dead run. He stopped when I arrested him at gunpoint but then tried to escape while I was about to handcuff him. My gun went off accidentally during the struggle, fortunately firing into the lawn. Other officers subdued the fugitive, who cursed and spit on me as he was being led away in handcuffs.

There were arrest reports, witness interviews, and crime scene photograph logs to type up. Hours of phone calls and typing reports filled the rest of my first week as a detective. My typing was slow and my camera skills needed work, but I went home every night satisfied and eager to start work the next day.

All of it was new and exciting, and every day went fast. It felt nicely strange to show up for work wearing jacket, slacks, and a tie instead of a uniform, and being addressed as "Detective" instead of "Officer" was hard to get used to after ten years in patrol. And working nine-to-five and then going home made me feel human again after all those years of rotating shift work; that I especially liked.

It was with an elated frame of mind that I finished my first week in detectives, and I wasted no time picking Sara up at her mother's home, and we went to church on Sunday as we usually did. After the service, I saw Ron and Kay Kinssies in the foyer. I had known them for about a year from home Bible studies around town and praying with Ron at a men's retreat. Because Ron and Kay were Catholic believers, I was surprised to see them at a Pentecostal church. I invited them to lunch.

"Why don't you come to our place instead?" Kay suggested, "that way the kids can play."

Ron and Kay's two kids were close to Sara's age, so I accepted.

The Kinssies' home was a four-bedroom rambler in a neighborhood of modest, well-kept, middle-class homes. Ron greeted us at the door, and together Sara and I stepped into warmth, love, and harmony that was so strong it felt like an invisible hug. Except for kids' toys in the living room, everything was tidy and clean. Theirs was a home where everyone received love, honor, and respect. Family portraits adorned the entry and hallway walls, and "Down By The Creek Bank," a Christian music tape for kids, was playing in the living room. A teapot was about ready to boil on the stove as Kay hustled about in the kitchen, and Ron stepped outside to cover his barbecue in case of rain. Even the aroma of the place was homey, and I was filled with admiration and respect for this family. I longed for my own home to someday be a sanctuary for family and friends like theirs.

"Ron's sister Kristene is staying with us for a few days," Kay said as she set cups, teabags, and honey on the table.

"She's engaged to this guy in another state, and she leaves Wednesday to move there and plan their wedding."

"Oh? I didn't know Ron has a sister," I ventured. Kay had my attention now.

"Yep," Kay said. "Kristene's been living in Seattle near her brother Richard until now. She went to a different church with one of her girlfriends this morning and should be back any time."

Ron has a sister? This should be interesting, I thought to myself. Out of curiosity, I decided to wait until she arrived.

Lightning hit me the instant Kristene breezed through the front door an hour later. As she crossed the floor toward us, I was smitten beyond any other time in my life. Like it had to have been the first time Jacob laid eyes on Rachel, so it was for me, and no less. And the Lord, knowing what I needed to understand about Kristene, gave me an open vision about her that appeared clearly and forcefully. I saw a horizontal line with Kristene perfectly centered just above it, and I understood that the horizontal line represented the spiritual things of

God; the deeper things of God were below the line. The Lord spoke to me then:

"Right now she is centered exactly right in Me. In past times she has slipped side to side without leaving Me but she has never gone below the surface to put down deep roots in Me."

I hoped I didn't show how awestruck I was when Kristene pulled up a chair and sat next to me, facing Kay and chatted light-heartedly with her. She was the rarest case of understated class, one of the most stunning women I had ever seen. She had a classic Adriatic look about her that is seen in top fashion models and film stars, but rarely in everyday life. So intrigued was I by her spirit that checking her out beyond mentally acknowledging her outward beauty and class would have to come later. All I noticed about her physically then was that she was unusually beautiful, in a way that photographs somehow are never quite able to capture. She wore a charcoal gray knit dress that clung to her in such a way that hinted well of a shapeliness that clothes could not obscure (I had an experienced eye for these things by now). She had large, dark eyes and luxuriantly thick brown hair, and her figure was trim and beautifully balanced. I was smitten with her beyond anyone else I had ever met. I heard myself talking with her, and she with me, but inwardly I had stepped outside the "me" who was talking and was absorbing Kristene's essence, character, and intense femininity. So radiant was she that I was entranced.

"You don't have to leave on Wednesday. You're welcome to stay with us as long as you like. You've got your own room here," I heard Kay say to Kristene.

Their conversation gave me the impression that maybe Kristene wasn't totally committed to her plans, or maybe it was just that Kay didn't want her to go. The four of us moved to more comfortable seating in the living room, and conversation continued to flow. I maintained an outwardly calm and casual composure, but inwardly I was smitten; really smitten. I hung on every word she spoke; her voice had a musical lilt that made me wonder if she ever sang. We talked and talked, eager to learn as much of each other as time allowed. She had never been married and had grown up in Seattle, the youngest of four and the only girl in her family, of which Ron was the eldest. Her parents were now living in California; her father had been a commercial fisherman in Washington before retiring. Her extended family was large. She had a German father and Croatian mother (I privately wondered how *that* could happen – those two nationalities don't get along)) She also had many aunts, uncles and cousins, all living either locally, or in Aberdeen, where she was born, or elsewhere on the Washington coast. Her interest in me seemed polite and modest, reserved, even. Although she gave me her full attention, she was self-possessed, expressing only polite interest in me and my words, her beautiful countenance denying me even the slightest tangible reason to hope that she was attracted to me at all.

Fading daylight caused me to check the time. I had overstayed my welcome and was already an hour late getting Sara back to her mother. I was sure it was near dinner time for Ron and Kay's household. I wondered if I would ever see Kristene again as I gathered Sara and her things into my red Toyota. As I backed out of Ron and Kay's driveway, I saw Kristene standing in the family room window, watching me. When our eyes met, she smiled and waved good-bye to me. As I waved back, a hook slipped into my heart. Neither of us could have known it then, but our lives would never be the same.

I drove Sara back to her mother's and went home. It was getting late, but I had no appetite. I skipped dinner and went to bed with my Bible, but I was just looking at the words; my mind was on Kristene, so enamored with her was I. I read out loud to force my attention on the words, but that helped for only a few minutes. I stared at the ceiling, reliving meeting and talking with her. After awhile I managed enough concentration to pray for the people and situations that were on my prayer list, but even then, thoughts of Kristene dominated my mind, and I apologized to God for being so distracted. I gave up reading and praying and eventually drifted into sleep; Monday would come soon enough.

CHAPTER THREE

A stack of new burglary and theft cases to investigate and a callout to assist patrol officers at a commercial burglary scene made for a routine Monday at the station. I was a rookie all over again, learning the ropes. Writing reports on a typewriter instead of by hand in a patrol car was problematic for me. My typing was painfully slow; the only way I could produce typed reports with few or no errors was to keep the writing pace to the slowest hunt-and-peck I could manage, have a bottle of correction fluid handy, and then maybe I would be done within a reasonable time. My photos from the dead body scene and autopsy came back; most were underexposed. I would need to add photography and typing to my needed skills list, but I was fine with that. I was happy; I was getting along well with everybody, and the other detectives were quick to help me learn. I was where I belonged, and that was a good feeling. The day passed quickly, and through it all my mind dwelt on Kristene.

After dinner that night, I called Ron. I was nervous as the phone rang.

"Hi, Ron, it's me, uh, John. Uh, well, would you mind if I asked your sister out to dinner?" I asked nervously.

"Okay by me, but you'll have to ask Kristene."

"Uh, well, uh, what I mean is, is she really leaving on Wednesday?" I persisted.

"You'll have to ask Kristene."

"But - Ron, do you think she would go out with me if I asked her?" I pressed him.

"I don't know. You'll have to ask Kristene," Ron said. "Here she is."

"Hello?" It was Kristene's voice on the line.

"Uh, hi. It's, uh, me, John. I met you yesterday at Ron's house," I ventured, fearing I sounded as oafish to her as I felt.

"Yes? I remember," Kristene said. *Her voice really does have a musical lilt to it,* I noticed. *She's **got** to be a singer.*

"Well," I stammered. "Uh, well, I—I know that you are planning to fly out of town day after tomorrow, but I thought maybe you aren't certain about it. So I thought, uh, well if you don't go that I might take you to dinner this Friday."

"I'm not going on Wednesday," Kristene replied, just like that.

Slow-witted me; the significance of her reply went right over my head at the time.

"Great," I said, "pick you up at 7:30?"

"That would be fine," she consented.

Only years later would I understand and appreciate that Kristene had dumped not only her prepaid flight but her engagement to a multi-millionaire just to have one dinner with me. As slow as I was to grasp what was happening, I was thrilled when I hung up the phone. So eager was I to see her again that I couldn't wait until Friday, so when I learned that there was a special guest speaker, Jerry Cook, at Neighborhood Church that Wednesday night's service, I called back and invited Kristene to it. She accepted and said she would come with Kay.

"Good. I'll save you a seat," I said.

The Wednesday night service was packed, and I was glad I got there early enough to secure seats in the middle-front section. Kristene and Kay came in and sat with me as the worship music began. Even though Kay sat between us, Kristene's presence had a magnetic pull on me. She was as exquisitely beautiful as I remembered her from Sunday, and I had to work at not looking at her too much; it was hard not to. When I did, I noticed again her thick, dark brown hair, which she wore in a ponytail, and that her eyes were beautifully dark, large, round, and hazel. As one having a good eye for these things, even though her dress wasn't form-fitting, I couldn't help but notice how perfect her figure was; it was impossible not to, such was her natural sensuality. And so we sat through the service, me staring straight ahead, trying my best to look calm and cool so as to hide the obvious: that so enraptured by Kristene was I that not a single word of the sermon I heard. When the service was over, we briefly said goodbye to each other, and I went home, and all that mattered to me then was that I had seen her again.

Friday night came, and at 7:30, I was parked in front of Ron and Kay's home, praying. "Lord, whatever happens tonight, don't let me say or do anything unless it is Your will," I pleaded. Ron answered the door when I knocked. This time she was wearing a rust-colored knit sweater dress. I was careful not to show how happy I was to see her again. *Better to be calm and cool than a crazy fool, even if that's what I really am,* I observed sardonically.

I took her to a fancy Mexican restaurant in Bellevue, the best in town; a white tablecloth, linen napkins, candle light, expensive kind of place. But, leave it to me to rain on the romantic ambiance we had begun by ordering only a single platter of nachos for dinner. I thought I detected a fleeting moment of discomfiture in her when the waiter left with our order. Hmm. Well, no matter. I made the move because I wanted to share dinner from the same plate to establish intimacy with her. Kristene seemed slightly irritated, but I didn't offer anything different. (Years later she admitted that she was annoyed because she thought I was being cheap). I had never done this before, but I wanted her badly, and keeping my desires in check wasn't easy. The idea just popped into my mind, and I wanted to be as close to her as I could get without crowding her, so eat from the same plate we did. My ploy worked; we talked all through dinner, exploring one another's thoughts, attitudes, ideas, and life experiences. Even though Kristene seemed a bit guarded at first, we became lost in each other for the first time.

After dinner I drove us east on I-90 to Snoqualmie Falls, the tallest waterfall in the Northwest. The falls are beautifully lighted at night, a romantic setting in any weather. We were alone there. We walked into the observation platform and stood next to each other at the rail, watching and hearing the gentle rushing waters of the falls. I slipped my arm around her waist. After some little time Kristene turned to face me.

"I think you're awfully nice," she said.

I kissed her then, softly but fully on the lips. Her lips were firm, full and intimated feminine energy and a deep sensuality pulsing quietly, on-hold, barely below the surface, and their effect on me was seismic. She smiled shyly at me, and looked down as we walked with my arm around her in silence back to the car. I knew from the strange peace I felt and the heat of my hunger for her that she was the right one, that we were right for each other. My thoughts were swirling, and yet in my inner man I also knew we were already on the path of union.

I took her back to Ron's, and we kissed again at the door, and as I went home, my heart and my mind were soaring like a schoolboy on his first puppy-love. But this was not infatuation. I had been down that road more than a few times before. No, this was different; it was solid and possessed an air of destiny unlike anything else in my life. What was it? Ah, yes: a sense of certitude, totality, belonging, and *rightness*—that was it. It was all of that, but I couldn't just plunge headlong into this. I had been hurt and disappointed before, and I really didn't know her yet, so caution would be the best policy. I would ask God to show me whether this is of Him or not, and if not, then I would ask Him to set me free from the wild passions accruing within.

I didn't know it until many years later, but that night Kristene went to her room at Ron's and knelt at the foot of the bed, and the Lord revealed to her that we would be married and have two children. At the time, though, Kristene pondered this in her heart and told no one.

On my bed that night, I relived each minute of our first date until I finally fell asleep. I called her on Saturday and she went with me to church that next Sunday, and we went out to lunch after that. I couldn't get her out of my mind, nor could I get enough of her, and I wondered how she felt about me. She was so calm and collected, I just couldn't tell. I realized I was deeply in love with her like never before, and I feared she might not feel that way about me.

Surprisingly I wasn't love-struck at work the following Monday; I was mentally at peace, focused, and clear-minded. I processed information and made decisions rapidly and well. Kristene was on my mind, of course, but she was at the *back*, as if she were there supporting me. I got through the day's tasks with a strong finish and went home.

That evening I visited with Kristene on the phone and arranged to take her to church again that coming Wednesday night. We went out again that Friday, followed by church again on Sunday. We came back to Ron and Kay's late in the evening. Everyone was already in bed, and Kristene started to make tea. Watching her move around the kitchen, I realized how hopelessly in love with her I was. I hungered for her. I had to tell her, but what if she rejected me? Win or lose, now was the time. I waited a minute, helping her set out the teabags and mugs. As she set the table, I took hold of her hand and gently pulled her toward me.

"Kristene, I love you. I mean I *really* love you. And I want to marry you. Will you marry me, please?" I asked.

Kristene smiled shyly and blushed. She hesitated, and I feared she would say no.

"Yes, I will. I love you too, John," she said.

We forgot about the tea and kissed deeply and held each other and talked excitedly in whispers. Kristene was blushing and smiling. She asked me to wait before telling anyone else, and I agreed.

At last she bid me go, and I went home with a happy heart and my head spinning. Had I gone nuts? I met her only two weeks ago and already I had asked her to marry me. I was trying to grasp that this gorgeous woman I had known for only two weeks, who dominated my heart and mind from the instant we met, really loved me, dropped her previous marriage plans to be with me, and was willing to be my wife. It was at once overwhelming and exciting. At long last I felt as though I had a future again, a destiny, and best of all, this time it was from God Himself.

The next weekend I went by invitation to dinner at Ron and Kay's where I met Kristene's youngest brother, Richard. Like Ron, he was handsome, virile, and fit. Richard was cheerful and quick witted, and having a most engaging smile, he was a born stand-up comedian, the life of the party wherever he went. Richard was not a Christian, and he loved to verbally spar with Ron about nearly everything, especially spiritual values, but it was easy to see their bantering was done in brotherly affection that brought them closer each time. We had announced our engagement to Ron and Kay the day before. To my surprise and disappointment, Ron was accepting of the news but not enthusiastic. Kay, however, was happy for us.

At dinner Kristene broke the news to Richard.

"Richard, I have some news to share with you," she told him calmly.

"Oh? And what would that be?" Richard asked while loading his plate with mashed potatoes for the second time.

"John has asked me to marry him and I have accepted," Kristene told him.

Richard's hands stopped midair, mashed spuds falling off the serving spoon.

"Oh? Really?" was all he could say at first, looking at Kristene but not at me. Other than a few bland, polite questions from Richard to Kristene, there was little discussion: Richard barely asked me anything.

I understood Ron's lack of enthusiasm; I was twice divorced, and statistically I was a bad marriage risk for Kristene, who had never been married. But I was not about to be put off. I had found in Kristene the woman who more than exceeded my dreams and nothing would keep me from her.

CHAPTER FOUR

Our love was nothing less than red hot; the chemistry between us was so powerful that we couldn't get enough of each other. I had swept Kristene off her feet, and yet there was more to it than that: we were onto something very special that was from God Himself. To honor God and each other, we agreed to have no sex until we were married, an old standard that seemed archaic in late twentieth century America. As Christians we understood that in the Bible, God intended sex to be within marriage only; that is how He wired us all. Sex outside of marriage is either adultery or fornication. We both recognized that obedience and sexual purity matter to God; we observed that our prior relationships had collapsed because fornication was the foundation. This time we cared enough and dared enough to wait in order to be right in God's eyes and have His blessing. It would not be easy; we knew that, but by taking the time to know each other first, we would be putting the horse in front of the cart. We were laying a proper foundation in our relationship that would last, and God would honor us because we were honoring Him by waiting. And so we began an old-fashioned courtship, the waiting-and-dating kind. The result of our decision was a romantic energy and purity unlike either of us had ever known before, and we were about to experience firsthand that God is the Author of human romance.

Enduring our self-imposed chastity until marriage would be agony for me, for I am a man, after all, and a passionate and romantic one at that. Kristene was one of the most beautiful women I had ever seen, and that she had drastically altered the course of her life to be with me enhanced my desire for her. Her dark hair was lustrous, so thick that its weight pulled straight its natural curls. Her skin was ivory with a tint of rose. She had a classic European look about her; her profile was reminiscent of nineteenth-century cameos. She oozed sex appeal no matter how modestly she dressed. She was naturally beautiful, with or without makeup. She was stately in the way she moved; the very essence of poise and class, her refinement was from an earlier time, and she was sensual too, so strong was her presence that she filled whatever room she entered, yet she wasn't full of herself. She fit me like a hand in a glove, and she wanted me as passionately as I wanted her. When we kissed, desire for each other burned within us. We wouldn't be able to hold out too long; of necessity, this *must* be a short engagement.

Our old-fashioned courtship was not only quaint, it was also fun. The humor of it was that here we were, two adults, Kristene was twenty-eight and I was thirty-four, each with multiple prior relationships, behaving as if we were virgins in our teens or early twenties, as if we were living in a more Victorian era, as if it were not late twentieth-century America. Because Kristene's parents lived in California, Ron assumed the father role; he was the one to whom I was accountable for where we went and what time I would bring Kristene back. This form of accountability helped build a strong foundation of trust, respect, and appreciation that would prove itself over and over in the tough times that would come later. We were building our relationship God's way, not the world's way, by putting first things first, so that when it came time for physical intimacy, it would be a fulfillment of what had been built between us.

On our next date after she accepted my proposal, we went to a very nice, white tablecloth and candlelight waterfront seafood restaurant on Puget Sound in Mukilteo. Kristene wore a dark green silk dress with a pearl necklace that night; it had long sleeves and was mid-knee length. It accented her natural beauty and refined elegance; in that dress she was class with an edge. Throughout the dinner as we talked about our dreams and plans, I kept noticing how she looked in that dress, the way it fit her, the way that shade of green perfectly set off Kristene's ivory skin, her large hazel eyes, and her heavy dark chestnut brown hair, worn that evening in a pony tail.

We saw each other on Wednesdays, Fridays, Saturdays, and Sundays, with frequent talks on the phone on the days in between. We had romantic picnics on the beaches of Puget Sound, in country parks, and at mountain creeks. We held hands at Sunday morning services at Neighborhood Church, visited Sunday night charismatic services held in the basements of Catholic churches in north Seattle, and saw visiting evangelists who came through town. We visited the Woodland Park Zoo in Seattle and the nearby house that Kristene's family lived in during her teenage years. There were long Sunday drives that seemed to go everywhere and anywhere — in the city, in the country, on the dirt roads of the deep woods — just to spend time together. We made the rounds of relatives, introducing each other to my parents and the many aunts, uncles, and cousins of her family.

Her people were solid folk, working-class stock of recent immigration from Europe. Her mother's parents were Vincent and Manda Domandich, who came separately to America from Croatia. Vincent was a patriarch, father of four daughters and a son, a strongman sort; tough, virile, of a large clan of commercial fishermen who had fanned out all over North and South America from Croatia in the early 1900's. Manda immigrated in 1910 when she was 16, to meet and marry Vincent, (whose family had already immigrated), in keeping with the old-country custom of marriages arranged between families. George Kinssies Sr. was a banker in Cologne, Germany when he and his wife Anna and their six children – four boys and two girls, were sponsored to come to America in 1926, to escape the civil convulsions gripping post- war Germany in 1926: rampant inflation fueled the economic, political and social anarchy. The communists and the Nazis and other factions warred with each other for dominance, and spelled doom for the descendants of Jacob.

These families were typical of the first-generation immigrants whose collective ethos made America great: hard-working, tight-knit Catholic families for whom the ties of blood and marriage were sacred and unbreakable, who did not divorce, who married young, had babies and survived hard times by living within their means, living out their lives in modest, well-kept homes with vegetable gardens and fruit trees in the backyard. Of crafts that benefitted the home both men and women were handy. The men were men, hardy, congenial and uncomplicated, dependable and deliberate, family men made rugged and hardened by their work in open ocean fishing, the shipyards and mills and the heavy construction trades. Their women were no less true to their gender, feminine, managers of their homes, bearers of the increase of family ranks, nurturers and trainers of their offspring, mates to their men.

None of her many relatives I was introduced to had the lasting impact on me as did meeting her Aunt Kate and Uncle Leo. Kristene brought me to their modest home in the coastal town of Hoquiam while we were yet engaged. Kate was one of four Domandich girls, all of whom had something of a Croatian accent, because though born in America, their immigrant parents spoke only Croatian in the home. Kate was about two years older than Matilda, Kristene's mother. When I met her, she was in a wheelchair, paralyzed from a stroke that had occurred many years earlier, yet she was constantly sweet spirited, bright, and cheerful, quick to smile and crack a friendly joke with the one side of her mouth that worked well enough to enable her to speak, though with difficulty.

Ever at Kate's side was the man whose life would greatly impact mine in the years to come, her second husband, Leo Swiergula (pronounced "swer-goola"), then in his seventies, retired from the Rayonier paper mill in next-door Aberdeen. Leo was a quiet, gentle man of average height and build; his broad face and high forehead that was appropriately wrinkled for a working man his age were the setting for deep blue eyes in which the selfless love of Christ could be seen, eyes that missed nothing; yet you had to really look to see this, for his overall features were so regular you wouldn't notice him in a crowd, but his outward ordinariness belied the great intrinsic strength and selflessness that pulsed below the surface.

Leo first saw Kate Domandich at Weatherwax High School in Aberdeen during the 1930s, where she was two grades ahead of him. He secretly loved her back then, but never told or dated her, for she was spoken for by Eric Kinssies, brother of George Kinssies, Kristene's father. Kate married Eric, and they had a daughter, their only child. Leo joined the Navy at the outbreak of WWII and was gone for four years. He returned home and went to work at what was then Grays Harbor Paper after his discharge from the Navy.

The postwar years were perhaps the heyday of commercial fishing off the Washington coast, for an economy and a hungry population on the rebound and few restrictions made it a lucrative business. A deckhand on a successful boat could make enough cash in a season or two to get started in just about whatever his calling was. And so it was with the men of the Kinssies and Domandich clans; because they were doing so well in these times, they went to sea often, on their own boats as well as boats owned by their friends. George and Eric Kinssies were to fish for tuna with their father-in-law Vincent Domandich aboard the trawler *Dorothy Joan* in the early fall of 1945 when George heeded a dark premonition to not go, but his brother and Vincent went. The *Dorothy Joan* was never seen again after it left Westport with its crew of five men. Newspaper accounts reported it mysteriously capsized off the shore of Newport, Oregon, leaving deckhand William Henry Weidborg as the only survivor, who would later tell Kate that a piece of heavy machinery became loose on the deck, eventually causing the boat to capsize, but this detail was not in the newspapers. Eric was the second of the Kinssies brothers to die at sea; Helmut previously perished by falling overboard not long before this happened.

Both families were devastated for a generation or more, leaving some with a lifelong fear of water, and Kate, Eric's widow, lived alone for several years, working and raising her daughter by herself until she began dating Leo Swiergula, a courtship that led to marriage in 1961.

After only seven years of marriage to Leo, Kate had a paralyzing stroke that left her unable to care for herself. Since then, Leo took care of the woman he had always loved, only leaving her to the care of Arlene, Kate's daughter, when he was at work. In addition to his job at the paper mill, every day he bathed and dressed and fed Kate, lifted her in and out of her wheelchair, in and out of bed, changed her bags of bodily waste. He shopped for groceries and cooked the meals, cleaned the house, and maintained a vegetable garden, the production of which they ate and shared with others. He took her to doctor appointments, and kept her company, cheering her with jokes and laughing at Kate's own brand of wisecrack humor that was hard to understand because she could only speak from one side of her mouth. This Leo did, lovingly, with never a word of complaint. Leo was a godly man, a devout Catholic, and it was not lost on me that the depth of his love for Kate pleased God greatly, and inwardly I decided I wanted to be on the far side of Heaven when Leo stands before the Throne to receive his reward from God, Who is greatly pleased with humble, selfless men who possess the inner strength to love sacrificially; men like Leo Swiergula.

Kristene took charge of cleaning my house at this time, which by now had deteriorated into a true bachelor's pit that had four year old baby food in the refrigerator, a coffee table that had a bullet hole in it, dust everywhere, rifles, shotguns, ammunition, and fishing gear stacked in bedroom closets, and weeds in the front and back yards. Kristene spent hours with rake and shovel, weeding in the front yard and as she worked, neighbors came over to meet the third Mrs. Hansen who would soon live in the same house with me. I was self-conscious of my poor marital track record, but even that was outweighed by my pride in being engaged to Kristene.

Like me, Kristene had a colorful past that stemmed from family turmoil. Though her family lived in Seattle, her mother's mental instability and physical violence against her necessitated her living with her Aunt Helen and Uncle Gene Hood and their daughter Helen in Olympia to finish high school, for by then Kristene was old enough to fight back; now that she could defend herself, Matilda wanted her out. Little Helen, as she was called in the family, was close to the same age as Kristene, and the two cousins were the sisters to each other that neither of them had. As adults they maintained their closeness over the years by telephone and personal visits as time allowed, for the distance between was a long drive and too short to fly.

The tragic discord and dysfunction that prevailed in Kristene's home was uncharacteristic of the rest of the Kinssies and Domandich clans. I would learn later it was unique to Matilda and George's household, due equally to the instability of the mother and the irresponsible passivity of the father, who was usually away deep sea fishing and wouldn't take charge when he was home, leaving Matilda as the undisputed dominant force in the home. What had made them this way is a mystery, but the result was unending chaos and financial distress that exacted a heavy toll on everyone, especially the four kids. Kristene told me about the shame the family felt when the landlord had to have sheriff's deputies forcibly evict the family, placing their belongings on the street in front of the neighbors because Matilda refused to pay rent, claiming the landlord had reneged on his agreement to sell her the house.

The details I would not know until later, but Kristene's home environment was worse than even this. Matilda was given to fits of anger that sometimes became a rage; she had a long history of mental cruelty and physical violence toward her three youngest children, especially

Kristene. By the time Kristene went to live with cousin Helen's family, anger, hostility and suspicion of others were the primary elements of her emotional foundation. Matilda and George's high-school graduation present to Kristene was a one-way ticket to New York City, a gesture that implied 'good riddance' because it was their only gift to her. In New York, Kristene lived briefly on Long Island with her brother Bob and his wife Angela and their kids.Bob and Angela were already Christians in 1970, when, at age 18, Kristene accepted Christ, received the baptism in the Holy Spirit, and somehow appeared on the 700 Club television show with its host Pat Robertson.

But Kristene discovered that living a committed Christian life as a single young woman living alone without a support network in New York City during the tumultuous 1970s was nearly impossible. Her beautiful face and figure enabled her to get a job as a Bunny, a costumed cocktail waitress at the New York Playboy Club. Playboy was famous for hiring only the best looking young women with the best figures to work for them, and they schooled Kristene in social skills beyond what she learned from the nuns in Catholic girls' schools: the art of being poised in all situations, how to graciously handle difficult customers, engage in polite conversation, and to be dependable and on time. Having a sense of adventure, she pursued job opportunities with other clubs along the East Coast from New York to Atlanta and Fort Lauderdale and back again, but always New York City was home base. Kristene also worked as a nightclub singer, a waitress at several five-star restaurants, and outside sales representative for a cosmetics company.

Her striking appearance attracted many suitors and even a few stalkers. The young heir of one of New York's wealthiest families was so obsessed with her that he threatened suicide if she didn't date him. On one occasion she was duped into visiting an apartment on the pretext of a job interview and was barely able to escape by fighting her way past several people who were trying to forcibly drug her into doing illicit sex films for them.

The early 1970's were a time of deepening economic recession that meant tough times for single young women living on the East Coast, and though Kristene was new to the survival game, she learned quickly and well. The school of life taught her that while good looks and a great figure could open doors of opportunity she might not otherwise get, she still had to know how to protect and provide for herself, to manage her money and take into account that appearances can be deceiving. There were costly lessons from roommates who didn't pay their share of expenses and were involved in criminal activity such as prostitution; some of them stole from her, and others were just plain dishonest. There were times when employment was so scarce that she often went without eating just to keep a roof over her head and times when she worked two jobs just to have enough to live on. Along the way Kristene refined the edge that her looks gave her in life by learning the finer points of makeup, dressing for the occasion, social graces, conversational skills, and practical know-how with which to earn her living such as culinary arts, bartending, record keeping, and sales.

Those tough early years on the East Coast were formative, for they awakened within her survival instincts common to all life; being a beautiful woman on her own, she knew she would be a target for male predators, and the ability to spot and deftly avoid troublemakers developed out of necessity. Laid atop the subflooring of suspicion that was her childhood legacy, the young and impressible Kristene, now a maiden, learned quickly to survive by assessing people accurately, by knowing how to spot and drive a bargain, and when to fold her cards and be reticent. One would never know it just to look at her, but beneath her breathtaking looks she was street tough, a survivor able to look out for herself without compromising her dignity, despite frequent pressure to do so.

That those unsheltered years never hardened her was amazing. The toughness was there, below the surface, ready to be called upon if needed, but the real Kristene, the woman people met, was warm, kind and sensitive. As a Christian she was well-read; the Book of Romans, regarded as the best theological treatise of the Christian faith, and the works of C.S. Lewis were her reading favorites. Her spiritual depth went even further: she had read the entire Bible several times, had received her personal prayer language through the Holy Spirit and had a firm grasp of the basic tenets of the Christian faith enough to be able to detect false teachers and their doctrines a mile away.

The more I learned about her, the more mysterious she became. Her life experiences and interests were so wide-ranging as to result in her being something of a paradox; Kristene was equally a woman of the world and a woman of the Lord; all her life she had teetered between the twain; for years the good dog and the bad dog within her warred for dominance. And always there was someone unseen, in the background, secretly interceding and praying protection over her in the Spirit. That someone was her brother Ron and Kay, his wife.

One afternoon while working in the field I stopped by Ron and Kay's to see Kristene for a minute. Kay and her seven-year-old daughter, Meaghan, were home. To Meaghan I was already Uncle John. Kristene gave a casual, uncommitted answer to my invitation for our next outing, and little Meaghan piped up.

"Don't let her fool you, Uncle John. Every time you leave here after dropping her off, Aunt Kris dances around the house singing, 'I'm in love! I'm in love!' holding her skirt out like this."

Meaghan waltzed around the kitchen, her arms fluttering bird-like in imitation of her Aunt Kris.

"Meaghan, stop! Stop it!" Kristene shouted, smiling and blushing beet-red and swatting the air at Meaghan.

But Meaghan only smiled an "I gotcha!" smile. Kristene quickly agreed to go with me on the outing, and I left, gloating in the firm knowledge that I really had swept Kristene off her feet.

Determined to keep up the momentum, I wasted no time notifying Pastor Rozell of our plans and applying for the pre-marital counseling the church required. It was no surprise to learn from Kristene's relatives that before me a number of other men had wanted to marry her. I knew I had to get her to the altar before she got cold feet and changed her mind. At the church office, we took the Taylor-Johnson Personality Profile test. The next week we met with Pastor Jack to go over the test results.

"The two of you are remarkably compatible for each other. Your ability to communicate is especially strong," he said.

"One concern I would have for Kristene is that the test reveals you have a hostility streak that you will need to address. The other is that you each show such a strong work ethic, you might not take time for play."

Pastor Jack's observations were spot-on: as our parents before us had done, both of us worked after school and weekends since we were fifteen. And I remembered that Kristene told me how as a little girl, she worked on the docks helping her dad and her brothers repair torn fishing nets.

We were sitting in the pastor's office. Kristene was dressed in white jeans and a long-sleeved, multi-colored plaid blouse, her thick, dark hair pulled back in a ponytail, her large hazel eyes contrasting against her creamy ivory skin. Her beauty and radiance continued to astonish me. Just looking at her melted me on the inside. I had to have her; no one else would ever do for me. She was the one I was meant to share my life with, and I was more than satisfied; when she was with me, I was complete.

Each of my parents was lukewarm when I announced our engagement. My father, himself married six times that I knew of, had the usual "so here's just one more he's bringing around" attitude. My Christian Scientist mother was ice cold toward Kristene.

"She's got a lot of miles on her, a long history of men, I'll bet," was Mom's only comment the next day.

But in spite of whoever was skeptical about us, we had a peace for which words were inadequate. We knew God was pleased with us, and in the final analysis, God's approval was all that mattered.

Kristene got a job as a sales rep for a small advertising publication in Bellevue. The pay was commission-only, and she put away whatever she made after expenses toward our wedding and honeymoon.

The church arranged for pre-marital counseling with lay ministers Dick and Sharon Shoop. My heart sank when I learned that the course would take twelve weeks; we couldn't hold out that long. We met with the Shoops weekly at the church and went through the written materials and workbooks they gave us. The problem was that the program was geared to younger couples who had no prior experience in marriage or intimate relations. Although it gave us a few useful techniques for resolving disputes and listening, it didn't begin to address nuts-and-bolts issues we would face as experienced adults, such as money, sex, past relationships and becoming a successful 'blended' family. We were pent up and about to explode.

I continued participating in the Saturday morning men's Bible study at Neighborhood Church, and Kristene participated in women's prayer group meetings that Kay hosted every week at her home, as well as other Christian women's functions. We prayed together a lot on the phone and when we were together. I seemed to know when Kristene prayed for me, and it seemed each knew what the other was thinking. This was the beginning of the process of two becoming one.

A red flag popped up one Saturday morning as I shared with the men that I was engaged to be married to Kristene, I sensed a check in my spirit. It was not a strong, forbidding check but a caution that there would be trouble ahead. I was puzzled, and although I kept it to myself, I asked Pastor Rozell about his courtship of his wife, Adel.

"I broke up with Adel during our engagement, just testing it to see if it was of God or not. It was brief, though. We came back together quickly, and my doubts were erased," he told me.

I decided to do the same: I wanted to test our relationship to see if it was really from God. Not only did the check in my spirit bother me, but so did what I knew of Kristene's off-and-on pattern of commitment to the Lord.

So the next Sunday afternoon when I brought Kristene back to Ron's, I told her that I felt we shouldn't see each other anymore, that I wasn't certain it wasn't just physical attraction rather than what God wanted for us. Kristene bolted out of the car in tears. I went home, feeling empty and uneasy. I prayed to the Lord that His will would be done. I had a wait-and-see attitude; what will be, will be, I told myself.

I got a call from Ron that very same evening.

"You really hurt Kristene's feelings. You were too abrupt with her," he said.

I explained about Pastor Rozell and being sure we were acting in God's will.

"That's all well and fine, but you didn't tell Kristene that, and she's hurt. Whatever you do, she needs to hear from you. Here she is," Ron said as he handed the phone to Kristene.

Tears in her voice; my heart melted. I couldn't live without her; no way. There was no longer any doubt that we were meant for each other. We quickly reconciled, and our energy and drive for each other were reinforced and renewed.

Kristene underwent water baptism at the very next Sunday night service.

"Ladies and gentlemen, tonight we present Miss Kristene Kinssies," Pastor Earl Goodman announced.

Kristene was standing in waist-high water in the baptismal pool with Pastor Goodman, wearing a white T-shirt, her lustrous dark brown hair worn loose to her shoulders. She was so radiant and beautiful.

"Kristene," Pastor Goodman said, "will you state before God and all who are present here your purpose in being here tonight?"

Beaming with a smile and rose-red glow, Kristene declared, "I am here to confess Jesus Christ as my personal Savior, to be baptized into Him and live my life for Him."

"Very well, then," Pastor Goodman said.

Kristene folded her arms in front of her and held her nose as Pastor Goodman laid his arm around her back.

"Kristene," he said, "by going underwater, you are signifying death to your old self, and when you arise, you are proclaiming your new life in Christ, for which you will live evermore. I hereby baptize you in the name of the Father, and of the Son, and of the Holy Spirit."

Kristene went beneath the water and emerged, soaking wet, more radiant and beautiful than ever. The congregation applauded as she came up out of the water smiling.

"Thank You, Jesus!" she exclaimed.

A history of family tragedies at sea. The Dorothy Joan was the fishing boat that capsized and sank off the coast of Oregon in 1945, killing Vincent Domandich and Eric Kinssies, Kristene's grandfather and uncle.

CHAPTER FIVE

Something happened next that accelerated the course of events. We were invited for a swim one day at my father's house, which had a pool. When Kristene came out wearing a low-cut one-piece swimsuit, seeing her figure sent my heart into overdrive, for she was perfection; stunningly voluptuous and buxom, exquisitely shaped and proportioned, and when I saw her tattoo of a cluster of three cherries inside her upper left thigh, a bold clue of wilder years, I was done with premarital counseling. I went straight in to Pastor Rozell's office the next day unannounced.

"This premarital counseling you're making us go through doesn't cut it," I told him without mentioning that I had seen Kristene in a bathing suit. "We're experienced adults getting counseling for eighteen-year-old virgins. In First Corinthians it says, 'It is better to marry than to burn with lust.' Pastor, we're burning with lust—*I'm* burning in lust. We're doing our best to honor God, but we can't hold out any longer."

Pastor Rozell, a quiet sort, calmly replied in his usual soft-spoken tone that the church required all couples to have premarital counseling.

"We're gettin' married, Pastor, with or without the church's blessing. Either you marry us, or we elope so we don't sin," I said.

The wedding date was set for August 1.

It was with a thin money clip that we prepared for our wedding and honeymoon, for I was paying child support, mortgage and car payments; the usual debt load for a divorced man. Without overtime, detective pay was marginal when it came to supporting two people and a household. We could only afford simple, thin gold wedding bands with mill grain edging at a jewelry wholesaler that was not open to the general public, but Kristene, my bargain hunter, somehow got access.

Kristene checked on and ruled out several fine local hotels as too expensive and not far enough away for the two weeks we wanted for our honeymoon. My dad offered to let us stay on Puget Sound beachfront property he owned a few miles south of Port Townsend, and we drove there to see it. It was a beautiful, rustic setting that would give us privacy and freedom if only we had something to live in. Except for a trailer that was occupied by a caretaker couple, the property was undeveloped, and two weeks in a tent was too much to ask of a city girl on her honeymoon. Stella Covey, an elderly Christian widow and a friend of mine, offered us her nine-foot camper mounted on a green, full-size older Ford pickup. The camper could sleep four in two single beds and a queen size bed over the cab. It was complete with toilet and shower, hot water, a kitchenette featuring a refrigerator and sink, propane stove, and dining table. We accepted Stella's offer, and I added the truck to my insurance policy and had a mechanic inspect the brakes and tune the engine.

Emotions see-sawed back and forth as our wedding day approached. We spent long hours shopping together for food and supplies and worked until dark each night cleaning the camper, laundering bed sheets, and stocking the cupboards. That last night before the wedding Kristene told me she had decided we should "postpone" the wedding. Right after I talked her out of it, we came dangerously close to giving in to our desire for each other. I told Kristene I was going to bed early and got into bed while she continued cleaning the house. When I heard her getting ready to leave, I called to her:

"Come kiss me good-night, Honey."

When she leaned over me to kiss me I pulled her into my arms. Our hormones raging, kissing and groping hungrily for each other, we came within a hair's breadth of breaking our vows of abstinence until we married.

"Stop, Honey. I'm leaving. Only a few more hours and then we can," she told me as she pulled away from my arms. She had been the stronger one that time.

The waiting would be over in just a few hours, and then our lives would change forever. But the next morning, it was my turn to get cold feet. I called her at Ron's and said I wasn't sure if we should go through with it.

"I tell you what," Kristene snapped, her tough side now on display "I'm going to be at the park this morning as we agreed whether you show up or not. If you're there, good; if you're not there, that's how it is." I showered and got dressed.

We were pinching pennies to get married: Kristene borrowed her dress from her former sister-in-law, and our wedding site was a cost-free small city park on the edge of downtown Bellevue on the morning of August 1, 1981. It was perfect weather, sunny and warm, and the sky was cloudless, a crystal-blue backdrop for the lush greenery of the park's trees and gardens. The air was scented by the musky smell of freshly cut grass and the fragrant perfume from overflowing flowerbeds that surrounded the park with bursting blues, reds, yellows, oranges, pinks, and every other color in the spectrum of light; everything was bathed in the soft golden light of the morning sun. It was the perfect setting for a wedding for two people in love; two people for whom God had turned back the clock and lovingly granted a new innocence, a restored innocence. Looking back at it now, I think Eden must have been something like this, but at the time, Kristene was all that was on my mind.

I arrived first, alone. I sat on a bench and waited, nervous that after all this something would go wrong. Minutes passed with no one else arriving. So nervous were we that each of us had called the wedding off once or twice and then recanted during the previous week. What if she stood me up now? I thought about the embarrassing judgment on me a certain couple had pronounced, and wondered if at the last minute they had scared Kristene out of marrying me. For two years I had been friends with this couple, who were about ten years my senior, and attended their home Bible studies, yet they refused our wedding invitation on the basis that it was against God's law, an act of adultery for Kristene to marry a divorced man. This couple, who were childless themselves (to the surprise of no one), warned us to not marry, saying further that I would not be scripturally free to remarry until both my former wives were dead. They then went so far as to tell us that our marriage would be adultery in God's eyes and He would never bless us or our children. My shock turned to anger when the man smiled as he said, "But we love you both." Kristene broke into tears, and we left their house. I was too angry to argue with him, yet I took no personal offense, for I knew he meant no harm.

While I waited, I pondered my mother's behind-the-scenes efforts to stop the wedding. For weeks she had been calling Pastor Rozell, demanding that the church not marry us. Pastor Rozell refused, of course, and finally had to stop accepting calls from her. I could only shake my head when I thought of my mother. A controlling one, she, but she was still my mom.

Members of my family arrived, followed by Kristene's brother Bob and his family and more of Kristene's relatives. And so we all waited for the bride.

I was relieved when Kristene finally arrived, brought there by her brothers Ron and Richard. She wasn't smiling. The ceremony was small and consisted of immediate relatives only. Kay was Kristene's maid of honor, Ron was my best man, and Richard was on hand to give the bride away. On the way to the park with Ron and Richard, I learned later, Kristene said to her brothers, "Let's just call it off and just have a party instead, okay?" Ron and Richard laughed as Ron, who had hosted Kristene at his house for three months, accelerated to the park. Kristene was visibly nervous, her eyes spacey, having a bunny-in-the-headlights, I-don't-believe-this-is-real look, saying little. She was so glowingly beautiful in the off-white, full length lace wedding dress that fit her form well, her long, heavy dark hair put up in turn-of-the-century style bun that the sight of her filled me with determination to get my ring on her and take her home. I knew that once that happened, I would ever be a blessed man.

We stood together before Pastor Earl Goodman.

"Today I extend John and Kristene's welcome to you in our joining with them," Pastor Goodman began in words that later proved to be truly prophetic. "As you witness this ceremony, it is their express desire that you will experience the same kind of love and joy they share today … Marriage was God's original plan from the very beginning in the Garden of Eden; it is the first human ceremony; it is in this same joy and spirit that we gather today in celebration of this marriage. And so after much prayer and considering all that is involved in marriage, and with godly counsel, John and Kristene believe today it is God's plan for them to be united in marriage. They desire that their marriage be a specifically Christian marriage that involves the characteristics of a love that only God can really give them to have, one toward the other. In 1 Corinthians 13 we find that the apostle Paul described this love, 'Love is patient, love is kind, it does not envy, it does not boast, it is not proud, it is not rude, it is not self-seeking, it is not easily angered, it keeps no record of wrongs. Love does not delight in evil, but rejoices in the truth, it always protects, always trusts, always hopes, always perseveres, love never fails.'"

"John and Kristene," Pastor Goodman addressed us, "I commend you for your desire for your marriage to be founded on this kind of love.

I challenge you that you will daily seek more and more of God's love into your hearts, and that you will share that, one with the other."

Led by Pastor Goodman, we exchanged the vows that Kristene had selected, I repeated the vows first:

"I, John Hansen, take thee Kristene Kinssies to be my wedded wife, to have and to hold from this day forward, for better or for worse, for richer or for poorer, in sickness and in health, to love and to cherish, till death us do part. According to God's holy ordinance, and thereto I plight thee my troth."

And led by Pastor Goodman, Kristene, her voice barely above a whisper and clenching my hand, repeated these same vows to me.

Pastor Goodman then gave me the ring for Kristene and said, "This gold ring represents endless and pure love. With it you are pledging yourselves, your possessions, and your love. John, take this ring and place it on Kristene's finger and repeat your pledge to Kristene: 'With this ring I thee wed, in the Name of the Father, and of the Son and of the Holy Spirit.'"

After Kristene repeated her vows to me, Pastor Goodman then prayed God's blessing on us, asking God to "give them many, many years of joy," and then pronounced us husband and wife. "Ladies and gentlemen, I present to you Mr. and Mrs. John Hansen," he announced.

As the gathering applauded us, my mind was on fast forward. *There's only one more thing left before it's a done deal,* I commented mentally.

The reception at Ron and Kay's was like a family reunion in which everybody really likes each other: genuinely friendly, intimate, eager to catch up on all the latest. Kristene had worked with Kay for weeks cleaning the house in preparation. I conversed with everyone there and received congratulations, hugs, and handshakes, but my eyes stayed with Kristene when she wasn't right next to me, and she was in the very front of my thoughts. At last the time came to leave, and the small crowd gathered outside. Kristene pulled up her dress; she had two garter belts on her thigh and removed one, which she tossed into the air. There were cheers when it was caught by a female in-law who was single. Everyone tossed rice at us as we made our way across the lawn to our car.

At last I took Kristene home, and when we reached the front door, I carried her across the threshold as an act of honoring her. It came to me then that God had truly restored "the years that the locusts had eaten," as the Bible says, for our innocence was renewed; the stain of previous marriages and romances for me and prior relationships for her were all washed away. No longer did they count or matter. God had given us a totally fresh start, a new beginning; it would be just us now. We were two redeemed people in love, and married. No time was wasted; I carried her straight to the bedroom, whereupon we repeatedly consummated our love, our marriage, our new life together as one person, and Kristene and I became as Adam and Eve once were when, in Genesis, Adam proclaimed Eve "flesh of my flesh, bone of my bone." And so the "we" came into being, and "I" and "me" were no more. Kristene was one heart, one spirit, one flesh with me. For the first time in my life, I felt absolutely complete as a man living upon the earth. No more would I be alone, and no more would my heart wander. Peace and joy, purpose and fulfillment were mine at long last. The only hunger I would ever know again would be that I would always hunger for her; a hunger that would be forever. I was a blessed man.

I rejoiced in Kristene's femininity and her zest for life; her unclad beauty was unequalled perfection, exquisite in every detail. Best of all was the knowledge that God authored our love Himself. He had hand-fitted us together. Because we had honored Him, He would honor us, and our love would therefore be enduring and inexhaustible. We loved and talked and loved and drank and slept and talked and loved more. I wondered if maybe this was what Adam felt when the Lord presented Eve to him, for Eve too was hand-fitted by God for him.

From this day on, we were never again two, but one.

CHAPTER SIX

A beautiful brunette with ivory skin slept next to me with one arm around my waist when I awoke the next morning, and I remained still, letting her sleep. Yesterday seemed like a dream, yet here we were. Kristene was now my wife; we had taken vows before God and consummated our love, and we were now one. It was a new life we were beginning. Only vaguely did I grasp then that there was an unusual permanence, an irreversible finality to our union brought about by our waiting; the depth of which would sustain us well in the tough times that lay ahead. She began stirring, and I kissed and caressed her until her eyes popped open and she smiled. I slipped out of bed and made coffee for us and brought it to her, and in bed we smiled much, sipped the strong aroma, soaking in our new reality. Later we dressed and went to a high-end hotel for breakfast. As we waited for our order I could read the disbelief on Kristene's face as she kept staring at her wedding ring, at a loss for words.

We returned home and finished loading Stella's camper. The pump for the running water was broken. There was no time for repairs. The propane stove, refrigerator, and electric lights worked fine, but there would be no running water for the sink or the shower. I added two two-gallon plastic buckets and a length of garden hose to our gear and climbed into the cab, Kristene snuggled up alongside me. We slowly backed out of the driveway, using the side mirrors to see behind us, and headed down the road to Hadlock the long way around, via Olympia. With the camper mounted in its bed, the big green Ford truck plowed through the air as if its purpose was to redefine wind resistance for the scientific community. No matter, we poked along in the slow lane, letting everyone pass us. We were happy and in no hurry.

It was sunny, and the traffic on I-5 and the 101 was light. We chatted endlessly and cracked jokes. What was not funny, though we joked about it anyway, was how fast the gas gauge moved from full toward empty. When we stopped in Black Lake for lunch I parked the rig as far as I conveniently could from other parked cars to allow us an easy exit. Four hours later, we arrived at my father's beachfront property a mile away from the tiny burg of Hadlock, where time had stood still since the '50s.

I parked right on the beach, as close to a large pile of driftwood as I could get. We were alone there, a rustic beachfront paradise of our own, the only sounds the lapping waves and seagulls that squawked as they hovered and dove to the water, competing for fish. The evening air was warm, and the fiery red sunset promised a fine day tomorrow. The tide was out, so we barefooted it across wet sand to the water's edge, into the cold water up to our ankles. We gathered driftwood, built a fire on the beach, uncorked a bottle of wine, and sat next to the fire, watching the sun go down in a blaze of orange glory, drinking wine, staring at crackling flames, listening to the sounds of gentle waves lapping nearby in the salt air blackness around us, talking until late.

My father's property was over thirty acres on a level beach on Puget Sound. It was undeveloped rural land except for a cavernous, turn-of-the-century gray concrete shell of a two-story building that once produced industrial-grade alcohol from the wood waste from local sawmills. Locals called it "the old alcohol plant." Built in about 1906, it had been succumbing to the elements since it was abandoned in 1921 and became the home of pigeons and wild animals.

On a bluff overlooking the bay sat the mobile home of the property caretakers, Dominic and Rita. I guessed them to be in their fifties, but their age was difficult to determine because their appearances were weathered from within, stamped with the look that long years with the bottle produces: haggard, permanent red veins about the cheeks and nose, grayish skin, the look of premature aging. They had a medium-sized cabin cruiser anchored in the bay, and a wooden rowboat on the beach to get to it. Next to their trailer they kept a large garden producing vegetables and berries, all of which were in full bloom.

We slept late the next morning. Warm sunlight, salt air, and cawing seagulls greeted me as I stepped out of the camper with dishes to wash. My bride had fixed a late breakfast in the camper, and I was filling the buckets with the hose.

"Hi ya, you two love birds!" called Rita as she crossed the meadow toward us. "I was by a little earlier to invite you guys to coffee, but your camper was rockin', so I didn't bother knockin'!" She laughed, winking at Kristene, who smiled and blushed. Rita looked at my crude dishwashing operation with curiosity; before she could ask, I told her about the camper's water pump. "No problem! I've got extra lengths of hose that'll reach here easy. And me an' Dominic would like to take you kids out fishin' in our boat tomorrow morning, okay?"

Rita dragged a hose with a nozzle from her outside faucet over to us. She invited us to see her garden. It was neat, organized, and well planned. The richness of the black, fluffy topsoil was expressed by row after row of flourishing produce: spuds - reds and bakers, carrots, beets, celery, cucumbers, radishes, bulb and green onions. There were berries too: strawberries, raspberries, and blueberries. And thick blackberry bushes lined the eastern edge of the property, overhanging with ripe berries. Dominic came out and joined us.

"Rita's the one got the green thumb. Ain't me. We got way more'n we could eat ourselves, so you two help yourselves to all you want. Just go to waste if you don't," he said.

Rita warned that sometimes black bears come in for the berries. "But bears'll leave if you toss a rock, make some noise, and yell at 'em—unless it's a mama with her cubs, that is, then you better get outta her way!"

Early the next morning a light fog filled the predawn blackness as the four of us boarded Dominic and Rita's crusty powerboat and motored out of the bay to Point-No-Point before sunup. Dominic throttled back the engine as we plopped our hooks set with fresh-cut herring as bait into the water. I only had to show Kristene once how to set the bait on the double hooks so that the bait wobbled in the water like a wounded herring. A fisherman's daughter, she mastered it right away and was able to properly set the bait, pay out line until the bait touched bottom, and then come back up ten turns of the reel and troll the bait just above the bottom. The sun came up. A few boats were landing salmon already. The water was calm and glassy; slow-rolling swells made it seem like oil. The boat's engine throbbed softly at low speed as we watched our lines in the water in silence.

"Got a fish! John! Quick! Help!" Kristene shouted.

Her salmon rod was bending up and down violently, and her reel was paying out line rapidly. I reeled in my line, stuck my rod in a pole holder, and stood behind Kristene, wrapping my arms around her arms to help her hold the surging rod. Whatever she had on line was huge, surging away from Kristene on the boat's port side. The line would either run out or break soon if we didn't go with it.

"Dominic, turn hard to port and don't give it more gas. Now!" I snapped.

The boat heaved to the left, bobbing slowly over gentle swells, enabling us to stay with the fish at the other end of the line. The line suddenly became slack.

"Honey, quick! Start reeling in your line as it slackens!"

Kristene responded immediately, keeping enough tension on the line to avoid a snarl. We followed the fish farther out into the bay and through several turns. It was headed for the deeper waters outside the bay. For what must have been an hour, I stood behind Kristene, pressed close against her back, the hands of each of us working the rod handle and the reel as one person. I could feel Kristene tiring, her arms beginning to shake from the long strain.

"Don't give up. We'll let the fish wear down, and then we'll reel him in."

She leaned her body back into mine even farther as she yielded to the strength of my hands and arms to handle the rod.

Eventually the fish began to tire, the strength of its surges weakening. Together we wound line back onto the reel, ever careful to maintain just the right tension, drawing it closer to the surface. By now, as tired as we were, after a good hour and miles of struggle, we wanted to see what we had on the line. A new surge of energy welled up within us as we worked the reel as one person. Then we saw it: about two feet below the water's surface, the dark gray shape of a large fish that plunged under the boat and away off the starboard side. We scrambled to swing our line around the stern and reposition on the starboard side. At first I thought it might be a shark, but the glimpse I got was enough to know better; I had seen its body. It was not a shark, as I had feared, and it wasn't a salmon. It rolled up toward the surface again, allowing me a second look. It was a large halibut, which often grow to weigh over two hundred pounds. The reel whirred loudly, paying out more line fast as the fish lunged to port side.

"Dominic! Hard left! Quick! Same Speed!" I yelled.

I welded myself to Kristene's backside again, my hands with hers on the rod handle as the boat heaved to starboard, rolling and pitching softly in the gentle swells.

"Honey, you okay?"

"Yes! Not quittin' now!" she beamed.

We were running out of line fast. The fish was heading into more open waters and going deeper. Dominic increased speed slightly until we began to regain line on the reel.

A large pleasure boat, gleaming white, with several over-dressed rich people in white tennis clothes and sunglasses, arrogantly sitting on patio chairs, laughing, coolly sipping their drinks, was ahead of us, coming from our right to our left, threatening to cut across Kristene's line. We yelled to them to turn aside, as we had a fish on the line. That we were following a taut line could be seen clearly. After staring at us for a few seconds, they made several derisive comments, laughed at us, and hoisted their drinks, smirking mockingly at us as if they were lords and ladies amused with the sight of peasants such as us, while their boat cut a small wake in front of us right over our line as a show of their disdain, but luckily without cutting it. Dominic cursed them openly for their mocking condescension as the hull of their boat passed over our line. Their insolence angered me for but a moment, for Kristene and I were focused on the chase at hand.

For another half hour or so, we followed our quarry in a northwesterly direction toward Indian Island with just enough speed to begin reeling line back in, closing the distance. Again the fish began to tire. We took in more line, and it appeared we might be able to boat the fish this time.

"Hand me the net!" I called to Rita. The fish was again just below the surface, a dark shape surging back and forth, obscured by the sun's flashing reflections on the water. The line was now straight down in the water and taut, indicating the fish was under the boat.

It headed straight down toward the bottom. Kristene carefully paid out more line. Dominic put the throttle in neutral. We waited. Tension on the line increased sharply to starboard. The fish was going under the boat to the other side.

"Slight forward speed, hard left rudder!" I called to Dominic. The stern swung around smoothly so the line wasn't chaffing against the hull. The line off our port side again where we were, we were back in business. Or so we thought. That brief pause at the bottom was all the fish needed to recover. With renewed energy, it plunged directly off the port side and then left so it was heading straight out, off the stern, line peeling off the reel quickly.

"Go hard left!" Kristene called. But Dominic, who had been drinking all morning at the wheel of his boat, swung right instead and the line snapped, most of it going away with the fish. Disappointment and disbelief produced a loss for words; Kristene sat down on a bucket, wordless. I gathered our gear in silence, and we began the long ride back.

When we got back to camp, we fired up the truck and drove to a late lunch at Nancy's Café, a small family-owned roadside eatery in Irondale and went to Fort Warden State Park on nearby Indian Island to use the campground showers. With an hour of daylight left as we readied to leave, Kristene noticed that the tide had turned so it was incoming.

"Honey, let's fish right here," Kristene urged me. I set up light tackle, hastily dug up some worms for bait, and we fished from the beach, facing the setting sun. Right away Kristene got a bite and jumped up and down, hollering excitedly as she reeled in a good-sized flounder. A small crowd gathered on the beach to watch Kristene's antics and gave her a round of applause as I waded into the water to net it.

Flounder, fresh picked potatoes, and veggies roasted over our campfire and white wine was our dinner that night, and as we ate, we laughed and drank a toast to the day's adventure, speculating back and forth about the size of "the fish that got away."

"That's a story for the books, and no one will believe us when we say how big it was!" Kristene mused, grinning and shaking her head incredulously as she sat staring into the orange warmth of the fire.

One idyllic day followed another. It was a time of intimacy and enchantment that neither of us had known; and always it was bright, warm, and sunny. We stayed mostly on the beach, sleeping in our camper, living on the fish we caught and what we harvested from the beach and Rita's garden. In accordance with the tides we sunbathed, napped in the camper and visited with Dominic and Rita. In our swimsuits and rubber boots, we dug clams and oysters and fished the incoming tide off the beach. Morning and noon, Kristene prepared gourmet meals on the stove in the camper; dinner we cooked by campfire at night. I had married a great cook. Kristene was creative in the kitchen; every meal was a new adventure. I was only too happy to do the cleanup with hose and buckets and a bottle of liquid soap. We shopped roadside stands for fresh fruit and corn and chatted with the vendors, soaking up the sunshine. Every night we built a campfire on the beach; some nights we steamed buckets of clams and oysters in a pot, roasted ears of corn wrapped in foil in the hot coals of our fire. Other nights we grilled our day's catch, and enjoyed buttered popcorn and wine for dessert.

A fairly short distance across the bay from us a riotous crowd at a rustic place called the Ajax Café often had a huge fire going on the beach, their noise wafting across the water to us. The Ajax Café had a dozen tiny 1930s-style wooden shanties that these people rented. Whoever they were, they brought us our evening entertainment with their huge beach fires, much yelling and laughing, large dogs barking and running around, in and out of the firelight. We never bothered to find out what it was all about; it wasn't important to know. We relaxed in the sand in front of our own fire, wineglasses in hand, holding each other, amusing ourselves with watching the show across the bay from us, their fire, their moving forms and shadows amid the boisterous banter and barking, until it was time for the camper.

We took trips to explore the region, driving the camper up to Sol Duc Hot Springs in the heart of the Olympic Peninsula for a day to swim in the pool, soak in the hot sulfuric spring waters, and use the showers. We poked around in charming, historic Port Townsend, where time seems to have stood still since the late nineteenth century. We relished the quaintness, the individualism, and the local color of this old waterfront town. Hand in hand we meandered through small shops, sampling food and delicacies in the many cafes and open-air fresh fish-and-chips stands, discovering colorful and rustic boatyards and moorages where skilled boatswains worked; salty men, bare-chested, tanned and tattooed, building or repairing wooden boats,

71

scraping barnacle-encrusted hulls, or mending canvas sails in the hot summer sun.

At a boatyard dock that is tucked away at the very north end of Port Townsend was the *Comet*, a huge old wooden power boat that might have been a Coast Guard boat when wooden hulls were in use. About sixty feet stem to stern, the *Comet* was a floating ark, practically crawling with scrawny, long-haired hippy types and their equally scrawny animals: wormy-looking dogs, cats, goats, chickens, even a sheep or two were wandering all over the top deck. Except for the lack of order and cleanliness, it was a veritable Noah's Ark. Locals told us the boat came up from California for the summer, and townsfolk were anxious for them to leave.

As the time neared for us to go home, Kristene became melancholy and withdrawn. I didn't know what the matter was, and she wouldn't tell me. On one of our last nights before we left, I was awakened by her quiet sobbing.

"Just go back to sleep," she whispered.

The next day we went into the camper for a siesta, and Kristene was crying again. I asked her what was wrong.

"I'm just holding you back," she said, shaking her head resignedly.

And she would tell me no more.

Kristene in our honeymoon camper on the Hadlock beach, 1981

Our Honeymoon Camper

The New Bride On Honeymoon

CHAPTER SEVEN

S ummer was ending as the bite in the air one morning foretold an early fall season. After two weeks of honeymooning, it was time to go home and face the daily grind. In a few days, Sara would be with us for the next weekend, so we kept the camper long enough for a brief return trip to Hadlock with her. We were not ready to go home; packing up and saying good-bye to the beach that had become our Eden, our private world that had sheltered and fed us from its bounty, saddened us. We bid farewell to Dominic and Rita. They had watched over us like personal caretakers, anticipating our needs and taking us out in their boat one more time the day before we were to leave.

We stopped at the Chimacum Café for breakfast on our way out of the Hadlock area. The café is an old-fashioned roadside rural eatery that has been owned by the same family since the late 1940s. The business does so well that every Christmas the owners close the café and take all their employees and their families on an expense-paid Hawaiian vacation.

The Chimcum has the feel of the '40s: pearl colored plastic topped, soda-fountain style lunch counter with mounted, swivel-seat stools, old-fashioned wood-plank floors, high-backed booths, and light green Formica tabletops. The food is Americana at its best: pies, mashed potatoes, stews, gravy, steamed green beans, chicken, beef and pork dishes, burgers and fries, everything is made from scratch, and the servings are country size, the atmosphere homey, rustic, rural, and hospitable. Sitting on the edge of acres of cow pasture, the Chimacum faces a two-lane highway and a gravel parking lot. To see tourists there is rare, for the Chimacum caters to locals, and most out-of-towners prefer the plastic fare of chain eateries. To sit at the counter there is to enjoy watching the seamless teamwork between the waitresses and the line cooks and to gaze at memorabilia from when Elvis Presley ate there while in the area to film one of his movies in the early '60s.

Returning to the city felt like we had come to another planet. It was crowded and noisy, even for a Sunday afternoon, the tall buildings, concrete and asphalt of the city an oppressive transition from the rural paradise we just left. Our home seemed small and cramped as we pulled into the driveway; just another suburban shoebox squeezed onto a tight plot of land. Inside the house was gloomy, with drawn drapes and full of hot, stale air from closed-up windows for two weeks. Kristene walked in, stopped in the foyer, and groaned, "Uhhh!" as she surveyed the evidence of my former bachelor lifestyle: dilapidated old leatherette couches and the coffee table with a bullet hole in the top, sitting on frazzled, dirty old shag carpet that stunk, the kitchen floor linoleum was cracked and peeling, and dated, dark wood paneling made dreary the entry, and none of the furniture was comfortable to sit on or pleasing to look at. Her silence spoke volumes. I thought of the pile of mail waiting for me at the post office and the bills to be paid, and that I had to return to work the next morning. *It can all wait a bit longer,* I figured. We opened drapes and doors and windows, unloaded the camper, and started laundry. To ease Kristene's dark mood, I made light of it all.

"The house needs to air out for awhile. Let's grab a bite somewhere and come back," I suggested, and out we went.

An apt title for our first week back would be Murphy's Law Week, because everything went wrong that could have. The little publishing company Kristene worked for had gone out of business while we were away and the owner skipped town, nowhere to be found, owing Kristene her last paycheck; my payday would be that week, but there would be no overtime pay on it, and after paying child support and the basic bills, remaining funds would have to be conserved to get us through to the next payday, when the mortgage was due. Kristene began job-hunting, a stress all its own; my mother kept dropping by unannounced and uninvited, and if we weren't home, she left either a ham or a loaf of rye bread in a bag on the front doorknob, whether we wanted it or not. My father and his wife stopped by for a visit, also unannounced and uninvited, and they got into a vicious fight right in front of us, as if we weren't even present. Then I was presented with Kristene's pile of unpaid bills that she didn't tell me about, four figures worth, and creditors were calling the house.

My caseload of burglary and theft cases went so well that I had no justifiable reason to work overtime, so overtime pay wouldn't be on my next paycheck either, which made it a case of Murphy's Law in reverse. We were short on cash, down to one income, and between paychecks; I was getting no overtime, and Kristene was unpaid, unemployed, unapproachable, increasingly distant and withdrawn. Reality had moved in with us like an uninvited in-law, accompanied by Buyer's Remorse, who handed Kristene a gift-wrapped package labeled "Second Thoughts," and to add to the pressure, my-five-year old daughter, Sara, was coming at the end of the week. "Timing is everything," so a folk saying goes. For a certainty we were in a trough of bad timing when everything turned out as badly as possible, seemingly with no room for worsening. All I could do was hang on and wait for another folk saying to unfold: "This too shall pass."

We returned to Hadlock in the camper with Sara and made a pleasant time of beachcombing, clam digging, kite flying, and campfire marshmallows. Sara was comfortable enough, but I could see that Kristene felt like she didn't fit in, like an extra left foot. When we got back, Kristene resumed job hunting, I worked my usual schedule, and we returned the camper to Stella. Funds were low. We pinched pennies, eating at home, counting the days until my next paycheck. Kristene was becoming more and more removed.

"Don't you feel exposed?" she asked me as she pulled away from me as I tried to hold her. I said I didn't.

"Well *I* do," she said and walked away.

Kristene landed a job the following week at a post office inside a local shopping mall and had to attend postal training before starting work. Evenings and weekends we went to detective division dinners at local restaurants and picnicked with Ron and Kay at Denny Creek. She remained distant and seemed no longer attracted to me at all. I wasn't about to give up on us; whatever was wrong, I would find out and fix it. One Saturday afternoon we went to the Seattle Aquarium. I had been silently praying all day about our situation. As we walked back to our car, I looked at Kristene as she waited for me to unlock the door. In just old jeans, sweater, and jacket, no makeup, her heavy dark hair around her shoulders, Kristene's natural beauty was so potent I could inhale it; she was breathtaking. As I absorbed her ambiance, the Lord spoke to me, "She loves you, but she is having difficulty with marriage commitment." It was a clear word of knowledge that strengthened me, and I kept it to myself.

What the Lord revealed to me that day prepared me for the shock when two days later Kristene told me she wanted to separate because she felt she had made a mistake. We hadn't yet been married thirty days, and already it was unraveling. Several times Kristene broke into tears as she told me she just didn't want to be married to anybody, that she had been comfortable with her single life, and she felt unqualified to have kids, which is what she knew I wanted.

"No one has ever loved me as much as you do," she said.

"Then why do you want to leave?" I asked.

"I'm too selfish to have kids. I'm just holding you back," she wept.

We married without addressing our differences on the important issue of whether we would have children. Our desire for each other overrode common sense. We hadn't finished laying a foundation before we began building our house. That was a mistake. On my insistence, we went to see Pastor Rozelle separately, Kristene first. When it was my turn to meet with Pastor Rozelle, there was hurt and disappointment in his eyes that told me he thought it was hopeless before he even said a word. His words to me were anything but encouraging as he said he only wished we had taken his advice to wait longer and complete the counseling program.

My heart sank when I learned that with her first paycheck from the post office Kristene had rented a one-bedroom apartment within walking distance of her workplace and got her furniture out of storage. She also bought a used bicycle to ride to work. I was heartbroken and pleaded with her not to leave when she kissed me good-bye and drove away in our little red Toyota. I went back inside the house, feeling crushed and empty. My mind was spinning. Had I heard from God correctly or not? If so, how could this happen? A sickening knot developed in my stomach. I had no appetite, and sleep escaped me. During the days and weeks that followed, I dragged myself to work. It was a blessing from God that my caseload became so light at that time that only the slightest attention was needed to do satisfactory work. I was too embarrassed to go back to Neighborhood Church. I continued weekend visits with Sara and what solace there was for me came from my time with her, being Dad, as always before.

A few days later, Kristene called me in the evening. She sounded thoughtful and cold, matter-of-fact.

"Just wanted you to know that I'm all right," she said. "I'm in my apartment, and I ride my bicycle to work. I want you to know there is no one else, nor is that the reason I left. I'm just not cut out for marriage or kids. It all happened too fast. If we had waited, this would have been over in about six months. I'm not the type for permanent relationships," she said. We talked for quite awhile longer, and she finally agreed to attend at least one session of counseling as long as it was at some place other than Neighborhood Church.

My hopes barely up, I arranged immediately for separate appointments for us at Burden Bearers, a Christian counseling service in North Seattle. The counselor I met with was an elderly woman named Alice. We talked about the crisis and prayed together for healing and restoration. A week later I met with Alice again, after she had met with Kristene. She had a long face.

"You didn't tell me your wife was so beautiful," she said. "It's no wonder you want her back. Uh—I didn't mean that the way it sounded. Of course you would want her back, regardless, but I didn't expect to see this. Your wife is one of the most stunning women I think I've ever seen. Unfortunately, Kristene had a hardened attitude about staying married when she came here, and it never changed. I'm really sorry, but I can't see any reason to offer you any hope on this. She's got her mind made up. And to be sure, I asked her if there was another man involved, and she told me there wasn't, and I am inclined to believe her," Alice said.

I withdrew socially from nearly everybody. Partly this was because so many people had an "I told you so," finger-wagging attitude; others had nothing encouraging to say. My own parents were the worst; they both had all sorts of unkind and uncharitable comments to say about Kristene, and I didn't want to hear any of it. I began working out with weights every day at home in the early evening, and when I wasn't doing that or working, I immersed myself in reading the Word and in prayer.

Two weeks later, I received a call at home from Alice, of Burden Bearers.

"I want you to know that I have been in much prayer about you and Kristene," she said. "I was praying for you both just now, and the Lord gave me a vision of a waterwheel that was steadily turning over, blade by blade, rotated by the water," she said. "I asked the Lord, 'Lord, what does this mean?' The Lord told me as clearly as I hear my own voice now, 'It means that life is an unfolding process. Tell John I showed you this.' That's what the Lord showed me and told me," Alice said. "I don't know anything more than that, but God doesn't give visions and messages without a reason. Pray and seek Him, and don't give up! As bad as it looks, all is not lost."

I thanked Alice for calling me and hung up.

The following Sunday night I was on the phone with a Christian woman, a friend, a prayer warrior who was known to operate sometimes in the New Testament gift of the word of knowledge. I told her everything and that it had been two weeks since I had heard from Kristene or seen her. We went into prayer together on the phone, asking God to heal the marriage. We were in prayer for long minutes when suddenly my friend became silent and I waited in silence for her to speak what the Lord had shown her.

"Luke 7:47, her many sins have been forgiven, and she who has been forgiven much will love much,' says the Lord. Whatever you do, don't give up! Don't you give up! Don't you dare give up! God is at work in this, no matter how bad it looks right now. I also sense that you are going to need revelation power as you go through this time, so I'm going to ask God to give you a special anointing for this occasion," she said. "Holy Father, in Jesus' name I beseech you to help my brother by giving him revelation knowledge for the days ahead, and I thank You in advance for saving this marriage. Amen," she prayed.

That night I went to sleep, my head swirling with thoughts about everything that had happened. I read and re-read Luke 7:47 and remembered what the Lord showed me when I first met Kristene. I resolved to stay the course, no matter what, but there was no denying that the situation looked hopeless. I went to sleep. A few hours later, I awoke from a very vivid dream that I knew was from God: a man came to my door wanting me to sign papers that he had with him. In the dream the Lord clearly told me not to sign the papers or say anything. I went to work the next day and came home at the usual time. It was getting dark very early now, and there was a knock at my door. A strange man was standing there when I opened it, he was the same man I saw in the dream, and he was holding papers in his hand.

"Mr. Hansen? I have here some papers for you to sign, please," he said. He was even smiling the way I saw him smiling in the dream. I asked him what they were. "Papers to annul your marriage to Kristene," he said. My dream really *was* from God, I realized.

"No, I won't sign," I told him.

"Oh come on, it's easy. Just sign!" he said, smiling a mocking smile at me. I refused again. He asked if he could leave the papers with me, and I told him no, and at that he left.

I closed the door, overwhelmed by how God had protected me and prepared me for this turn of events. *Now I know firsthand that I have heard from God and that He is ever faithful,* I thought to myself.

Two nights later, Kristene called, and her tone was angry.

"What's the idea in not signing the annulment papers?" she demanded. "If you think you can save this marriage by stalling, think again: I want out! Now I'll have to have a divorce on my record. Because you did this, it's gonna cost you. You'll regret you did this," she said. "Just you wait."

"Okay, go ahead, take your best shot. Knock yourself out, Baby," I said as I hung up.

The following weekend I was served at home with divorce papers, and the ninety-day countdown began for the third time in my life. . In spite of the signs I had received that God was with me in this, I was consumed with despair. I felt embarrassed to face my fellow officers and detectives to whom I had been witnessing for so long now, but there was no way out of it: I still had to work. I couldn't handle the pitying stares of my family and friends. Alone and ashamed, my faith on the line, I withdrew.

"Turn to me and be gracious to me, for I am lonely and afflicted.
The troubles of my heart have multiplied; free me from my anguish."
Psalm 25:16,17

CHAPTER EIGHT

Time was against me. While the legal clock was ticking, I blocked out social events, friends, and family, everything that wasn't essential for survival and victory, like a prizefighter training for the championship title fight. I had no tolerance for distractions; my new lifestyle was stripped down, an austere routine that could best be described as a tunnel. I arose early every morning and sought God in prayer for more than an hour; I went to work during the day, but I was in prayer every minute I was alone. I came home at lunchtime and prayed again, eating only a light meal. Every night I came home and worked out with weights, ate, read the Bible, and prayed all night until I fell asleep.

I kept to a lean diet and drank a glass of red wine once a week for the benefit it would do for my blood. I lost weight—a lot of weight; more than twenty pounds. I have always been naturally strong without having to work out much, but now it seemed the clock was being turned back on my body as it hardened and became as lean as it was in my early twenties.

Reading the Word as much as I was at that time resulted in sharper mental clarity and a quicker grasp of everything I heard or read. I only left home to work, buy groceries, and do things with Sara. I avoided calling or seeing any of Kristene's relatives, not wanting to involve them. No one in my own family was of any help; my mother made it worse by crying and saying, "Oh! I just *knew* she wasn't the kind who would stay home! My heart *aches* for you!" My father was cynical. "Too bad you lost such a pretty package," he said. I avoided being around anyone who would distract my focus on getting help from God.

During this ordeal, I was led by the Spirit to pray actual prayers found in the Bible. I knew that God honors His Word and watches over it, so three times a day I prayed over Kristene from Ephesians 1:17–19a and 3:14–19, Philippians 1:9–11, and Colossians 1:9–14. One week rolled into another without any word about or from Kristene, and the days were clicking away. One night while cleaning up around the house, I had an overwhelming impression that God was calling me to fast seven days. I had never before fasted more than a few hours, so I was doubtful that it was really God I was hearing from. But the impression upon me was so strong that it could not be denied: God was calling me into a fast. The next day I began fasting, taking only liquids, such as water, coffee, or tea.

The first day of fasting was easy. I wasn't hungry; I was actually enthusiastic, especially because God called me to do it, which I knew meant that He would bless my efforts if I obeyed Him. But food was all I could think about on the second and third days. I told no one what I was doing; it was too private. On the fourth day I was no longer hungry, and my prayers were on fire. But when the fifth day ended, my bowels turned to water, and I couldn't get more than a few steps away from the toilet. This went on all through the early evening, and I told the Lord I couldn't do it anymore. I couldn't work the next day like this, and I would have to eat something if I were to work. I was just about to eat a banana when my brother-in-law Bob called.

"Hi, John, how's it going?" he asked. I said I was okay.

"Well," Bob said, "the Lord told me very clearly tonight to fast for you and Kristene for two days. I can't do any more than that. You know I do my own work and the Lord knows I need my strength. So I'm starting right now," he said.

I thanked Bob without telling him that the Lord directed me to fast seven days, of which I could only finish five. Once again God's mercy and grace were shown to me when I most needed it and least expected it.

More days rolled by. Nothing changed. For some reason, I had read mostly in the Old Testament since becoming saved, possibly it was because I have always enjoyed reading history, but I hadn't read much of the New Testament. One night after dinner I was sitting on the small couch in the kitchen nook, reading the Old Testament, when suddenly I had an open vision of two men sitting side by side on a bench with their backs to me. They were in a jail cell, and the cell door was made of wide metal bars crossing each other vertically and horizontally. Their feet were in stocks, and they were singing hymns, praising God. I saw a large human hand to my right, pointing at the men, and a voice said, "This is the Philippian jail that Satan got Paul and Silas into." I knew this was the Lord speaking to me. "This is what happens when it is My time to act," the Lord said. I saw the jail cell shaken by a great earthquake, and the stocks on the men's feet fell off and the jail cell door fell open, hanging only by the bottom hinge.

I burst into sudden laughter when I saw the truth about how puny Satan's power is, but my laughter stopped abruptly as now I saw a another vision: this time I saw two different people on the same bench, a larger person and a much smaller person sitting closely side by side. Both had their backs toward me and the Lord. I saw that there was a thick cord running from the tailbone of the larger person to the tailbone of the smaller person. Again the Lord's hand appeared on my right as He said "This is you and your wife. The cord between you means that the two of you are one flesh and one spirit in My sight. Keep praising Me and thanking Me, for if you do, this is what I will do." And I saw the earthquake shake the cell door open all over again. In a state of total awe I have never before experienced, I slipped off the couch to my knees and thanked and praised God in a loud voice for a long time that night.

I had heard from the very throne of God like few men have, and with it came a promise from God Himself.

That open vision not only changed how I prayed, it changed my life and my grasp of the spirit realm. It would not be until years later when I read the Books of Acts that I understood the open vision was of the exact scene of Paul and Silas in the Philippian jail in chapter 16, verse 25. For the present time, I knew only to pray about my situation without letup, and I learned from the vision to praise and thank God for results in prayer *before* I realized the results. I told no one about the vision; it was just between the Lord and me and was too private. Still, as the weeks went by with nothing happening that I could see, my hopes faded a little.

Out of the blue, Bob Kinssies called me again, this time to invite me to an evening midweek service at a church in Seattle. I rode with him and Angela in their car, and we talked and enjoyed seeing each other again. I avoided talking about Kristene, and they respected me by not asking questions. Bob and Angela's church was called Northwest Tabernacle, a small Pentecostal church that was probably descended from the great Azusa Street Revival in Los Angeles in 1906 that all the Pentecostal churches in America could trace their roots to. The church was located in the heart of Seattle's Central District, one of the oldest neighborhoods in the city. It was a time-worn, traditional wood-frame structure, painted white, with double front doors, and inside were wooden plank floors that creaked, wooden pews scarred with age and use and the musky scent from decades of being packed with earnest believers.

I was surprised to see that the pastor, Reverend Wood, was white, yet the congregation was almost entirely black. I admired how dressed up black people are when they come to church, an expression of genuine respect and honor that white churches have been losing for some time now. That week there was a guest evangelist from out of town, someone I had never heard of. The organ and piano music and the drums were pounding out rhythmic Gospel music to a hand-clapping, dancing crowd of young adults and their kids, with quite a few elderly grandparent types sitting patiently in the pews, impeccably dressed, some of the men holding canes in their hands.

Then the music quieted to a soft whisper as a signal for everybody to be seated. Pastor Wood then introduced the guest evangelist, a stoutly built, balding, dark-skinned black man who appeared to be in his mid-forties. In a guttural, raspy voice that reminded me of the legendary jazz musician Louis Armstrong, he smiled broadly as he said, "Well praise the Lord, everybody! Praise the Lord! Y'all praise the Lord? C'mon, let's show the Lord we love Him! Show Him we are thankful that He has saved us from the fires of hell! The Good Book says to enter His gates with thanksgiving and His courts with praise! Give glory to God! Thank You Lord that I'll go to Heaven when I die! Thank You Lord that You protect my life, my home, my family and all I touch! Thank You Jesus that because of You, no weapon formed against me shall prosper! Glory, glory, glory, glory to You, God!" With open hands lifted shoulder-high, he paced up and down in front of us, his gravelly voice rumbled into a deep vibrato and his eyes half-closed as he went on, giving thanks and praise to the Most High.

The air was electrified as the congregation jumped to their feet as one person, some clapping, some raising their hands in the air, smiling and laughing with genuine joy. Piano and organ music filled the air with shouts and cries of laughter, exclaiming over and over, "Hallelujah! Thank You, Jesus! Glory to God! Oh glory, glory, glory, glory to God! Praise Your holy Name, oh Most High!" Others rattled off exuberantly in tongues, and a few danced around the sanctuary. My own home church, Neighborhood Church, itself a Pentecostal church and often a hotbed of fervent worship, was nothing like this. In a short while, everyone returned to their seats to listen to the sermon.

He preached powerfully about the necessity of absolute faith and trust in God if we want to be of use to Him, and I knew God was speaking to me through him. He cited specific instances from the Bible about the lives of Abraham, Moses, and David, how they were called, how they answered, yet they went through long, dry periods of waiting for God to fulfill His promise to them. The waiting times were God's way of testing us, he said. Fiery trials are God's furnace to purify and refine our faith, and he stressed that it is our duty to be quick to repent, to consider others better than ourselves, to believe God no matter what. This man knew his Bible. Without notes, without a lectern, with only a black leather Bible in his hand, he paced back and forth, his face beaming with joy, preaching powerfully, accurately quoting Scripture in a resonant, guttural baritone with gravel in it, rhythmic, never stumbling over a word. No namby-pamby, cheap grace here; this was pure Gospel, coming not in lofty, wimpy words, but real blood-and-guts stuff that reaches forcefully into the human heart, and I was spellbound, for the words coming out of him were meant for me; I was hearing from Heaven itself. All through the congregation encouragement poured forth to him like waves lapping and pounding at the shoreline: grunts of agreement and mutterings of, "That's right," "C'mon now," and "Amen" punctuated his pauses.

He preached on and on about how faith in God was required of these men to be able to stand long enough to receive and see God's promise fulfilled in earthly terms, and that trust in God was required of them to be able to act on the instructions of a God they could not see. His words established a cadence early in the sermon, a rhythm was building into a mighty crescendo that I swear shook the walls.

"Like Abraham, you gotta trust Gaaaaaawd to keep His promise no matter what the circumstances look like! Ohhhh yeah! Abraham left his home, everything he knew, amen, and he set out, amen, knowing not where Gaaaawd was taking him! Amen. And Abraham was an old, old man but he believed Gaawd when *Gaawd* told him, 'I will bless you and make you the father of many nations! Your wife Sarah will have a son!' And praise Gaawd, Abraham believed Gaawd! Oh thank You, Jesus! Amen and amen! Without Abraham havin' faith, without Abraham trustin' God to do what He said, God couldn't have used Abraham! Amen? Do I hear tonight? Anybody here? Amen!" Mopping the sweat that gushed from his head and face with a white handkerchief and holding a microphone in the other, he paced back and forth, his eyes searching the faces in the congregation.

"Now Moses, he left his known world too! He had safety, wealth, position, a certain future, all his needs met. But he considered right standing with God with suffering was better than the best the world had to offer, and he shunned the world. When God called him to go back, Moses obeyed God - he left his home to go back to Egypt where he was a wanted man, to conduct what seemed impossible—to free Gaawd's people out of their slavery! Now if Moses had no faith in Gaawd, could Gaawd have used him? No! God would have had to find somebody else! Now does anybody think that Moses's faith was perfect? No! He wavered like us-uh, but Moses, like Abraham, though he wavered a little because he was human like all of us-uh are, *he staked it all on what Gaawd said because it was Gaawd that said it!*"

Those very words shot through me like a rifle bullet. His arms were waving now as he looked up at the ceiling and paced up and down past the mourner's bench.

"Gaawd-uh, the Gaawwwd that always comes through-uh, the Gaawwwd that *never* fails-uh, the Gaawwwd that is always right on time-uh, helped him so that the faith of Moses *was* enough! Hallelujah! God used that man of faith to do one of the mightiest deeds ever done! He humbled Pharaoh and led the children of Israel out of slavery! Hallelujah! Somebody give Gaawd the glory!"

And the congregation began shouting praises to God and rocking side to side, nodding in agreement.

"And now comes David," the preacher man continued, "after he was told that he would be king over Israel, after he killed Goliath, he still didn't become king! God tested him by makin' David wait! David waited fifteen looooonng years before God's promise came to pass-uh. During that time David trusted God to help him decide which battles to fight, where to go, and what to do. David had that kind of faith that pleases God by always seekin' God's advice *first* on everything, ummmm-hmmm! So God was so pleased with David, God made him the greatest king Israel ever had! See that? From a mere shepherd boy to the greatest human king in history, all from trustin' God! You see, brothers and sisters, without faith, God cain't use ya!" Then the preacher looked right at me and said it again, "Without faith, God cain't use ya." Suddenly I felt goose-bumps covering my skin.

His preaching had formed a rhythmic cadence early on that was now building into a throbbing crescendo. "Without faith, brothers and sisters, Gaaawd cain't use ya! If you don't trust Gawd when your back is against the wall, when the chips are down, if you don't really trust His goodness, don't believe Him, if you believe the situation as it appears in the natural and not Him who maketh all things, can do all things, in Whom nothin' is impossible, if—you doubt Him, He cain't use ya! Anybody here feels they got too little faith? C'mon down to the front on my right so I can pray for ya. Anybody here tonight got their back against the wall and you see no hope, c'mon down. Anybody here sick? C'mon down to my left and me and the deacons will pray for ya in the name of Jesus!"

People streamed forward from the pews, hands upraised and weeping as they came down the center and side aisles, gathering at the front as the praise and worship poured forth from all over, and the piano and organ played softly and solemnly. Such was the power of the moment, that I could feel the Holy Spirit and angels in the room; in my mind's eye I could see demons scurrying out of there like terrified rats in a room when the light switch is flipped on. I went forward to pray with a couple of other men who were praying over others and put my hand on the shoulder of a man in front of me. The evangelist walked by us, pacing back and forth with Bible in hand, exhorting us and praying aloud when he stopped. Looking right into my eyes, he said, "God says to remember what He told you to do. He will do for you just what He said He would. Don't give up. *Don't give up!*" He then moved on to pray for others, and I knew I had heard from God again.

I was quiet when I rode back with Bob and Angela. At home that night I lay on my bed, the power of the worship and the message still coursing through my body. I tried to digest the evangelist's sermon and personal message. Although I couldn't see anything happening, I had already seen enough of God's care and attention to me that I was way beyond not trusting Him. I also realized I had nothing to lose. I knew from Bible reading that God hates divorce and that He created marriage and the family. I read in 1 John 5:14–15, "And we know that if we ask according to His will, he hears us. And if we know that he hears us, we know that we have the thing we ask of Him." From this I knew that my requests regarding our marriage were His will also, but how Kristene's free will affected what God was able to do was confusing to me. I determined to tough it out, and wait.

But there wasn't much time left.

CHAPTER NINE

Christmas and New Year's came and went. Despite my depression, I managed to do a credible job of going through the motions for Sara's sake. We bought and put up a tree, drank hot cocoa, and played Christmas music while we decorated it with ornaments, strings of colored lights, and tinsel. On Christmas Eve after Sara was asleep, I placed many small gifts I had wrapped under the tree for her to find when she awoke. Those moments were bittersweet. They were warm and loving, yet the reality was that here I was, going through another Christmas alone except for a brief visit with my daughter and Christmas Day at my mother's. The honeymoon joy of just a few months ago seemed like nothing more than a nice dream.

I accepted an invitation from some of my buddies from the men's prayer group to form a small team from Neighborhood Church to go to the maximum-security unit at the state penitentiary at Walla Walla to share our testimonies. As down as I was, I still wanted to do the Lord's work, though I had to admit that my testimony at that point wasn't likely to encourage anyone considering Christianity. The time to go was set for February.

Life's routines regained their normal stride after the New Year. The inflow of new cases slows down right after the holidays, but I had a volume of unfinished cases from the previous year to work. I kept to my spiritual and physical regimens and avoided social contact, with few exceptions. I wasn't attending church anywhere regularly, and I felt bad about that. I couldn't face the pitying stares at my home church; the few times I did go, I went to churches where no one knew me. I wanted anonymity. And as always, Kristene was at the front of my mind all day, every day.

The second Monday in January was cold, drizzly, and gray—typical Northwest weather. Late that afternoon I was driving back to the station from an interview when the police dispatcher radioed to me to call the dispatch center. I went to a phone booth, and the dispatcher called me there. The message was to call Pastor Jack Rozell at his home immediately. This was highly unusual. It was Monday, the day pastors have off, so of course Pastor Jack would be at home. Concerned for what it could be, I called Pastor Jack from the same phone booth.

"John, I hope I am not interrupting you. I told the dispatcher this was not urgent," said Pastor Rozell when he answered the phone.

"That's okay, Pastor. What's going on?"

"John, I have been praying today for you and Kristene, and I have an overwhelming sense that I believe is from the Lord - that you should write Kristene a letter, stating only something to the effect of, 'I still think of you often and I wonder how you are.' Don't say anything about whatever your problems were, and especially don't mention religion. Then you should end it with, 'I love you'" Pastor Rozelle said.

I thanked him and promptly went to a stationery store for a blank card and matching envelope. I wrote the suggested words on the card and mailed it to Kristene's workplace.

I wondered if Kristene would even get my letter or if she would respond at all. I didn't know any other address to send it to, just her workplace, which I had to look up. How sardonic it was, that here we were, still newlyweds, already separated, and I didn't even know Kristene's phone number or her address. Some testimony we were of Christian marriage, I thought. That we were separated so soon and I didn't even know where my wife was, I realized, would make all the smug, churchy naysayers think they were justified in saying we were a hopeless case. Mentally I shrugged my shoulders. I thought, *everything that could be done by me for this, I have now done, so she either calls or she doesn't; whatever will be, will be.*

Two days had passed since mailing the letter, and I put my mind on other things, figuring life would have to go on. That night the home phone rang. I answered it on the second ring.

"Hello, John." It was Kristene.

"Hi. How are you?" I asked.

"Well, I am okay. How are you?" I said I was alright. "I did get your letter," she said, "and yes, I think of you often too. I am thinking I would like to see you."

I was totally clear minded, but still, I could hardly believe my ears. "Okay, how about tomorrow after five?" I offered.

"Sure. I'll be closing up the post office at that time. See you then," she said.

The next day flew by so fast that the next thing I knew I was arriving at the strip mall where Kristene worked. *"Lord, don't let me say anything that isn't given me by You to say. Let Your will be done,"* I prayed as I parked in the parking lot. I checked my hair and straightened my tie in the mirror. I walked into the post office, and there was Kristene behind the counter, waiting on the last customer. She blushed and smiled lovingly when she saw me, evaporating any doubts I had that she still loved me. We went to a local place to eat and then to her apartment, where she fixed me a cup of tea. We sat across the living room from each other and talked, but not about our issues; it was just a gentle circling of each other. Her heavy chestnut hair was in a ponytail, and she wore a tan wool sweater and a pleated plaid skirt, her large dark eyes luminescent. Her beauty was breathtaking. I was still inhaling her persona; I couldn't help it, such was her beauty and her intense femininity as I sat across from her. I left early and kissed her lightly on the lips at the door, and she gave me her home phone number. As I drove home, I talked to God about it. This was no dramatic reunion one would see in a movie, but it was a huge turn of events, and God's hand was evident.

I decided to wait a bit before calling her. Two days later, it was Friday, and it was not my weekend with Sara. I went home after work, exercised with weights, ate my usual bowl of Campbell's Chunky Beef Soup, showered, watched a rerun of *The Beverly Hillbillies*, (I needed *something* to laugh about) read until I was tired, and went to bed early, planning to go shooting the next day in the mountains around North Bend. At about ten, I was dozing off when there was a knock at my front door. I opened it, and there was Kristene.

"Hi," she said. "I was out at dinner with a couple of my girlfriends and wondered if you'd let me stay here at home tonight."

I let her in. The fact that she called the house "home" wasn't lost on me. She looked around the house, checking up on my housekeeping. I could just about hear her wheels turning, but she made no comment. We went to the bedroom, where she undressed quickly and slipped under the sheets and said, "Let's not do anything. Just hold me." Of course it was difficult to honor Kristene's request, but I did. We just held each other all night, and I lay there in a state of joy mixed with disbelief. In the morning, I made coffee for us before she left for work. I didn't know what to expect next, but I went to work that day with calm and a great peace within from seeing firsthand that God was at work.

During the next two weeks, Kristene spent every night with me. She never formally said anything about coming back, and I sensed it would be unwise to press the matter. On her own initiative, she set up counseling sessions for us. She picked a woman counselor, a psychologist, who operated her practice out of her condominium. The woman was not a Christian; her walls were covered with posters espousing New Age values, such as reincarnation and the goodness of all humanity, and slogans and goofy platitudes that reduced God from being the holy and sovereign Creator that He is to a smiling, benevolent cloud floating in the sky, a Santa Claus sort of being whose only purpose is to be at the beck and call of us humans. Nowhere was there any mention of Christ or the Cross.

"There are many options available to you, Kristene," the counselor sniffed. She was a thin woman in her late fifties with rather manly, close-cropped gray hair and a gray, pinched, prudish face and furrowed brow from too much reading and frowning, dressed in an equally gray plaid pantsuit, sitting in a big leather chair, leaning forward with her knees pressed together, bony hands clasping a notebook in her lap. Just to look at her was to become tense. She didn't even acknowledge me when we came in.

"You can keep your marriage and live apart in separate places and see John as you wish. That would be okay, and also you would be free to see others too, and so would John—if you think he would do that," she continued, never once looking at me. "Or you could let your divorce go through and still see each other as friends. As the powerful woman that you are, Kristene, that's another option you might consider."

I didn't like her. Talking about me as if I wasn't in the room and never addressing me at all was clearly intended to demote me in Kristene's eyes. I struggled to hold my anger in check. *This can't be from God, but if He has brought us this far, I will trust Him for the outcome,"* I thought to myself. Still, it was anything but what I expected. The counseling dragged on for an hour without the counselor making one mention of our being together in one home as a married couple. I noticed the 'counselor' wasn't wearing a wedding ring: *So the professional marriage-wrecker is single! Hah! That figures,* I smirked mentally.

Without even looking at me she handed me the bill for the "counseling" and scheduled Kristene for a second session in two days. She did not want me to be there. "My husband comes with me, or I'm not going," Kristene said flatly.

"All right, then, he can be here too if that's how you want it," she said, snatching my check from my hand without looking at me or giving a word of thanks. She never once looked at me or spoke to me, and I wondered how many marriages she had ruined.

We drove home in silence. The counselor's contempt for our marriage and for me as a man was so blatant that Kristene rose to defend it. I had encountered women psychologists in the counseling business like her before through my police career: snide and aloof, with a sneering scorn for traditional values. They make a point of it to undermine the male and the male role at every opportunity, until of course they themselves needed protection from a burglar or a stalker. *Then* they usually wanted a *male* police officer at their door. This lady's bias was so bad that there was no need for me to say anything in protest; her agenda-driven approach would lead to her hanging herself with Kristene if given a little more rope, for Kristene was male-oriented, something that would not compute for the so-called counselor.

The next morning I was home when Kristene received a call from the post office where she worked to call her attorney. The ninety-day clock was running out on the divorce action Kristene had filed; only days were left. Kristene returned the call while I was there. Her attorney told her that the divorce papers had been lost or misfiled by either his office or at the courthouse and he would have to file them over again. He felt confident the court would not require another ninety-day wait if he personally appeared before the judge with her.

"I'm not going through with it. I have moved back home. I am back with my husband, and this is where I am staying," Kristene told him.

"Why are you doing this? Is there something wrong?" I could hear the attorney ask her.

"I'm staying married. That's all you need to know. If there's any more money you need or papers for me to sign, you can send them to our address," Kristene said as she hung up the phone without saying good-bye. I slipped my left arm around her waist and held her tight as I phoned my supervisor with my other hand.

"Roy? It's John. Look, something's come up here at home and I won't be coming in for about another hour, if that's okay. It is? Good. See you soon. Thanks, Roy."

CHAPTER TEN

A new dawn began for us. Kristene cancelled further sessions with the woman counselor and found a Christian marriage counselor at Bellevue First Presbyterian Church named Dr. John Ortmeyer. The second I saw him, I relaxed in the knowledge that this man would help us. He was about my age, middle thirties, and was dressed casually in slacks, loafers, and a loose dark blue sweater. He was of medium height and a tad overweight, with dark hair and a neatly trimmed beard. He exuded calm competence and a desire to help. His remarkable listening and questioning skills enabled us to bare our souls and speak from the heart and had the effect of double doors and window shutters being flung wide open at once, flooding us with the light of understanding. Any doubts about our love for each other or whether we were right for each other were forever dispelled, for Kristene broke down sobbing as she declared her love and desire for me, and we came away resolved that our love would last for all time and our marriage would work, no matter what.

We each had one individual session with Dr. Ortmeyer after meeting him together the first time. During my session, I learned more about the extreme trauma Kristene suffered as a child at the hands of her mother, a harsh, brutal woman frustrated by the passivity of her husband who was absent from home most of the time as a commercial fisherman. Her mother's physical beatings and emotional abuse had imprinted Kristene with a resistance to strong mindedness so that the previous men in her life were weak, passive types. Now I could understand her comment to me, "You remind me of my mother." My years of military and police experience had stood me well in times of crisis but also made me hard-edged, something I hadn't seen in myself and to which Kristene reacted negatively when she didn't want to. I saw that in spite of my best intentions when I came to Christ, I still lacked true gentleness, patience, and compassion for others, and I needed to work on that.

My love for Kristene made me want to change, to make loving kindness and putting her first my priority. I needed help to do this, and I appealed to the Lord, the essence of my prayers for change being like this: "Please make me conscious of my hard edges. I want to be gentler, like You were when You were here on earth."

"Don't pressure Kristene about having kids," Dr. Ortmeyer counseled the last time I saw him. "That will come with time. She is aware of how much time she has biologically for child bearing. Be patient; she wants a family with you just as much as you do," he told me.

Right after this, Kristene took a sales job close to home at a small children's boutique in Bellevue Square called Tyke Place Market, the name being a clever word play on the historic and famous Pike Place Market on the Seattle waterfront. Its owners were three married couples about our age with little or no business experience but who were from solid, upscale Bellevue families who believed in helping their kids get started in life. The owners were impressed that Kristene's sales know-how boosted sagging post-holiday season revenues out of the red ink.

It was late winter, the nights remained dark, long and cold. Many nights when I came home from work, Kristene had already fixed a large Caesar salad using the best quality olive oil, Greek olives, fresh Romaine and feta cheese, croutons she made herself, garlic bread, and red wine. I built a fire in our living room fireplace, and we spread a picnic cloth out on the floor in front of the fire and ate dinner by firelight, talking, flirting, and seducing each other with our eyes. We pushed our plates aside and played poker, substituting our clothing for chips to its inevitable end, each rejoicing in being either winner or loser in front of the flickering flames.

Meanwhile, the time for my trip with the church team to share our testimony with inmates at the state penitentiary at Walla Walla was postponed from mid-February to late March, and I recognized this as the Lord's timing, giving us more time to settle in, to build the foundation of our marriage and home.

We returned to Neighborhood Church. As hard as it was for Kristene to go back, we already had roots there, and the people were so loving and accepting and wanted us to feel accepted, at home, and not judged. It was a true homecoming. I resumed going to the Saturday morning men's Bible study meetings at the church, where I knew the men had been praying the intercessor's prayer for us all those months, and Kristene went to women's prayer meetings at the church and at Kay's home.

Our marriage was back on track now, surging forward at full speed at a time of a great move of God, an incredibly exciting, historic time to be a Christian; the revival in the Pacific Northwest was in full swing. People from all walks of life were flocking to Neighborhood Church in large numbers, hungry to experience the supernatural power and love of God. The perception that the Holy Spirit was in the sanctuary was just as strong as it was the first time I went there. After most services the space between the front row of pews and the pulpit was packed solid with people responding to the altar call. Dramatic conversions and the gifts of the Holy Spirit of prophecy, tongues and interpretation, word of knowledge, word of wisdom, and physical healing were commonplace. Sermons I heard then still burn within me today, decades later. Word of the happenings there spread everywhere in the community. So well attended were the Sunday services that there were three morning services and one evening service, and the overflow section was always filled. Even the Wednesday night service was so well attended that it was necessary to arrive at least a half hour early to get a seat. It was during these mighty times that we resumed building our marriage, our home, on the foundation of the Gospel, and over the years to come, the foundation laid then would prove itself over and over to be in line with a stanza of that great old hymn, 'The Solid Rock':

"My hope is built on nothing less
Than Jesus' blood and righteousness;
I dare not trust the sweetest frame,
But wholly lean on Jesus' name.
On Christ, the solid Rock I stand,
All other ground is sinking sand."

We attended a dinner for our prison outreach team at the home of Bob and Louise Calvert. While we men relaxed in the den, the wives gathered in the kitchen, where they embraced Kristene and assured her that she was one of them and they were glad to see her back. It felt good to us to be Christians, to belong to God's family, to be restored, and to have the Lord leading us through circumstantially open doors to be where we should be, for we were being "led beside the still waters" and "made to lie down in green pastures" as it says in Psalm 23. We had reached a place and time of peace and restoration.

Sadly, my parents' reaction was a different story. Instead of being glad that Kristene and I were together again, my parents seemed disappointed that Kristene was back. My father and his wife Jeanne were skeptical about us, as if it wouldn't really last, for after all, *nobody* could really be this happy. My mother could barely bring herself to be civil to Kristene and began spreading negative comments about her to other members of my family, including my daughter, my father, and my father's wife. To her credit, Kristene was gracious to each of my parents, seeking them out on the phone and inviting them to dinner at our home often, ignoring their spiteful behavior and instead "heaping burning coals on their heads" with kindness, as it says to do in the Bible.

An unexpected dark side to Kristene working at Bellevue Square was that stalkers seemed to come from out of nowhere. At first it was an expensive gold heart necklace encrusted with genuine diamonds and rubies that was sent anonymously to her at work; even my fellow detectives were unable to identify the sender. Then there were anonymous calls Kristene received at work just before closing. The calls were from at least two or maybe three different men, but there was one caller in particular who called her the most and knew her work schedule, repeatedly asking her to meet him after work.

We ignored the calls until Kristene was followed home one night after closing the store, then we worked with mall security to identify the man. When he called again, Kristene agreed to meet him by her car after work in the upper floor of the parking garage. Mall security officers staked out the parking garage while I loosely followed Kristene from the store through the dark, nearly empty parking garage to our car. As I approached, I saw a man I recognized from years ago standing a few feet away in the shadows near our car; when he saw me, he fled on foot before anyone could react, disappearing into the darkness. The next day I learned from mall security that this man (whose name I knew) worked at a certain store in the mall a short distance from where Kristene worked. I went there, but he was not in. I went back at the end of the day, and he was there, ringing up sales at the cash register.

I stood staring at him in the doorway. He instantly recognized me and became visibly frightened. He nervously hurried through a sale with a customer and then disappeared into the back, leaving the other customers standing in line, hiding until I left. A week later I learned from mall security that the man quit the store on short notice in the middle of their investigation of him. After this I had Kristene quit her job.

A new unity began taking root in our extended family at this time. That period, looking back now, was the greatest of times, a golden era. At first it was between the four couples: Kristene and me, her three brothers and their wives. We were in our thirties, the prime of life. Every week someone was getting together: family dinners and holiday gatherings in each others' homes, frequent phone calls, picnics at parks, weekday breakfast and lunch meetings at restaurants. There were lively dinners when all eight of us were together, with Bob and Richard sharing food and cooking ideas, Ron and I talking about politics and the economy, Bob and Ron, the construction men, talking tools and materials' costs, and the women talking about kids, food, what wine Richard brought this time, and beer and specialty breads, and the kids played together. When we met at restaurants, it was just us adults, it was always at a small out-of-the-way place with ambiance and great food, and we dressed up for the occasion. The meals were long and leisurely and consisted of several courses, and happy conversation flowed gently like a brook. Each of these times was an individual tapestry, the fact and memory of which was woven for all time into our family fabric.

And so the eight of us became as one through our camaraderie and the bonds of blood and marriage, the deepest of all ties: Ron and Kay, Bob and his wife Angela and Richard, the life of the party, and his longtime girlfriend Barbara. It was a golden time of harmony, caring and genuine interest in one another, beaming smiles and hugs when we met, and laughing, joking, and ribbing, and the result was a strong sense that we belonged to one another.

But there was more yet: the flourishing roots of this new family dynamic spread outward to include uncles and aunts, nieces and nephews, and cousins all seeing each other not out of duty as in funerals and weddings, but out of preference. Kristene was the leader in building this next level of family cohesion; she did it through personal visits, phone calls, remembering birthdays, and staying in touch out of genuine love and acceptance; sowing the seeds of honor, building unity.

March arrived before we knew it, the month of my birthday, and Kristene was so quiet about it that I was wondering if she had forgotten or if she had made surprise plans; she hadn't given the slightest hint. On my birthday, I went home right after work, expecting to see her, but the house was empty. I noticed a large cardboard box with a shipping label on it in the living room, and there was a note taped to the kitchen phone. I read the note, written in Kristene's rounded cursive style, that read, "Darling, I got called back to work this afternoon. See you later tonight. Love You, Your Wife." Disappointed, "Oh, no," I groaned as I walked toward the bedroom.

Suddenly the box in the living room burst open at the top, and out popped Kristene, her hourglass figure clad only in a one-piece blue swimsuit.

"Happy birthday, my darling! Happy birthday to my love! Happy birthday to you!" she sang, arms uplifted, smiling and laughing, embracing me. Dinner came much later.

"So Jacob served seven years to get Rachel, but they seemed like only a few days to him because of his love for her."
Genesis 29:20

CHAPTER ELEVEN

The jolly mood of our band of five men from Neighborhood Church evaporated the instant we arrived in our borrowed passenger van at the Walla Walla State Penitentiary. The six-hour drive enabled us to become better acquainted, and laugh and joke as well as pray together on our way, but the gray morning cold and an eerie gloom enhanced the grimness of the brooding gray prison walls and buildings when we arrived, silencing friendly banter. After brief introductions with prison officials, we were taken on a courtesy tour that included seeing the pack of Bloodhounds kenneled outside the prison wall, kept and trained to track down escaped prisoners. Seeing this in the Northwest surprised me, for I had only associated dogs and their handlers tracking down escaped prisoners with the Deep South.

A stout, stern-faced uniformed guard escorted us through a series of security procedures and electronically controlled steel doors.

"Okay now, which one of these men is the cop and which is the ex-con?" a grinning Bob Calvert asked the deadpan guard. Monte Christensen was standing with me inside a glass partition, waiting for the sound of the buzzer and the metal clang to let us proceed to the chapel. Pointing at me, he said,

"Hah – that's easy," he said, pointing at me, "that big one, he's got cop written all over him. That other one, though, he don't look like he's been in."

Another burley guard with forearms thick with muscle, and meaty hands like hams met us at the last door and escorted us across the prison yard to the chapel. One whack from either arm could put a man down, I concluded. The guard strolled casually alongside us and exchanged friendly greetings with some of the inmates by first names. Inmates pumping iron in the exercise yard stopped to stare as we walked by; cold stares, hard faces. I felt eyes upon us from everywhere, not only the yard but from cell block windows and the guard towers where riflemen watched with binoculars. In the eyes of all who saw us, we were fresh meat. In spite of the daylight, the atmosphere felt dark, heavy, permeated by evil and oppression. Knowing that we were in the bowels of hell on earth, knowing we were ward to a few and prey to others, gave me a cold knot in my gut, yet I sensed God's favor. My being here now was His will and timing.

My attitudes against these men were hardened by years of helping crime victims, who were usually betrayed or forgotten by the criminal justice system in favor of the criminal. I considered for a moment that an inmate might recognize me, but I shrugged it off: so what, I concluded. As we neared the chapel building, I reminded myself that I was there to reach lost men. I took my biases into account and set them aside, and determined to accept and strengthen these men as potential brothers in Christ.

"The ex-con and the cop, brothers in Christ" was the theme of our visit to inmates in the oldest and most notorious prison on the far side of Washington State. Tall, lean, and handsome as a movie star, Monte was a Montana boy who wound up serving multiple life sentences for a list of drug-related offenses when he received Christ as his Savior. Over a remarkably short time and against overwhelming odds, Monte was paroled to his wife, Holly, and their little son, Jared. I met Monte and Holly through Neighborhood Church, and in spite of our opposing backgrounds, we bonded quickly. When they came to Bellevue, they lived in a little yellow rental house, a house where I was guest of honor at many a dinner, where I spent hours fellowshipping with Monte. Monte supported his family as a finish carpenter, but his heart yearned for men in prison to know Christ as he had and he took every opportunity to volunteer in every jail and prison ministry that opened for him. Over time Monte's incredible story of God's love, forgiveness, and renewal was told in a book entitled *70 x 7 and Beyond* that has been reprinted many times and continues to win souls to Christ.

The chapel was completely packed; standing room only. Inmates of every race and age group, clad in blue denim prison uniforms, sat together, their faces reflecting eager anticipation. Quite a few of the men had brought their own Bibles with them, and the openness and acceptance of the inmates was a surprise to me.

I briefly told of my two-fisted lifestyle that resulted in personal upheaval and broken relationships until I came to the end of myself, repented, and asked Christ into my life, earnestly seeking change. The men relaxed and laughed with me when I told them I was a living example of God's grace: if I had been caught for half the things I had done, I would be seated among them now, listening to Bob, Monte and the others. They listened intently as I related how for three years I lived alone after coming to Christ, practically a hermit, seeking and serving God, my old friends leaving me, until eventually the Lord blessed me with a wife of His choosing. "I couldn't have done better if I had designed her myself, boys," I said. The men smiled and nodded, savoring the fact that a stranger bearing Good News was also sharing something of his personal life with them.

Perseverance in Christ rather than going my own way had paid off over time for me, I told them, proving that the Lord's ways are higher than ours. It took time, I related, but my new life now in every respect exceeded my best hopes. I urged the men to do the same: come to Christ, repent of your old ways, receive the Holy Spirit, and follow Him wholeheartedly; persevere no matter what. I was surprised and humbled when these men applauded me as I finished, and I felt a new satisfaction in being used by God to reach men for Him.

Monte Christensen spoke to the men as one of them, a former prisoner locked up for life without hope. Men leaned forward in rapt attention as Monte shared the details of his crimes, the grip of demonic influences on his mind and heart brought on by drugs, the severity of multiple consecutive sentences, and the agony and devastation he had caused his family. The men hung on his every word as he told of receiving Christ in a wrenching conversion experience, the peace that followed, and how God worked behind the scenes to preserve his family and soften the hearts of the parole board and ultimately the release he thought would never happen. At the altar call at the end of Monte's sermon, nearly every man stood up to accept Christ, either for the first time or to rededicate himself.

We spread out to pray individually with the men. The inmates who brought their Bibles helped us pray with and for their fellow prisoners. The chaplain explained later that these men assisted him as elders and deacons of the body of Christ at Walla Walla.

I prayed with man after man, leading each one in the sinner's prayer, asking forgiveness of sin and to receive Christ as personal Savior and the Holy Spirit. As many inmates waited patiently for us to pray with them, the verse from Matthew 9:37 came to mind: "The harvest is plentiful but the workers are few."

I was amazed to see how many times the facial expressions of these men changed as emotions broke through upon receiving Christ. Lives were being changed dramatically. As I observed how good I felt then, it occurred to me that giving is better than receiving.

I called Kristene from a pay phone to hear her voice before the long drive home. She had been praying for me and the men with me, that lives would be changed as a result of our outreach. Hearing Kristene's voice was like cool water in scorching heat; just the few minutes of the call replenished and strengthened me.

Indescribable peace and satisfaction flooded us when I returned home. We were in the very center of God's will. God was pleased with us. He had hand-crafted our marriage; He had personally fitted us together; it was a seamless fit that anyone could see. We were pleased and satisfied beyond words to have each other, and the world before us was fresh and new and clean.

Spring arrived in western Washington. Warmth and soft breezes came, along with some sunshine now and then, and we began fixing up the house. It troubled me that I had been through two previous marriages that failed in that same little house, but not Kristene. She rolled up her sleeves and went to work, making it *our* home. With warmer weather coming, we began planning our first project, to repair and repaint the exterior.

I thought of the men in the penitentiary as I returned to work. My fellow detectives paid only polite interest in hearing about my experience at Walla Walla. Like I was before my trip, their sympathies ran toward the victims the violators left behind them. But as a result of going to Walla Walla, I saw criminals not as enemies but as lost men at the bottom, men God wanted to rescue.

My supervisor tossed a stack of new theft and burglary cases onto my desk as he walked through the detectives' office, which we called the bull pen. I stared at the new stack and the unread stack from last week. Getting back in the groove would be tough. My desk phone rang, and I picked up.

"Hello!" shouted an older-sounding male voice.

"Is anybody home there at the Bellevue PD? Do you guys do anything besides take reports?" I calmed him down enough to talk.

"I'm David Sullivan. Two weeks ago I reported the theft of all of our belongings from a storage facility here, and no one has called me. Your records people told me our case was assigned to you."

I found his theft report and met him and his wife at the storage facility. The two empty units that had once held their belongings were twelve-by-twelve-by-twelve feet; each had been filled to the ceiling with handmade furnishings from twenty years of living in the Middle East.

I photographed the units and arranged with the facility management to view the security video tapes in a few days.

Working shoulder to shoulder with Kristene on house projects, I learned more about her strong artistic talents and planning skills. The wood exterior of our home still had the original "harvest gold" stain, a popular color of the early '70s era when the house was built. Red-brick fascia was on either side of the garage that had been filled in to make a family room. Wet Northwest weather had cupped and cracked the siding on the south and west sides, and everywhere the stain was almost completely worn through, even green with mold in places, making the house look small and dumpy. Gray was a popular color in home decorating in the early 1980s, along with red oak and ceramic tile. We worked together prepping the house on weekdays after work and Saturdays, pressure washing the exterior, treating the moldy areas with bleach. I replaced cupped and cracked siding with new boards, filled minor cracks and holes with silicone caulking, and applied primer to the whole exterior with a brush.

Kristene tried different shades of premixed solid gray stain on the wall, but none were quite right. She took a chip of brick from the front of the house to have the paint store custom mix a medium-gray solid stain that was cut with stain the same red as the brick. How such a simple move caused the resulting shade of gray to fit so perfectly with the brick front was amazing, yet the red itself was indiscernible to the eye. Simple me, I laughed at myself: she must be amused at how easily impressed I am. I was just beginning to learn that Kristene was a woman of many talents, and how much I was a blessed man.

We had to wait for my next payday to buy enough stain and supplies to paint the whole house. As the weather warmed enough to open the pores of the siding for staining, my request for two weeks of vacation was approved. The timing was perfect.

We began the work; money was tight. Buying the stain, primer, brushes, and other equipment consumed our disposable cash and some of our grocery money. Oatmeal was cheap; it and black coffee was our breakfast every morning before we began painting, and often it was our lunch too. We were up with the sun and worked together until it went down, applying the stain by brush instead of roller or sprayer so we would have a long-lasting, quality job. So in love were we that we often slipped back inside the house. Something about seeing Kristene standing on a ladder, paint brush in hand, dressed in paint-stained grubbies yet intensely feminine, her long, dark hair pulled up under an old ball cap, and paint spatter on her ivory cheeks, made her irresistible.

Often I would take the brush out of her hand, set it on the bucket, and help her back down the ladder, she softly protesting "What are you doing, Honey?" and "Where are you taking me?" (As if she didn't know). I led her inside the house and onto the living room carpet.

"Shhh, just be quiet and do everything the nice policeman tells you," I suggested.

Removing her ball cap and shaking her heavy, dark hair onto her shoulders, Kristene smirked, "Oh! Well, if you say so, Officer."

Every night after the sun went down we fixed simple, cheap dinners, usually green salad, oil and vinegar, bread, and the cheapest red wine Kristene could find, and we talked and flirted and loved until sleep came.

The final touch to the project was to paint the metal front door the same terra cotta red as the brick trim. It was a labor of love, and the result was magnificent. The medium gray siding, with window and door trim painted a darker gray, all of it cut with the terra cotta red of the brick trim, gave our home a snap of crisp and clean, colors and subtle hues masterfully fit one another in a harmony pleasing to the eye. It had a sense of *rightness* about it. It was warm and snug and intended to be, like our marriage.

Our home looked brand-spanking new as I backed out of the driveway to return to work. Small as it was, our labor of love had transformed a simple little tract house into the house that people noticed when they drove by, and it made me feel pleased and satisfied. Tan and feeling fit from outdoor work, I settled in to work the Sullivan case. Leads were piling up. The security video tapes revealed a large rental truck occupied by two men and a blond woman making multiple trips in and out of the storage facility between Christmas and New Year's. The total estimated worth of the stolen furnishings was almost $200,000. It might be just a property theft, but my instincts told me this case was big and would lead to bigger things. To the near exclusion of other cases, I pursued leads on the Sullivan theft case daily.

We spent a lot of time with Ron and Kay that summer. There were frequent dinners, barbecues, and picnics, to which we brought Sara with us as often as we could on visitation weekends. We went to the beaches of Lake Washington after work on warm days, swimming out to the wooden lifeguard's raft and back and laying in the sun, basking in its heat and the smells of warm lake water and green grass and the laughs and yells of swimmers and boaters and the water softly lapping the shore.

Ron and Sally Mebust, a handsome blond couple from our church, invited us to go ocean charter boat fishing with them, and the memory of this trip gets me grinning to this day. We went to Westport, a small fishing town on the Washington coast where Kristene's family was living when she was born. We checked into a small, two-story motel there that had acquired a rustic look from the weathering of its cedar siding. The four of us rented motor scooters and raced around the beach and along the narrow roads. Kristene led us to the house that her family lived in when she was born at the hospital in Aberdeen, several miles away. We ate lunch and dinner at a little mom-and-pop place right on the waterfront that served the freshest fish and chowder, the best I had ever had and at the cheapest prices. We checked into our room early and made love before falling asleep.

"Everybody up! Everybody up! Boats are leaving in twenty minutes. All fishermen be at your boat, report to your skipper in twenty minutes!"

I looked at my watch: 3:30 a.m., still dark. I looked out the window as the message was being repeated. A man wearing a flannel shirt with a battery-powered bullhorn was standing in the bed of an older pickup truck that was idling along the street in front of the motels.

"Time to get dressed, Honey," I said.

We met Ron and Sally outside and grabbed a quick breakfast of dry toast, coffee, and hard-boiled eggs. I took a pill of Dramamine for seasickness, and we boarded our boat with about ten other passengers. The sky and the water were both a cold black-grey as our boat busted through white-capped waves, heading for the mouth of the harbor where the famous and dreaded Westport Bar lay at the bottom.

Beyond the bar the waves were higher and steeper, and the boat pitched, rolled, yawed, and then fell straight down like a free-falling elevator racing to the bottom and crashing mightily when it got there. I could feel myself getting sick. To avoid it, I stood at the bow, facing into the wind, and kept my eyes on the horizon that was just now becoming visible. Meanwhile my wife, the fisherman's daughter, was thoroughly enjoying the ride. I had moved back to a place on the forward deck where I could sit leaning against the pilot's cabin, too woozy from nausea to stand, struggling to hold down my breakfast. Kristene, dressed head-to-toe in a yellow rubber rain-suit, took my place at the very forward end of the boat. Every time the boat would slip off the face of a steep wave and fall through the air, crashing onto the bottom of the trough so that salt spray drenched us, all she could say was, "Oh wow! How awesome was that!" while clutching the bow rail, completely drenched.

"Hey, Honey! You're green! Are you okay?" Kristene called to me.

I was now curled almost in a fetal position on the deck against the cabin, watching her, my embarrassment competing with my seasickness to see which could make me throw up first.

I raced to the rail and began throwing up as we reached the fishing waters, and the skipper slowed the boat to an idle. In my mind's eye, I could just see the fish below the surface racing to get to my last meal as

I white-knuckled the rail. The bait boy went to work helping us bait our hooks with fresh herring and letting out the right amount of line, and of course I was continuing to draw the fish. I saw my breakfast followed by last night's dinner come up and hit the water. With meekness did I lower my baited hook into the water, and with even greater meekness I saw my bride immediately land her first large king salmon. Ron's wife Sally was just as sick as me and sat next to me after her line was in the water. Kristene and Ron thought this was very funny, but I was too sick to care; my pride went overboard into the water along with my last donation. Both Kristene and Ron quickly caught their limit of fish, Kristene's second salmon being another large king. To add insult to injury, even Sally caught a fish while her pole was in the pole holder. Hours passed, and I was beginning to feel better. At last the tip of my pole began jerking up and down, and I grabbed it from the holder. I reeled in a small silver salmon that was barely big enough to legally keep. The sea had fortuitously pitied me and granted a nice little token. Photographs were taken of each of us holding our fish; mine being the smallest and me being the joke of the day. It was all great fun among good friends, and it is a treasured memory to this day.

Fishing boat dock at Westport. Our charter
boat left here to fish the open ocean.

John suffers seasickness and jokes alongside Sally Mebust while Kristene
and Ron Mebust laugh and catch fish.

The end of male ego. A happy Kristene carries her large salmon over her
shoulder; John's tiny fish in a bag on top of small cooler.

CHAPTER TWELVE

Heating your home with a wood-burning stove was all the rage in the Pacific Northwest during the 1980s. Just about everybody was using a freestanding stove or fireplace insert, and firewood, especially alder, was so cheap and plentiful in the nearby public forests that significant savings in home heating costs could be had with a modest investment. Burn bans and air quality alerts were unheard of then. During the summer we bought a Jotul brand stove on sale with our tax refund. It was made in Norway, sturdily built of double-walled cast iron, painted cranberry red, and was our first major purchase. We set it up in a nook near the kitchen table, out of the way yet centrally located so its radiant heat would warm even the bedrooms on a cold day. As much as we liked hot weather, we were eager for cooler temperatures to justify lighting the stove.

A born bargain hunter and deal driver, Kristene brought home beautiful high-end accessories for the stove at absurdly low prices.

"Look what I found, Honey!" she would say.

Heavy rustic handmade solid brass buckets, one large one for the large firewood, a smaller one for kindling, a copper teapot and matching trivet to keep the teapot off the stove as water boiled to humidify the air, just sort of followed her home. I had seen some of these accessories at retail stores and knew what they cost, so I was shocked when I saw the receipts showing Kristene had paid a pittance.

When I learned how far she had driven these deals, out of embarrassment I quit asking, figuring the best way to protect my reputation in the community was to stay as ignorant as possible and not be seen with her in stores.

Our finances then were a case of squeaking from payday to payday, between which we could barely put two nickels together, because everything we brought in, we spent making our house a home. Our first arguments were about money. Kristene often spent beyond our bank balance, to which her defense was almost always something like, "But, Baby, it was on sale!"

Of course, Kristene's explanations were about as plausible as if she had said 'How could I be overdrawn? I still have checks!' She was too beautiful to resist, and I loved her too much to win a fight on principle, so I arranged with the manager at our bank for Kristene's checks to be covered by overdraft. That done, my ignorance-is-bliss policy, though not very responsible of me, worked well nonetheless. In my chosen state of deliberate ignorance, I could go about my work and be able to concentrate and enjoy our evenings and weekends together.

Work was going well, and the Sullivan theft case was no exception. After exhausting all leads, I asked the Lord for a break. Two days later, David Sullivan called me to say that his adult daughter found their couch and a chair in a West Seattle antique store. I immediately met the family there. The furniture pieces were as described in detail in the theft report, and they were returned to the Sullivans. The store owner's purchase records identified the seller as Joe Burns, with a Bellevue address. A records check indicated Burns had a history of felony charges and convictions. Further investigation revealed that Joe Burns had recently returned to Washington from California with his wife, Connie. I found them living in Ocean Park, a small town on the Long Beach Peninsula of the Washington coast.

I obtained arrest warrants for Joe and Connie Burns and arranged to meet with Deputy Staudenraus of the Pacific County Sheriff's Office in Long Beach. The Sullivans agreed to meet me there to identify and recover any of their belongings we might find. Because this was a weekend trip, I obtained permission to bring Kristene with me as my assistant.

Ocean Park is a small beachfront community on the Pacific Ocean that is entirely dependent on tourist trade. We met Dale Staudenraus at the Pacific County Sheriff's substation in Long Beach. Over six feet four inches tall, lean and solidly built, sporting a thick black mustache, his dark green Stetson accentuating his height, Staudenraus' imposing presence personified the Law in this rural county. We followed him to the small rental house in Ocean Park where Joe and Connie Burns were staying. The front yard was littered with trash, old car and refrigerator parts, and broken furniture. Another uniformed deputy joined us, and we went to the door.

A gaunt but still attractive woman appearing to be in her late thirties with neck-length wavy blonde hair let us in. The deputies knew her as Connie Burns. She looked hard and older than her actual age. Her thinness was the kind that hard drug use produces; in her case it was heroin. Joe was not home, she told us, and she didn't know where he was, or when he would be back. After she was taken into custody on the basis of my arrest warrant, Connie told us that she and Joe and a Seattle friend named Rocky stole the furniture in Bellevue and sold it to Mexican gang leader in return for heroin. She gave us written permission to search the premises, and then she was taken away for booking. I let the Sullivans in to walk through the house with me; they identified several rugs and artifacts that had been stolen from them. Kristene assisted me in logging and photographing the evidence and taking written statements from the Sullivans so they could take it home with them. At the end of the day, we were hungry and wanted to see the beach.

Always ask a cop where to eat when in a strange town. The deputies directed us to a ramshackle mom-and-pop seafood joint for dinner.

"Don't let the condition of the building fool you—the food there is the best," they told us. We weren't disappointed. The building looked as if it was built in the 1930s and not maintained since then. Gray rotted wood clapboard siding looked ready to slide off onto the ground, and old wood plank floors, covered with threadbare area rugs, sagged and creaked as the waitress guided us to our table. But O, the food! Oyster stew made the right way, a bucket of steamed mussels and clams, salmon, wild and fresh, grilled over an alder wood fire, done to perfection, all with chilled white wine. Stuffed, we checked into a new hotel on the beach and drove out as far onto the beach as we dared to watch the sunset before going back to the hotel, where we opened windows to catch the sound of the pounding surf, and the ocean breezes, us loving passionately.

In the morning we joined the Sullivans for breakfast and walked with them through the antique shops in Long Beach. The first shop we went to had several small rugs, called kilims, and wood furniture pieces that the Sullivans identified as theirs. While we waited for Deputy Staudenraus to arrive, the shop owner refused to give us any information regarding how he acquired the property. When Deputy Staudenraus walked into the shop, the short, slight, bespectacled owner wouldn't answer his questions either.

"This is an invasion of my privacy. I'm terribly sorry for these poor people, but I bought these things legally, and they're mine now. If they want them back, they'll have to reimburse me," he said.

His thumbs hooked into his gun belt, Staudenraus stared down at the short, slight, bespectacled proprietor. The deputy dwarfed him in both stature and presence, yet there was a kindly patience and firmness in his voice when he spoke next.

"Okay then: you're done doin' business today. Close 'er up right now and tell your customers to leave, as a police investigation is underway. You do it or I will," the Law said. Customers had overheard the confrontation, and had begun easing silently out of the shop on their own, like mists that fade away when the sun rises.

"Now, now, now, Deputy, wait! *Wait!* You—you just can't—I mean, you can't! You just can't!" whined the nervous shopkeeper.

"I can't?" echoed the Law. "You're knowingly in possession of stolen property that you're tryin' to sell while the rightful owners are standing right here. You're runnin' an illegal operation. It's called fencing. Keep talkin' and we'll see what I can and can't do."

The shop owner sighed loudly as he threw up his hands in surrender. "Okay, Deputy, but what about the money I paid for this stuff—cash money! How can I get my money back if you're taking the property?"

"I'm not *taking* the property," the Law corrected. "You are *voluntarily returning* it to the owners it was stolen from. And you're *voluntarily* giving me copies of your sales receipts and a statement regarding your purchase of these things. If you can't get your money back from the Burnses, or the judge in Seattle who hears this case, it's your loss," Dale said.

"Yeah, I guess so," sighed the owner.

The shop owner admitted that he and other merchants had been buying merchandise for their antique shops from Joe and Connie Burns for months. Joe and Connie Burns were locally known as unemployed drug addicts. That and the volume of property they suddenly came into plus the low prices they were asking made all the shop owners suspect it was stolen, but no one dared or cared to ask. We found and recovered more property belonging to the Sullivans in other antique and second-hand shops in Long Beach and Ocean Park, all of it purchased from Joe or Connie Burns. The Sullivans rented a moving truck to haul everything back to Seattle. Kristene worked with me taking statements and itemizing the recovered evidence. Before the day ended, we were all invited to dinner at the Staudenraus home that evening.

Stiff ocean winds buffeted our car as we followed Dale's directions to his beachfront home, where he and his wife Margaret greeted us warmly at the door. We removed our shoes to avoid tracking sand inside, and Dale took our jackets. It was a traditional Northwest-style home with cedar shingle siding, a steep-pitched roof, high ceilings, and enormous picture windows facing the pounding surf of the Pacific Ocean. We followed the aroma of simmering spaghetti sauce, pasta noodles boiling on the stove, and garlic bread warming in the oven into the kitchen. Wine was served in the adjoining great room as wind gusts shook the windows, peppering them with sand and salt spray. Before we could ask, Dale told us the windows were double layered tempered plate glass, able to withstand ocean storms.

We settled down to an unforgettable evening of good food, good wine, hearing the Sullivans' stories of life in the Middle East, and how each piece of the furniture they brought home with them had a story behind it. Dale, it turned out, had lived and worked in Bellevue as a butcher in his younger years and knew some of the officers who were now my superiors. Margaret Staudenraus, a very pretty and perceptive brunette, picked up on our honeymoon glow and asked us many questions with an admiring and genuine interest that made us feel special. And so we relaxed into one of those rare evenings that you never forget, that you wish would never end; sharing and laughing with new friends at the end of a shared adventure, good food, and the warm ambiance of a loving home like the Staudenraus's. Life was good.

We fairly floated home the next day in our happy state with loads of evidence logs, written statements, notes, and rolls of undeveloped film, all of which was used to charge and convict Joe and Connie Burns for felony theft and possession of stolen property. At home we resumed our enjoyment of a lazy summer, weekday afternoons on the beaches of Lake Washington, church on Sundays and Wednesdays, barbecues and picnics with Ron and Kay, visiting relatives, sneaking our own popcorn and soda into matinees at movie theaters, living on the cheap, sharing meals at restaurants, and meeting at home for nooners instead of lunch. Frugal Kristene shopped sales and clipped coupons, and we saved and planned all summer for our next home renovation project, the interior.

We were dead broke and between paydays when we celebrated the miracle of our first wedding anniversary, but it didn't matter. We were happy just to go to the lake, share a pizza, and exchange cards. We felt blessed to have each other and a home, loving relatives, good friendships, meaningful work, and the knowledge that we were at the right place at the right time. There would be other anniversaries when we could afford to celebrate more elaborately. We were on the receiving end of God's special grace to us, and it was more than enough. I was a blessed man.

The first bite of fall weather came at the end of August. Crisp, cold mornings became warm, sunny days followed by cool, clear evenings; the woods were alive with vibrant colors as leaves changed to red and gold, a time of harvest, a season-within-a-season that usually lasts until mid-October. I was gathering firewood from public and private forests, cutting, splitting, and hauling alder and Douglas Fir logs in my big Dodge pickup, stacking it on the south side of the house where the weather would dry and season it for burning. Kristene made trips into the countryside, where she bought fresh local produce, Indian corn still in the husk, pumpkins, and gourds that she used to adorn the front door and entry and the rest of the house to honor the season.

Every morning I loaded the stove and started the fire, refilled the water kettle and the brass buckets with more firewood and kindling, and then dialed down the fire to a slow, steady burn once the fire was hot enough that the smoke coming out the chimney was invisible. We were able to leave the furnace off even on the coldest days. The logs would burn slowly and evenly all day while we were at work, and the dry warmth that filled the house felt like a warm hug when we came through the front door at night. Our heat bills fell below fifteen dollars per month for nearly six months on a single cord of wood that cost less than forty dollars. It was fun and rewarding to heat our home this way.

I was working more overtime as we entered the holiday season and the extra pay made it possible to hire professional help to do the work on our home that was beyond our skills.

We ripped wood paneling and fake brick from the walls, replacing it with subtle and sophisticated wallpaper and paint that Kristene carefully selected. I tore into one bathroom and then the other, each time installing waterproof sheetrock and sealant, then putting up new tile in the shower stall and the tub surround that we selected together. Tiling was painstakingly slow work for me, but the end result was well worth it: the tiles were level and straight, grout and caulking lines clean and crisp. I installed the latest in European linoleum on the floors, but new countertops and sinks I left to a professional. We worked weekday evenings until late and a few hours on Saturdays, but on Sundays we honored the Sabbath by dressing up for church and resting and visiting with family and friends.

God kept surprising us with new ways to honor us for honoring Him: there was a harmony and a sense of right timing about everything we did or undertook. In our home remodeling it seemed an unseen hand was making sure that deadlines were met, people kept their word to us; opportunities and blessings of all kinds seemed to find *us* and fall into our laps. Our money somehow seemed to go farther, and people with the right skills and materials prices seemed to come to us from out of nowhere, so that the end result was a beautiful home interior, exquisitely appointed wood plank flooring, kitchen tile work, custom countertops and wallpaper. As our home took shape, we entertained guests there more frequently than before, and we were content to just spend time there ourselves.

Our hunger for God and our interest in spiritual things increased as a result of His blessing us. The sanctuary at Neighborhood Church continued to be completely filled four times on Sundays and again on Wednesday nights; many services ran overtime as the area between the front pews and the pulpit was packed with mourners who knelt, sat, or lay face-down on the floor, prostrate before the Almighty, weeping and pouring their souls out to God, pastors and elders moving gently among them, praying over and laying hands on them. We also attended Catholic charismatic services around the Seattle area, usually on Friday or Sunday evenings. Because the Catholic Church didn't officially recognize the gifts of the Spirit, these meetings were mostly in the church basement or an auditorium if the church had a school, but never in the church sanctuary. On a few occasions, we went with Ron and Kay, who were in the process of being led away from the Catholic Church, but most of the time we went by ourselves.

While attending these services with Kristene, I saw in her the truth of the saying, "Once a Catholic, always a Catholic," as tears flooded her eyes as we joined throngs of charismatic Catholic believers who worshipped and even danced before the Lord in the way I imagine King David must have danced when the ark was being returned to Jerusalem. The gentle sweetness of the Catholic believers opened my eyes to the power and mercy of God and the diversity of His Kingdom. Theirs was a deep faith, founded upon years of formal training to accept what the priests taught, and their tone was decidedly softer, more meek, and reserved compared to the fiery zeal of black and white Pentecostal congregations.

As we hungered for more of God, I wanted to experience a Messianic Jewish service in order to understand more about the Lord and His Kingdom. I found just such a congregation in Bellevue, and we took Sara with us when we attended the first time, when a unique Christian rock band called "Lamb" was playing. "Lamb" was a group of Jewish rock musicians, and their music somehow blended Jewish traditional music with messianic worship and rock and roll. The lyrics inspired joyful worship, and rhythmic beat led to everyone hand clapping followed by everyone dancing, hand-in-hand, in a big circle; it was great fun that went on for hours, and the presence of the Holy Spirit was palpable.

As we grew spiritually and savored the things of God together, our love deepened in ways we could never have imagined. For one thing, a romantic paradox developed between us: The peace and sense of belonging we had with one another was like an inexhaustible well in a dry land that continually refreshed us with the deepest satisfaction, yet at the same time we thirsted insatiably for each other, desiring to literally crawl inside each other, if possible, so strong was our desire to be not two but one. We were so powerfully drawn to each other, we were like a pair of magnets, but then how could I not be with someone as stunning as Kristene?

It was not lost on us that our persevering in the spiritual disciplines of time in prayer, Bible reading and fellowship had a cumulative effect on our relationship, making our devotion and love for each other as dependable and unconditional as the rising of the sun every morning. It was beyond mere physical attraction now; my love and desire for Kristene would never be lessened by ravages of sickness and old age, should they come, and her love for me was the same.

A byproduct of our being so spiritually united was that no matter how far apart we were at times, each always knew the thoughts of the other. We became able to perceive approaching danger, tragedy, and seasons of blessing. We called this phenomenon, "One mind, one heart, one spirit," and we knew the Lord's protection was upon us.

"Those who trust in the Lord are like Mount Zion which cannot be shaken but endures forever.

As the mountains surround Jerusalem, so the Lord surrounds His people both now and forevermore."
Psalm 125: 1,2

'May 1981. Our courtship included working together on the house

Back together. Our first portrait after reuniting. 1982

Our first home. Kristene with Kaiser in driveway

Kaiser and Jaeger enjoy a warm stove on a cold night

CHAPTER THIRTEEN

Having Kristene with me on the trip to Ocean Park worked magic on the outcome of the case, for when Joe Burns was arrested and transferred to the King County Jail in Seattle, the details of his confession exposed previously unknown Mexican Mafia drug activity that was buying up small businesses with its heroin and marijuana profits. A local pimp, drug dealer, and heroin addict known as Rocky had introduced Joe to the leader of the gang. Joe described Rocky's apartment in the Capitol Hill area and said he and Connie traded several rugs and paintings there to Rocky for heroin. I began working with Seattle undercover detectives Milo Walker and Duane Lewis, both of whom knew Rocky as a heroin addict, drug pusher, and pimp with an extensive history of drug-related offenses.

Armed with a search warrant, Detectives Walker and Lewis and I stepped into the dark gloom of Rocky's apartment on Cherry Street in the Capitol Hill area of Seattle, where on a sunny afternoon the drapes were drawn, the walls were painted dark brown and red, and table lamps emitted a weak, evil, yellowish glow. A musty-smelling, busted-down sofa and chair and the pungent odor of burning incense gave the place the feel of an old-time den of iniquity where entering souls were lost forever. A very beautiful young girl in her early twenties was sitting in the middle of the living room floor; her only interest in sleazy Rocky could be his dope. Another bad sign for Rocky was that he knew both detectives by name. Rocky verbally challenged us in an irritating nasal whine intended to impress his female prey that he could handle the cops; he posed as her protector. But the girl wasn't buying it. She was panicked by our arrival and begged us to let her leave. Walker and Lewis checked her for warrants and let her go. She left in a hurry without a word to Rocky. It angered me to see such a young girl starting down the heroin road that would lead to prostitution and an early grave, all under Rocky's guidance, and I wondered where her parents were, and if they knew or cared.

In his thirties but old before his time, Rocky was a thin slip of foul flesh. He was short, gaunt, and stoop shouldered, with thin, greasy black hair that flopped over his forehead, dark circles under his eyes, and loose skin having the grayish yellow of a longtime drugger. As soon as the girl scurried off, he whined, begged, and groveled, offering to work as an informant for us in a nasal tone of voice. There was no one Rocky wouldn't snitch on to get himself out of trouble.

The stolen property listed on our search warrant was in plain view in Rocky's living room, and I arrested him for it on the spot. They were all small items: rugs, lamps, and Middle Eastern paintings in antique wooden frames. As I lugged the property out to my car, Rocky became a tough guy again; he wouldn't talk to us without an attorney. When I handcuffed him, Rocky reverted to offering to turn in lesser dealers in return for his freedom. None of his deals held any interest for us. He said he was afraid to give up "the Mexican Mafia guy," whom Rocky said was "seriously federal." We booked Rocky into the King County Jail, knowing it wouldn't be long before his habit would drive him to see things our way. I logged in the evidence, made out my report, and went home.

The long hours I was working were a test of the strength of our young marriage. I was working overtime almost every night, riding the streets of Seattle with Milo and Duane to establish Rocky's reliability as an informant as he made controlled drug buys. Rocky agreed to the prosecutor's offer to work off the stolen property charge in return for setting up the Mexican drug dealer he had introduced to Joe and Connie Burns.

Kristene never complained about my being away so much; she knew it was temporary. Instead, she found ways to draw closer to me without interfering with my demanding schedule: quick meetings for coffee or lunch, love cards left for me at the station, "I love you" and "I miss you" phone calls. She would get up early with me for coffee and iron a fresh shirt for me while I was in the shower. She would look me over before I left the house to see if everything was right. She always ironed my dress shirts, and if she thought my shoes weren't shined enough, she polished them with me standing in them. So here was this beautiful brunette, kneeling in front of me, polishing my shoes out of love for me, her man.

"Don't you dare tell those guys I do this for you!" she would warn me. I just grinned; I was a blessed man indeed.

The months peeled away like pages of a calendar being thumbed through quickly. Every hour I wasn't working I spent with Kristene. To be with her more, I suspended men's fellowship meetings and church activities except for Sundays. I hungered for *her* and wanted to be with *her*. The overtime pay was enough that I rebuilt our savings, and when time permitted, I could afford to take Kristene out to dinner at a nice restaurant, a movie, or a play.

As busy as I was, I made a point of keeping up my daily prayer life, for without that all effort was for naught. Rising early to be alone with the Lord before Kristene got up, I prayed and gave thanks for Kristene and our marriage. I asked God's help to be a better husband, father, son, and brother. I prayed for the salvation of each one of our unsaved relatives and close friends. Kristene often prayed with me over my caseload, case by case. As there are thirty-one chapters in Proverbs, the book of wisdom for daily living, and thirty-one days in most months, it was my custom to read a chapter a day of Proverbs and the Psalms, and I made it my practice to pray aloud whenever I was alone in my detective car.

It now became clear to me that an immutable law of life, the Law of Reciprocity, was working to my benefit. In James 5 the Bible says the prayers of the consistently righteous are powerful and effective. I had focused on living the faith consistently for five years, and perhaps the most obvious effect was that God was answering my prayers quickly and powerfully, and it seemed that every case I prayed over unfolded swiftly, and in unexpected ways. New developments in the Sullivan case were happening every week. The drug dealer who received the Sullivans' property, identified as John V., was from Mexicali, California, and Yuma, Arizona.

John V. must have felt like he was in top of the world on the last morning of his freedom. He was the head of a criminal gang composed of his several brothers and cousins, and under his leadership the clan had prospered well enough in the short time since coming to Seattle that they were beginning to pour the profits from selling heroin and cocaine into buying legitimate businesses. Cash talks. The first of these was a gym with state-of-the-art equipment in South Seattle. John V. was a body builder; he was in his mid-30's, mustached, lean and heavily muscled, the picture of masculine health, and a veteran of the U.S. Army in peacetime, before Vietnam. But his life and his fortune were destined to change this day; he was beginning his warm-up routine on a rowing machine when me and a team of detectives swept through the door and I arrested him on the spot for trafficking in stolen property. He was speechless from shock as I handcuffed him and took him away, leaving his former prostitute, exotic dancer girlfriend there, just as speechless. I read him his rights; he clammed up on us; no talk. We booked him into the county slammer and went about our work.

Further investigation by us while John was locked up, which left his gang in panicked disarray, yielded spectacular results: the day before John V. was released on bond Detective Walker and I seized by search warrant a large blue wooden chest stored in a storage facility in John V.'s name that contained a fully functional submachine gun with the serial number drilled off, and a number of other stolen guns, and enough ammunition to start a small war. One day after his release from jail, I arrested John V. again, this time at his apartment while he was fixing himself breakfast, for possession of yet more stolen property and federal firearms violations. We booked him right back into the county lockup he had just left, for a longer stay this time. It certainly was a bad week for the rising crime king. We now had the bad man at our mercy.

Through a deal with state prosecutors, John V. personally surrendered all of the Sullivans' stolen property to the police station in a single large truck shipment. The investigation was over a full year in duration when David Sullivan came to the station to identify and pick up his recovered property. The chief and several top brass came out to see the huge haul and meet the Sullivans. It is a rare event in police work to see a 100 percent recovery of a huge loss of stolen property a year after the theft, especially when it is personally returned from across the country by one of the crooks.

The Sullivan family was overjoyed that their property was fully recovered. Kristene and I had bonded with this family since those summer days at Ocean Park and we allowed them to treat us to an appreciation dinner at one of those fine restaurants, the starched white table linen, candles, sparkling stemware, soft music, tuxedoed waiter kind of place. Over a luxuriously long five-course dinner, the Sullivans admiringly asked about our marriage, how we met, and how the investigation came to be such a complete success. They listened intently as we shared with them how the Lord brought us together and how we had prayed together over the case, briefly explaining the principles and tenets of Christianity and what the Bible teaches about the power of agreement in prayer.

"Wonderful! And now, we have something very special for you two special people," David Sullivan beamed as he reached under the table and handed me a gift-wrapped medium-sized box with a card tucked under the satin ribbon. The card was a simple yet elegant expression of thanks from the entire family. In the box was a Middle Eastern–looking brass urn with a hinged lid and a handle.

"We knew that you are Christians, and this urn that you recovered for us now belongs to you. It is made of brass with copper and silver inlay by a Jewish Christian coppersmith who lives above his shop on Straight Street in Damascus, the same street the apostle Paul was sent to by Christ to have his sight restored," David explained. I was speechless. Kristene gulped back tears and tightly squeezed my hand under the table. After dessert and coffee we parted amid hugs and hearty handshakes and much well wishing.

At home that night I placed the urn on my nightstand and lay in bed, staring at the ceiling and pondering how dramatically my life had changed. God was honoring me personally and us as a couple beyond comprehension, and I was overwhelmed. Not only did I have my wife back against all odds, and better than before she left, but God was literally blessing everything I set my hand to do. In just five years, He had totally transformed by life for the better. The difference was dramatic, and I noted and reflected upon it that the changes had come not all at once, but in small increments, as I persevered in my Christian walk. And I pondered that before my rebirth how wearied I was by the pointlessness of life; since then it seemed as if every day God Himself *went looking* for new ways to bless and honor me, and I could scarcely take it in.

As I ruminated on the many changes the Lord had wrought, into my mind came foreknowledge of an important but positive event that was on its way. I was mentally tired after an intense year-long investigation that had paid off handsomely for me, but left me feeling drained when it was over. And though I was quiet about being exhausted, my supervisor, Lieutenant Roy Gleason sensed I was tired and gave me some much-needed some time off.

The hours Kristene was working I spent pottering around the house, leisurely fixing this and that, and catching up on my reading. When she was home we either visited relatives and friends or went for drives in the country. All this time I was secretly waiting for the 'event' I had foreknowledge of to manifest. It occurred to me then that we had been married almost two years, yet I had never met Kristene's parents other than in phone conversations. George and Matilda had been living in California all this time, and they announced they were coming up for a visit in a couple of weeks. Kristene had told me earlier that her father had been battling cancer for two or three years.

But the news of their coming visit sent Kristene into a funk, and I didn't know why. My best efforts to draw her out and get her to talk were to no avail. She withdrew and worked feverishly around the house inside and out, polishing and vacuuming inside, weeding and painting and raking beauty bark outside, exuding a tight-lipped nervous energy I had never seen in her before.

I was emotionally and physically cut off from her without knowing the reason. Her invisible walls were up, and I couldn't penetrate them; I felt alone even though she was physically with me. We were two isolated people living in the same house. Bummed, I was weeding in the front yard when a word of knowledge from the Lord revealed to me the harshness and physical brutality of Kristene's childhood at the hands of her mother, that He had protected her and preserved her through those years, and now He was bringing her parents up to Kristene for there to be healing for her. There were no words, just a knowing that could only have come from God.

But as I would soon learn, even revelation directly from God couldn't prepare me for meeting Matilda.

CHAPTER FOURTEEN

"Hi, Mom. Hello, Daddy. Meet John, my husband," Kristene said as we met them at SeaTac Airport. Short and stocky, a gnarled stump of a woman in her late sixties with thick glasses, leathery, suntanned skin, her upper lip set in a permanent snarl, and short, thinning gray hair, Matilda Kinssies exited the plane into the airport and bolted right past us without saying a word. She was looking straight ahead, headed for baggage claim. I was shocked. But her husband, George, smiled and opened his arms when he saw Kristene. A handsome gray-haired man in his early seventies who bore a remarkable resemblance to the '40s movie actor Gary Cooper, George radiated an eagerness to reconnect with his children. He hugged Kristene warmly.

"Good to see you, Dolly. You look wonderful!" he said in a guttural German accent, wet eyes beaming lovingly at his only daughter. I sensed that Kristene's love for him was bittersweet. Her little girl needs for her daddy only partially met, never fully. She grew up loving him and needing his protection, especially from her mother's violent rampages, but he was never there for her, even when he was at home.

Turning to me, George said, "I'm pleased to meet you, John!" A tanned right hand, huge, veined, thick with muscle, was extended to me. My own hand got lost in it when I grasped it. You would never know he was battling cancer by looking at him. He had sky blue eyes set in an always-smiling, strikingly handsome face that was tanned and weathered from years of wind and sun, a face that radiated kindness and acceptance to me. It was easy to see that Kristene got her looks from him. We liked each other immediately, and I was impressed with this man, for he exuded both gentleness and bravery in a way that few people appreciated. His lifetime of toil at sea had stamped him so that he was like a book you wanted to read, to know his story, for even in retirement years and fading health he was masculine and rugged, with a full head of thick gray hair, high cheekbones, bushy eyebrows, a strong, tight jaw line, and deeply weathered skin. Here was no pencil pusher. A man of medium height and stature, that George was still physically hard, lean, and strong yet equally quiet, wise, and gentle explained how he seemed to stand out in a room full of people. George would be the one you noticed in a crowd, the one you knew would be really interested in you, the one you would want to know and who would gladly be your friend.

George was away at sea for most of his married life, unreachable while his four offspring were being traumatized by their emotionally harsh and unstable mother. Given to fits of rage and anger, Matilda often resorted to physical violence. She made Bob and Richard pick off branches from the tree in the backyard that she would use to whip them with. As the only girl and her daddy's favorite, Kristene bore the brunt of her mother's abuse. I had heard the stories that Matilda often punched and slapped and dragged Kristene by her hair down the hallway, and crept into her room while she was sleeping and cut off her hair and cut up clothes Kristene made for herself. Although this abuse went on for years in the Kinssies household, Matilda's abuse of her children was never reported to the authorities. This was the 1950s and early '60s, a time when domestic violence was more or less accepted, perhaps in the interests of privacy or preserving parental authority. Certainly it was a time when children were not thought of as having rights but should be seen and not heard.

During the weeks of George and Matilda's visit, more of the grim details of this aspect of family history that I had only learned a little of from counseling now came out in small chunks as I listened to Kristene and her brothers reminisce about their childhood, the cruelty of their mother, and their absent father's timidity. It spoke well of all of them that all four had not only survived but had turned out so well, that they were neither bitter nor angry but instead could laugh and joke about some of their parents' behavior. All three brothers were successfully self-employed and of good reputation; of the four siblings, only Richard was not a Christian.

Yet for all their forgiveness and good-heartedness toward their parents' failures, the years of childhood trauma had mentally and emotionally scarred each of the Kinssies kids. For Kristene the scars were manifested by a deep-seated tendency toward hostility and a tendency to see people and situations in a suspicious light first; Kristene was quick to believe people were out to get her.

As the oldest child, Ron filled in for his absent father as the male head of the household, a willing self-expenditure that cost him his youth. Not only had he had been both brother and father to Kristene all of her life, but he had also done no less for Bob and Richard, teaching each of them to drive, taking them to social and sports activities, and doing his best to hold the fractured family together. Perhaps because she needed him for his strength and stability, Ron was the only one of the children Matilda never emotionally or physically abused. The volatility of the home environment took its toll. Ron the adult was godly, loving, and devout, yet overly serious, long faced, and brooding much of the time, his handsome countenance often seeming sad even when he wasn't.

Bob and Kristene were seemingly tied for receiving the worst of Matilda's abuse. As a little boy, this second-oldest son was often whipped by his mother with a switch or spanked and confined to a closet for hours at a time for even the slightest infraction. His mother's abuse resulted in Bob having lifelong issues with authority. As a child Bob frequently ran away from home and got into trouble with the police, the family making multiple trips to the juvenile detention center to pick him up. When he was seventeen, the juvenile court gave Bob the choice of either the Navy or the Green Hill juvenile reformatory; he chose the Navy. Tough, strong and wiry in the same mold as his father, Bob was never able to grasp the necessity of military discipline and was often in the brig. While stationed on the East Coast, Bob married Angela, a brash New York girl who was even tougher than him. Bob was given a general discharge from the Navy in about two years.

While raising their family of three kids, he and Angela became Christians under the ministry of a rogue pastor named Parfetta who reportedly had been expelled from the Assemblies of God and was later charged with financial crimes. Bob and Angela moved to Washington during the 1970s, where Bob ran a successful home remodeling business. Ambidextrous and marvelously skilled with his hands, Bob was known for superior craftsmanship in anything to do with building, and he had a heart for God. For a time he became a full-time preacher. Even then, Bob had a bifurcated personal struggle, a fixation with authority that marred his life: he had learned from his mother and the military to hate authority over him, and this he did with great vehemence, yet he craved the recognition authority brought to those it had either been bestowed upon or had earned it, yet authority of his own, he had naught, whether bestowed or earned. To hear him preach or talk with him would be to often hear the phrase 'as one under authority,' which was his way of asserting that he had such a special relationship with God that God had given him authority over others, therefore his was the final word in any discussion. That almost no one accepted Bob's claims that he was God's special mouthpiece distressed him, and adversely affected many of his relationships with others. Of the three brothers, Bob was the most severely scarred, mentally and emotionally, by childhood under Matilda.

Richard was the most urbane of the brothers. A handsome bachelor who had been married and divorced once, of which a daughter was the only offspring, Richard was at once masculine and refined, an innovative businessman and gifted writer and speaker. While working at a Seattle

Safeway store, he educated himself on wine and wine production and convinced store management to create a separate section in the store devoted to featuring a variety of wines. The concept was such a success that he opened his own business, the Seattle Academy of Wine, wrote a daily column on wine in the *Seattle Post Intelligencer,* and even had a daily five-minute radio spot on a local FM station. Beneath his ready smile and friendliness, Richard seemed emotionally cool; friendly and very genuine, he seemed to deal with the trauma of his childhood by emphasis on the positive and remaining reserved when it came to emotional commitments and priorities.

During their visit, George and Matilda spent daytime hours visiting at our house and evenings at one of their sons' homes. Having Matilda overnight was too stressful for Kristene.

"You sure got the big house, Dolly!" she said with a trace of Eastern European accent. "You sure got more than I ever had, Dolly! Who taught you to dress that way, Dolly? Where did you learn to cook like this? I never taught you that!" Matilda would repeatedly remark in a loud, scolding voice, pacing through the house, coldly inspecting the furniture, decorations and fixtures in an up-and-down review, that, without verbal comment, conveyed disapproval. There was never a compliment or a thank you. There were only cold comments made in high-volume, disapproving tones. One of five children of Croatian immigrants, though born and raised in America, Matilda had never lost the accent of her parents, so that words ending in "ing" were pronounced breathily as "ink" instead. "Ohhh, I'm tellink you!" was one of her favorite expressions, for which she was mimicked often by her children.

Matilda's open jealousy toward her only daughter was grinding me down already, and I was amazed at Kristene's ability to absorb such mental and social abuse. What was most aggravating to me was Matilda's show of nice behavior toward Kristene when her sons and their wives were present. As bad as my own childhood environment was, I had never seen such malice by a parent toward a child's success, nor had I ever seen the target of the abuse display as much grace as Kristene did.

Matilda never allowed George to have one-on-one time with Kristene, despite Kristene's many efforts to be alone with her dad. It wasn't my place to intervene, although I tried to help. Matilda made it evident that she didn't like me enough to be alone with me, and so I could do no more than to feel hurt for Kristene.

Kristene was never one to repay evil with more evil. No, instead she organized a large family reunion at our home to honor her parents. Everybody came who physically could—cousins, nieces and nephews with their husbands, wives and children, grandchildren, old folks, young folks, toddlers, and shirttail relatives. Beforehand, Kristene spent hours cooking in the kitchen, with me working 'til late to clean up the house inside and out. When the day came and people began arriving with their own special dishes of food and favorite wine, our sparkling clean little house was jam-packed full of boisterous, happy relatives, hugging, pinching, jostling, teasing, loudly greeting, and even arguing good-naturedly with each other. Good food, red wine and beer, and goodwill flowed like a river in our little home. Little ones played with each other around the house and in the yard, wives swapped recipes and gossip, and men talked business, sports, and politics. Every room was full: the family room, kitchen eating area, dining room, living room, and even the wrap-around deck outside, and the aroma from the kitchen seeped into even the bedrooms. In the midst of this family tapestry, I checked on my wife. She was busy in the kitchen, smiling and chattering away, fixing and serving platters of appetizers and main course dishes, preparing dessert, and keeping things organized. Kristene was in her element: busily serving her many loved ones who surrounded her; radiant and happy, she was.

Trying to the melt the ice between us, I cornered Matilda in the living room and asked her why she and George always called Kristene Dolly.

"Oh yaaah, that!" she shouted, (though I was standing right in front of her), waving an arm at me in a pushing away gesture. "I went into the hospital not long after Kristene was born. And George, he was so proud to finally have a little girl, that she was all he talked about when he came to visit me. Every day, I tell you, every day George would come to my hospital room, saying, 'The little doll did this today,' or 'the little doll did that today.' So she was called Dolly because of her dad."

Everybody ate, some of us overate, and before dessert we crammed into the living room as Grampa George opened a violin case and took out his musical saw, a carpenter's handsaw of high-grade steel that his father in Germany taught him to play. It was amazing to watch. Sitting down, George nestled the wood handle between his knees and placed his left hand over the small end of the blade, bending it slightly. With his right hand, George held a violin bow, which he drew across the flat edge of the blade, making the most angelic music, like a woman soprano singing opera. The entire house became reverently silent as George played that great old hymn "How Great Thou Art," and then Kristene sung the next tune with her father playing the saw in the background. It was a scene that brought many to tears, it was so beautiful. I knew from hearing Kristene singing next to me in church that she had a beautiful voice, but I was mesmerized hearing her sing alone for the first time, with such a wonderful vibrato. As dessert was served, Uncle Clyde asked everyone to quiet as he played a tape of Kristene singing as a guest amateur on *Evergreen Jubilee*, a local television show on Channel 4.

"Ladies and gentlemen, our next guest is twelve-year-old Miss Kristene Kinssies, who will sing 'Sad Movies Always Make Me Cry.' Please give her a welcoming hand." The audience applauded as a younger version of the voice I knew and loved sang:

Sad movies always make me cryyy …
He said he had to work, so I went to the show alone
They turned down the lights and turned the projector on
And just as the news of the world started to begin,
I saw my darlin' and my best friend, walk in

141

And I saw George and Matilda were looking down at the floor, teary, their minds and hearts in the past, as the song ended.

A young George Kinssies with his musical saw

George and Matilda Kinssies with Kristene, age 2

Kinssies family at Bob's graduation from Navy boot camp

Kristene: crowned beauty queen at age 15

CHAPTER FIFTEEN

"So, John, Kristene tells me you're Norwegian! That's a good nationality to be, you know. Yahh," George reflected. "When I was up there fishing in Alaska, all those Norwegian and Danish guys on the boats, yeah, they were strong! Even the old ones, they were stronger than most of us younger men, never sick!"

George was stretched out on our living room couch, his eyes looking at the ceiling as his mind savored past sea adventures. Kristene had taken her mother out shopping so George could take an afternoon nap, but he kept talking out of a desire to bond his life with mine.

We had a huge sectional couch in our living room, and I was on the section across from George. I wasn't sleepy when I first lay down, but with the house so quiet and warm, I would have fallen asleep in minutes were it not for George wanting to talk.

"Yahh, you'll live a *good* long time being Norwegian," he predicted fondly. I had come to love and admire this gentle man; the bond of love and respect between him and his sons, the way his grandchildren flocked to him whenever he came around, how he treasured Kristene like a rare and beautiful flower. His life at sea was a life lesson that bravery comes in many forms, and here was one brave man.

I was just beginning to nod off again. "Yahh, that Kristene, you know, when she was a little girl, she'd sing with me playing the saw, and the crowds would love her," George said drowsily.

Now I was awake. "Crowds? Play where?" I asked.

"Yahh, you know, we'd practice at home a lot and then we'd perform at USO shows at Fort Lewis, at Democrat Party picnics, and amateur talent shows. She even sang 'God Bless America' to Bobby Kennedy when he came to Seattle for the 1968 presidential election campaign. Yahh, that Dolly, she'd be cuttin' records today if she had stayed with it," George reminisced. The thought occurred to me that she wouldn't be married to me if she had stuck with music. Lucky me, I thought to myself.

"Why did it stop?" I wanted to know.

"Her mother stopped it," George said simply, and that was it; no more was said.

Everybody loved George. Somehow he always became the center of honored attention at every family gathering. He was warm and friendly and always interested in others. Women doted on him, men were eager to talk with him, and grandchildren hovered hungrily around him, hoping for another story or a magic trick. He and Matilda were just visiting at this point and still had their apartment in California. George was seventy-one and had already been operated on for intestinal cancer, about which we knew little except that he wasn't getting better. None of us wanted him to spend his last years away from us, especially the grandchildren.

Kristene took the initiative by finding the Moe Elbert House apartments for the elderly just as construction was completed and the first residents were moving in. Best of all, it was conveniently located in Bellevue between our house and Ron and Kay's. The four households contributed to the setting up and furnishing of the apartment, and George and Matilda were soon set up in a new, nicely furnished home close to their kids and grandchildren within easy walking distance of a shopping center and bus routes.

For nine months everything went well. Warm traditions were established, and old ones were expanded upon. The four households included George and Matilda in our life routines, with frequent visits and trips around town, small dinners, and family feasts that included uncles, aunts, nieces and nephews, live music, and lots of food and wine. Grampa George played his musical saw and began teaching the young ones to play it, his huge hands an expression of his gentle kindness as he held little hands in his, drawing the bow across the bent blade, making that rich, sweet music. Life was good, life was rich, and there was something wonderful and complete in having all the family generations living close by each other, harmony overriding differences, everyone getting along, with no one left out. This culture of belonging and honoring of marriage and blood ties was new to me, and I couldn't get enough of it.

I couldn't get over the contrast between Kristene's family and mine. Whereas hers was as I describe here, my family gatherings were cold and dysfunctional. In my family the axiom, "If you haven't anything good to say about someone, better not to say anything at all" had been twisted around to, "If you can't say anything bad about someone, better to say nothing at all." I saw that the negative energy was generated and perpetuated by my parents; after more than twenty-five years they were still selfishly dragging everyone around them through their divorce. And so I anticipated and savored every minute of Kristene's family gatherings because this is how it should be: a large family of siblings, sons and daughters, aunts and uncles, cousins and nephews and nieces, jokes and laughter, and always much food and wine.

Kristene was especially grateful to have her daddy again, graciously overlooking her mother's obvious efforts to deny her time alone with her father with a variety of ploys and excuses. I understood Kristene much better when I saw for myself Matilda's jealousy toward her only daughter and George's timidity in terms of his failure to stand up to his wife on behalf of his children, especially his only daughter. I came to understand his timidity better when I learned that the backyard fence of his family home in Germany adjoined the backyard of the local police station, where George and his siblings peered over the fence to watch police firing squads execute prisoners. But of Matilda's hostility and lack of love toward Kristene no understanding was to be had. For all her trying for her mother's approval, it was painful for Kristene that even after so many years, Matilda still disapproved of her, never thanked or complimented her for anything as she did her sons, and still she never let Kristene be alone with her father, always finding ways to block their relationship, allowing only their sons the privilege of being alone with him.

The time George and Matilda were here helped my understanding of Kristene. George was a very nice man, but niceness by itself isn't enough when it comes to being a husband and a father. The needs his wife and children had of him could never be met with niceness alone. What his family needed from him was loving strength; strength that assumes authority as the head of the family, takes the lead, establishes order and peace and admonishes peace-breakers even if the violator was the wife. His family needed him to be a deliberate man, but George was not up to that; perhaps it was just never in his wiring.

At this point the damage was done, and I could do aught else but admire all four siblings for the way they had made the best of the hand they had been dealt, forged ahead in life and succeeded, never assuming a victim mentality, showing their parents love, acceptance and respect. It was awesome to see.

The family unity we all enjoyed so much ended abruptly when Kay visited George and Matilda and noticed loaded boxes stacked in the living room. Without telling anybody ahead of time, they were moving back to California, as if sneaking out of town. The reason Matilda gave was that California offered better healthcare benefits for George's cancer treatments, but that wasn't the whole of it. The whole story was that Matilda was constantly getting into conflicts with the management and neighbors in the building, making it necessary for either Kristene or Kay to intervene so they weren't evicted. But eventually the patient former nuns who ran the Moe Elbert House could take no more of Matilda and insisted she and George leave. The sorrow and disappointment we all felt at their going would not have escaped anyone's notice. Not allowing

George a say in the matter, Matilda declined offers of a farewell dinner. They left on a plane, their boxes having been shipped ahead of them, leaving all their furniture behind, without a word of thanks for all their kids had done for them. Deprived once again of her daddy, Kristene grieved quietly, and I nurtured Kristene.

To make the best of it, we kept in frequent phone contact with George and Matilda and each other. Ron started his own commercial construction business at this time. It seemed like everyone in greater Seattle knew or had heard of Richard. He was on the radio and the local newspaper every day, educating or giving inside tips about wine. Ever loyal to her brothers, Kristene wore a white sweatshirt bearing the name and logo of Richard's 'Seattle Academy of Wine' everywhere she went and sometimes called in to Richard's radio show using an assumed name to promote his business. The weekly Bible study Bob and Angela had hosted in their home for several years grew to the point that Bob took the big plunge by closing his home remodeling business and going into ministry full time as an independent preacher, and at first Kristene and I attended their services regularly to support them. Bob's kids provided musical backup: oldest son Bobby played the drums, Johnny the guitar, and Angel, their only daughter, sang. Bob proved to be a fiery and effective preacher, his sermons often rising to a rhythmic, pitched crescendo, his face flushed and neck veins bulging. Tanned and ruggedly handsome like his father from years of physical outdoor work, dressed in a dark suit with white shirt and tie, Bob had film star charisma. On Sundays the tiny congregation of about thirty people met in a rented hall near Kirkland and at Bob and Angela's home during the week. Services were sometimes wild events that were without a schedule; they just ended when they ended.

A new season of adventure opened for us. In the manner that one thing always leads to another, it began when we bought two German Shorthair puppies that were brothers from the same litter with the idea of bird hunting together. The smaller one was the runt but was the alpha male of the two, so we named him Kaiser, meaning "emperor" in German. The other pup had strong hunting desire and instincts, but his timidity overshadowed these qualities. We named him Jaeger, which in German means "hunter." We bought shotguns intending to hunt pheasants and ducks together with the dogs. With training whistles and a book on gun dog training, we trained the dogs in parks with canvas training dummies covered with pheasant feathers and drenched in liquid pheasant scent. We enjoyed many hours following the training steps in the book and teaching the dogs to respond to hand, voice, and whistle commands.

Then, as the momentum of events we were caught up in would have it, we bought an orange and yellow Volkswagen camper van and were taking the dogs with us on many weekend outings. Over time the dogs got so they didn't get along. Kaiser was dominating Jaeger so severely it was ruining him. We found Jaeger a new home with a young couple who lived on a small farm and everyone, both dogs included, was happier.

Next thing either of us knew was the surprise discovery that having a camper van brought out the vagabond in me. Yes, Me! You read it right – Mr. Police Officer, has a gypsy soul. Imagine it! Then, armed with a worn first edition of the book *Of Men and Mountains* by William O. Douglas, the Supreme Court Justice of the 1930s who grew up in Yakima on the east side of Washington, we spent most of that summer retracing the routes of Douglas' expeditions through remote regions of the Cascade Mountains in search of places he chronicled in his book.

We found as many of the hunting and camping sites as we could reach by vehicle, and camped at each one. At night, by light of lantern and campfire, I read aloud his descriptions of when he camped there long ago, the people he brought with him and others he met by chance, and how their camp was set up. So vivid were his descriptions that by being there as I read aloud, we were conveyed mentally back in time to those bygone camps of yesteryear, to simpler times when the nation was younger and values were more clarified, and we envisioned ourselves being in camp with Douglas when he was there, meeting the other characters in his stories, backpacking with him through mighty pine forests and alpine meadows, eating and sleeping where he ate and slept. Our historical explorations and campfire readings in the deep woods made for new romantic adventures for us, for we were still newlyweds, and little did we know then that in following Douglas's footsteps, we were building a lasting legacy of our own, a marital legacy, campfire by campfire.

In the era before and during the Great Depression, Douglas wrote firsthand of mountain men, hunters, train-riding hoboes and hermits, snow blizzards, deer hunts, and horseback expeditions. A self-taught botanist and climatologist, he wrote knowledgeably about the climactic and botanical aspects of this mighty mountain range that provides a cultural curtain between east and west in Washington and Oregon. Nearly fifty years later, Douglas and the people he wrote about had all taken the final journey, but he would be pleased to see that the places he loved and wrote about remain wilderness today; visited, yes, but protected and still unspoiled by civilization.

Many of the areas Douglas depicted possessed bodies of water, each having a distinctive name and a personality that we discovered when we found them ourselves. Provided we were alone when we found such a place, we made it our custom to go skinny dipping in whatever river, creek, or lake that Douglas mentioned in his book. Upon arrival, we would strip down, and with Kaiser standing guard, we braved the chilly waters just to say we had been there, done that. One such place was Bumping Creek, and just getting there was a hair-raising experience, a brush with possible death. Following a hand-drawn map in Douglas's book and a Forest Service map, we wound up driving along a soft dirt narrow path cut into the steep side of a mountain. With the upside of the mountain on my left, I could touch the mountain by merely extending my arm out the window. The van was as far to the left as I could get it, and on the right side was a steep drop, the first obstacles being huge old-growth fir trees about a hundred feet down. The bottom was somewhere far below that. There was no way to back up or turn around, and the path got narrower as we went along. It didn't help that the forest was so dense that the midday sunlight was dimmed to the point that it might has well have been just before sundown. Creeping along at less than five miles an hour in low gear, strapped into our seats, the thought occurred to me that if we slipped off the path into the abyss below, we would never be found. It was white-knuckle time, an occasion to "pray without ceasing" as the New Testament admonishes, which we did every inch of the way.

Eventually we emerged onto a broad meadow, flat and grassy, with Bumping Creek at the far side and more pine forest beyond the opposite side of the creek. We camped near the water at a bend in the creek where the water was slow moving. We were totally alone and the sun was very hot, so we plunged into the cold water, soaking, washing, and playfully splashing each other. When the water had cooled us to the point of chills, we spread out beach blankets and fell asleep in the sun.

We built a campfire before dark, grilled burgers in the flames, heated a can of baked beans in the coals, and talked until late, sleeping on the ground in the cool night air, beneath a cloudless, pitch black night sky studded with countless constellations. Next morning we slept in late, and fixed a cookstove breakfast of sausages, toasted canned brown bread and hobo coffee before breaking camp and moving on. I dreaded going back out the same way we came in; it was too dangerous. Looking around the meadow, I found a level dirt road that looked as though it could be an easier way out; following it, we found our way back to the main dirt road and headed north.

I decided to check on a twenty-acre piece of land that we owned in the mountains above the small town of Peshastin. The dirt road up Derby Canyon to the property was maintained by the county for the first five miles, and made for an easy drive. For the next five miles the road was steep, rutted and rough from snowmelt and seasonal rains, winding higher and higher through uninhabited pine forest, and our faithful camper chugged slowly uphill in low gear, laboring through ruts and over rocks until at last we reached our land. We walked around on the only part of the twenty acres that was level, an area of maybe five acres; the rest of the land was steep alpine meadow, dotted with Ponderosa Pines.

This was a remote place with no utilities or even a maintained road. For years I envisioned someday clearing the level area and building a retirement cabin there. Living here full time would be a primitive life; too primitive for Kristene. A man and his elderly mother already tried and failed to live there full time, the winter and other hardships were too much. They returned to town, abandoning their shack to vagabonds and drifters. Indeed, we later discovered that day that the shack was inhabited by several rough-and-ready mountain man types. A weekend getaway here might be a better idea, if we do it at all, I concluded.

As I watched Kristene walk through the trees with Kaiser, I remembered that years ago I had seen her in a dream on this very spot. I didn't recognize her because we had yet to meet, but I knew she was my wife. She was wearing a two-piece swimsuit because of the heat, and she was helping me stack the logs that had been felled to build our cabin. Her long, dark hair was pinned up out of the way and sweat streaked down her body from hard work in the heat. I said nothing to her about it until later, but remembering that long-ago dream reaffirmed that we were each other's destiny and that God had a plan for our lives together. Before leaving the property, we talked about where the cabin would go and where we would dig a well and put in a septic.

Kristene was content to let me do the driving in the mountains. As much as possible we stuck to remote routes on these trips, two-lane roads of crumbling asphalt and barely distinguishable old dirt logging roads that got us into the backcountry where, like William O. Douglas, we too met a variety of colorful characters: back-to-the-land types, two former attorneys now living like societal drop-outs raising llamas in the mountains, and rugged woodsmen living off the land, throwbacks to an earlier century, freelance loggers and wilderness guides, even a community of Amish believers.

It was a time without equal for us. We were constantly alone together with only the barest of life's necessities to sustain us: an extra change of clothes, a cooler to store our food, Coleman camp stove and lantern, soap, toothpaste, toothbrushes, and a thermos were all we needed. We purposely left behind the fol-de-rol of city life: television, telephones and newspapers, wardrobes, accessories and equipage, household furnishings and bric-a-brac. It was a formative time; such simplicity enabled us to grow together at an easy pace, talking for hours on end about everything under the sun, laughing much, enjoying periods when talk wasn't necessary, exploring new places, encountering new people, finding and setting up the next camp, going about camp chores - gathering firewood, cooking and cleaning up before moving on again; all this deepened our bonds of trust and understanding. Our interest in each other never flagged; we preferred to talk with each other even when we had radio reception or tape cassettes to play, and I was especially pleased that Kristene went without her usual makeup on these trips, something I always said she didn't need; she was so beautiful. It was a romantic, magical time; every day was a new adventure; we were as a pair of roving gypsies, roaming mountain back roads in a VW bus with our dog. It was a time that produced inner healing and emotional mending for this city girl as she settled into our love and our belonging to each other, and for me it was a time of healing of old wounds from childhood trauma and failed marriages.

CHAPTER SIXTEEN

Although it was never our intention, the salient thing about
our vagabonding in the Cascades was the depth it gave our
communion, for from that time on, each seemed to possess
an unusual awareness and foreknowledge on behalf of the other, to
a greater extent than before. Our roaming came to a close when the
weather changed; shifting gears, we settled back into work and home
life, not knowing that the season just ending was divine preparation
for the ugly upheavals we would face together, the first of which was
soon to come.

We had reached a new level of confidence about the strength and
durability of our marriage at this point that we savored, like a hot drink
in freezing weather that warms the insides all the way down. It was
the first time for either of us that we felt so free to pour ourselves into
another so unreservedly. Our differences were added spice to the mix,
and we were on top of the world.

Our home, once the scene of two prior marriages that failed, now
mirrored the love between Kristene and me; it had never looked as
beautiful, as warm, and so well cared for as it became under Kristene's
care. She had transformed a mere tract house suffering from neglect into
a real home, where guests always stayed longer than intended, friends
dropped by often, and all around the ties of blood and marriage were
strengthened. And so I was pleased, rather than disappointed, when
Kristene preferred to nest at home instead of bird hunting with me and

Kaiser that fall, for when I returned from the hunt, my slippers were at the door with a towel for Kaiser's feet, and food was ready on the stove. Kristene knew the finer points of cooking from working in five-star restaurants, always using new combinations of herbs and spices and just the right side dishes to make the gamiest bird a dining experience. With her in the kitchen, every meal was a new adventure.

We tired of wild fowl after awhile. Our freezer was so full of plump game birds that we traded with friends for their deer and elk meat and wild salmon. The trading visits made for lively conversation and great stories of hunting big game in the forests, charter boat fishing in the rough seas off the Alaskan coast, tales that I added to my own stock of stories that I told at our family wild game dinners, held in the dead of winter at season's end at Ron and Kay's house, with the children listening to my narratives of gun dogs and hunters in the field while they ate.

With the spring came news that George's cancer had taken a turn for the worse. He had been admitted to a hospital in Santa Rosa, and Matilda wouldn't let any of their kids talk to him, saying he was asleep and was not to be disturbed. Kristene spoke with one of the doctors by phone and learned that his condition was deteriorating. She also spoke to a nurse who told her George had been very sick but was conscious and able to talk most of the time; she put him on the phone with Kristene. George sounded drugged and in denial that there was anything serious going on.

"I'm coming down to see you right now, Daddy! I love you!" she told him with tears in her voice. We loaded our van with clothes and food for the road, arriving in Santa Rosa in about fifteen hours. We took turns driving and stopped only for fuel and the restroom. After the first eight hours I gave her the wheel and stretched out on the camper bed, feeling tense and tired. I watched Kristene in the driver seat as I drifted off to sleep, absorbing her, and admiring her strength and depth of character. I was a blessed man.

George had been released from the hospital just hours before we arrived in Santa Rosa. He was delighted, but Matilda was irritated to see us. George looked gaunt, weaker than when I last saw him. Kristene sat next to him on the couch. "How are you feeling, Daddy?" she asked.

Taking her hand in his, George nodded and said "I feel great, like a forty-year-old man, yeah."

Father and daughter were together once again. As always, George was intensely interested to learn everything about everything we were doing, plus all the latest about his boys, their families, and their work. Matilda rustled loudly in the kitchen, banging pots and pans in angry anxiety, seeming to time the noise so it would override Kristene's conversation with her father, but Kristene patiently ignored her mother's efforts to disrupt her visit, holding hands with and talking to her dad, with me admiring her inner strength.

From the very start, my relationship with Matilda was strained; we struggled to be civil to each other. What I had been told of her abusive treatment of Kristene, and what I had seen of her obvious preference for her sons, and her brusque mannerisms made me feel defensive for Kristene and interfered with my efforts to warm up to her. It may not have been true, but Matilda seemed intimidated by me, and a thin civility was the best she could manage. Many times Matilda's mental cruelty toward Kristene offended me, but it was Kristene's turning the other cheek that really got to me. Her consistent patience, kindness, and overlooking of genuine wrongs against her started me on yet another path of self-examination, a quest for more change within myself that I needed. On this visit, I did my best to engage Matilda in friendly conversation so Kristene could visit with her daddy, but she would have none of it. Matilda was openly angry that Kristene was talking to George and wasn't interested in anything I had to say. We ate in strained silence and left when Matilda insisted that George needed his rest and said she wasn't interested in talking to us.

We met with George's primary doctor at the hospital that same night. He was a boyish looking young man in his thirties, clean cut, professionally polite, empathetic, and wanting to help.

"Your father's prognosis is that he could live another two years if he opts for surgery that would bypass the colon again, if he accepts the regimen of chemo and radiation we recommend, and he doesn't smoke anymore," he told us. He went on in detail about the spreading cancer and the effects that chemotherapy and radiation could have on him. The good doctor was pulling no punches: both treatments were drastically toxic, akin to fighting fire with fire; even combined they could not save his life, only extend it, and at the price of excruciating pain to George.

In the morning we took George and Matilda out to breakfast, a drive around Santa Rosa, and a little shopping. We rented the movie *The Man From Snowy River* and enjoyed watching it with them in their apartment. The day on the town and the movie had been a pleasant escape for all of us, but it tired George. The following morning we stopped by for coffee and to say good-bye. When I shook his hand, I sensed it would be the last time I would see him.

Kristene was quiet for the first few hours of the drive home; when she talked, she avoided the subject of her father. When we arrived home, Kristene called her brothers to report what we learned from the doctor and how much George's condition had changed. The knowledge that a loved one would soon be gone made returning to life's routines difficult. The major components of our lives: home, family, work, and church were outwardly the same as before, but now we were waiting and dreading that which must come. And yet I sensed there was something else that was headed our way soon, a future event that gnawed at me. What it was I knew not, only that it wasn't benign like George's imminent passing; instead it forebode evil that was just ahead.

In a sidelines sort of way I was learning from Kristene's examples of love, grace, forgiveness, selflessness, and judging not. Because of her parents' abuse, rejection, neglect and failed love, Kristene's childhood was a nightmare of parental abuse and neglect, and her maidenhood was similarly scarred, yet she chose to love her parents as if she had never been hurt at all. And in so doing she lived out the verse in Psalm 27 that says: "though my father and mother forsake me, the Lord will receive me," for God was at work within her all that time, thus she could endure injustice nobly, suffering without complaint, in keeping with true Christian character. How remarkable, I thought. It impressed me greatly that instead of being angry and bitter, she had taken the high road and shown them love, compassion, generosity, and acceptance. They were now old, weak, and poor, living only on Social Security income, yet Kristene never failed to treat them like royalty. She never kept a record of wrongs or bore grudges. I arrived at the conclusion that she was a better person than me, a knowledge that I was all right with; I was more than happy to be her student in these things.

Both of us were working to achieve family unity, like we saw in many Christian families we knew. It had started with one person, and we were determined that in my case it would start with Kristene and me. Since coming to the Lord I had been praying steadily for my family to be saved, especially my parents. My mother was so self-righteous and self-deceived that she had convinced herself that Christian Science was merely another Christian denomination. Eventually I gave up talking with her and stuck to praying for her salvation. My father had become much more open to Christ after his latest drinking binge was nearly fatal. He was honest about his bad behavior, even acknowledging his abuse of his wife Jeanne all this time. We invited Dad to come with us to the Billy Graham crusade at the Tacoma Dome, and he came. He sat intently listening to every word of the message, and when the altar call was given, he stood up and said, "I'm going down there. You coming, Jeanne?"

"H- - - no, I'm not going down there, and you aren't either," Jeanne said. And my father sat down again and nothing I said could persuade him to go forward. He would resume his lifestyle of hard drinking, abusive behavior and foul talk until the end of his days. About two years before he died, a local minister and a neighbor led Dad in the sinner's prayer, but in his behavior and talk there was no change for the better, and if anything, he took the Lord's name in vain even more after that.

Life wasn't all roses for us either, but we had the Holy Spirit in us, and that made all the difference. We did have fights; you could have sold tickets to them; intense personalities are bound to clash, as ours did. Kristene still had a defensive hostility streak in her that developed from enduring her mother's cruelty and learning to survive life on the fast track of the East Coast. She was quick to believe that other people were out to get her and put her walls up. My temperament was shaped by military service during the unpopular Vietnam War and being a uniformed cop during an era of strong public anti-authority sentiment. I was hardened to being disliked for making unpopular decisions, for holding the line, and for doing the right thing no matter what.

At first it was always Kristene who broke the ice. "It says in Ephesians not to let the sun go down on your anger. So come on, Baby, its' getting dark, so come to me," she would say.

Our love and unending desire for each other always prevailed over episodes of negative emotions because that was the choice we consciously made. From Kristene I learned to focus instead on the preciousness of our marriage, and this put helped things in a right perspective. In the course of time I assumed the role of peacemaker from my teacher. As sensitive to her feelings as I was, I was ever the clumsy oaf who said or did the wrong thing at the wrong time that upset her. Even then I marveled at her, for when there was fire in her eyes from anger, she had a certain aura of sensual hostility about her that was mesmerizing. We always reconciled, but it wasn't easy, for our spats were draining.

The frequent mending our volatile love required taught us to overlook perceived offenses and focus on the fact that we belonged to each other, that we were one flesh, one spirit, and no separation could happen; that was the big picture.

Neither of us had ever had it this good: our home was beautiful, we had the support of a large, loving family and many good friends, our health was excellent, we were active in church, my detective career was blossoming, and we were prosperous and more in love than ever. We stayed in constant touch with George and Matilda by phone. George was holding his own while undergoing chemo and radiation treatments. Kristene became active in women's ministries at church, often making meals of spaghetti, lasagna, or beef stew to deliver to shut-ins. I was active in men's groups and met every Tuesday morning with my brother-in-law Ron at a local restaurant for Bible study and prayer.

At work I developed the Mexican drug dealer who had returned the stolen furnishings in the Sullivan case into an informant on a missing persons case that we believed was a double homicide of a married couple, Gary and Laurie Crabtree. In the process of working with him almost every day, I shared my faith with him and eventually led him to asking Christ into his life.

One morning as I was home taking the trash out, the Holy Spirit revealed that the Crabtrees were dead but they would be found. The disappearance of the Crabtrees was a high-profile mystery in the news. The case was outside my department's jurisdiction, but I was assigned to it by special request of the King County Prosecutor's Office, a huge honor for me and my department. In the course of investigation, I met with Gary Crabtree's ex-wife and son and Laurie Crabtree's parents. Based on what the Holy Spirit revealed to me, I boldly promised them that Gary and Laurie would be found.

After months of sifting evidence and dozens of witness interviews, a jail inmate turned informant strengthened our case by disclosing that he was present when the murders of the Crabtrees was planned. Dumping the bodies into Lake Samamish was part of the plot. As a result of this and the same information from another witness, King County Police divers began searching portions of Lake Sammamish, a large body of water. One morning I was shaving before going to work when I received a word of knowledge that the Crabtrees bodies were on the bottom of Lake Sammamish and would be brought to the surface.

The area of Lake Sammamish the informant said the bodies of the Crabtrees were to be dumped was near the southeast shore of the lake, where the two killers lived in a trailer. This was where two-man teams of county police divers concentrated their search, a few hundred yards away from the trailer. The lake bottom there was 80 feet deep and muddy; the water temperature at that depth was 34 degrees year-round. The cold and poor visibility limited diving time to about 30 minutes.

Police diver Zsolt Dornay was about to conclude what would be the last dive on the last day of the search (and three days after I received the word of knowledge that the bodies would be recovered from there) when he beheld what looked like a woman's body lying on the bottom. On closer inspection by pressing his mask against the leg because of the darkness and following the leg to rest of the body, he determined it was a woman wrapped in a weight-down sleeping bag. When he sat down as his diving partner approached, he sat in the lap of yet another body – a man's body. He had found the murdered bodies of Gary and Laurie Crabtree weighted down on the lake bottom, and my partner Bob Littlejohn and I were on the beach as teams of police divers labored through much of the night to float the bodies to the surface and ashore.

The dramatic finding of a missing couple on the bottom of the lake, weighted down with chains and concrete blocks, was headline news. For me it was a powerful example of the power of prayer at work in the course of human events. At the time the bodies were found, the two men responsible were already in the county lockup on robbery, theft and weapons charges as a result of our ongoing investigation. My partner and I, with other detectives, arrested them at gunpoint in their lakeshore trailer a month earlier.

It would later turn out that the weapons the men stole and still had when they were arrested were taken with the intent to murder the Crabtrees and were used for that purpose. Now both men would be charged with two counts each of first degree murder.

During the next year, the killers were tried in another county in which the victims lived. The trial lasted six weeks. It was hotly contested; the lead prosecutor had me and my partner following up on leads through most of the trial. Kristene prayed earnestly all through the trial for a successful outcome.

"The Lord showed me that you guys will win," she said, "but you will have to work for it. The real enemy in this is unseen and very strong."

The killers, David Simmons and Billy Dailey, were convicted by jury of two counts each of first degree murder and one count each of conspiracy to commit murder, each receiving three consecutive life sentences. The case was written up in The Seattle Weekly newspaper, and for a time after this, my partner Bob Littlejohn, and I became not famous but locally well-known.

The Crabtree case and its courtroom outcome put my career in overdrive, as well as everything else in my life. Before the trial was ended, Dennis Wyatt, the captain of detectives, came to the trial and waited until a recess to talk to me.

"Take two weeks off on me after the trial is over," he told me. "When you come back we're putting you in the Crimes Against Persons Unit. It's a waste to have you working thefts and burglaries."

Rapes, assaults, robberies, missing persons, suicides and homicides became my caseload when I returned to work. I attended autopsies often and developed working relationships with prosecutors, medical examiners, detectives from other agencies and developed informants. I was sent to a variety of schools and training seminars and was making lots of overtime. Everything was on the upswing. It seemed we were on top of the world and nothing could go wrong.

Then it started. After several months in my new position; something began to haunt me, a sense of foreboding, of coming damnation. I couldn't shake it. Someone close to me was going to die soon and would spend eternity in hell. The sensations of hell I felt were terrifying. It was worse at night than any other time; sleep was impossible. These were not dreams, I was always wide awake. These were open visions, imparted knowledge from another realm, terrifyingly strong and clear. I could see only blackness, horrible blackness, and I understood that the blackness was there to prevent me from seeing what was on the other side. I didn't hear anything, but I sensed intense heat and suffering were on the other side of the blackness. I knew that I was standing at the edge of Hell itself, with only a veil of blackness between me and it, and the horror beyond the edge, beyond the blackness was unspeakable. I knew that once there, no one comes back, not ever.

At first I was so fearful that it was me who would die that I slipped out of bed and went into the bathroom, where I would kneel on the floor and repent and beseech God with all the earnestness I could muster. I did this out of fear that God was telling me that I was about to die and I wasn't really saved. Of course, that was pure fear on my part, and Kristene talked it over with me and we prayed together in earnest. This forewarning of doom with no possible escape came and went, night and day, for about two weeks. Only partial relief came when finally I prayed in the Spirit, but not completely. Whatever it was, it was still coming.

A week later I was at home, settling into a quiet evening with Kristene when the phone rang. "John, I need you here right away!" my mother said.

"Why Mom, is something wrong?" I asked. Her voice was urgent.

"I'll tell you when you get here," she said.

"Mom, first tell me what's going on," I insisted.

"Come!" my mother shouted and then hung up.

I drove alone the ten-minute drive to my mother's. As I pulled into the circular driveway, I saw two young men in military uniform following my father and his wife from my mother's house. My mother was trying to stop my father, but he was angrily pushing her away as he walked toward his car. Forgetting the military men, I immediately assumed my dad was drinking and everyone was trying to stop him from driving. Dad tore out of the driveway past me with his wife seated next to him. Fearing he was drunk and might be arrested, I followed him to his apartment in Bellevue and confronted him in the parking lot.

"Dad, what's going on? Have you been drinking again?" I asked him.

My father angrily brushed past me toward his apartment, without speaking. I stopped him physically; he had not been drinking, but he was angry and badly shaken.

Suddenly he turned toward me.

"John, go be with your mother," he said. "You be a good son to her."

Then he walked away, leaving me standing there speechless.

Dad's wife Jeanne looked at me, intensity in her eyes, and in a broken voice shouted, "Your brother has killed himself!"

CHAPTER SEVENTEEN

Jeanne's words slammed into me with the force of a sledgehammer blow. What!? My only brother dead? Killed *himself*? Shock froze my mind. For a second I stared uncomprehendingly at Jeanne, mouth agape, disbelieving, my feet frozen to the ground.

"Go to your mother, John!" my father shouted again.

I ran to my car and drove back to my mother's house in a daze, running red lights, trying to grasp what I had heard. When I arrived I was relieved that the Air Force men had not left my mother alone. Mom was bravely holding her emotions in check, remaining calm, getting a grip on the situation as she served them tea and talked with them. They told us there had been a police investigation because my brother died in his apartment off base and that the Air Force was conducting its own inquiry. My brother David, whom the family nicknamed Buzz, a captain at age thirty-two, had been in the Air Force for twelve years after college graduation. He had never dated that I knew of and never married. He lived alone. We were seven years apart in age; we were friendly but never close.

I called my father. He had started drinking already; his words already slow and slurry.

"Dad," I said, "this is not a time for you to be drinking. We've got to pull together. We need you. Please stop drinking and come back up here."

I called Kristene at home; she was waiting by the phone. When I told her the news, she said she would be ready to spend the night with my mother.

When my father and his wife returned to my mother's, the Air Force men left, and the four of us sat in the living room in shocked silence. Within minutes my father began blaming my mother for my brother's death, accusing her of smothering him, not allowing him to have a girlfriend, become a regular man, and so on. My mother went on the defensive, and a fight started, each blaming the other. My father stormed out, and I followed him to his car. As he got into the passenger seat, he broke down, stammering, "I—I failed, I failed. I let him down. It's my fault." It was the first time I ever saw my father as a beaten man, inwardly on the ropes. It was true at least in part; he had verbally beaten Buzz down for all of his life so that he had no self confidence. But Buzz was gone, and there was no point kicking a man who is down. So to console my dad, I told him that whatever he did wrong happened too many years ago for him to be blamed for this; my brother was an adult, and he chose to do what he did. I told my father to get some sleep, and he left.

Even when Kristene arrived a few minutes later, weeping and hugging her, Mom showed no outward emotion. We talked until late and retired to the bedroom across the hall from my mother's room, keeping the door cracked open to be able to hear Mom. During that long, sleepless night, we heard Mom crying and sobbing beyond her closed door.

As I listened to the sounds of my mother mourning the death of her youngest, my mind went back to how I had tried to bond with my brother over the years, especially after I became a Christian. Our mother always ran interference, never letting us be alone together. My brother was the only one of the four of us who remained in the Christian Science church; everyone knew he only did it out of dutiful obedience to his mother's wishes. I thought of all the many times I witnessed to him, which he dutifully reported to his mother, who in turn dissuaded him from listening to me. Now he was tragically gone, and that it was by his own hand was a shock to all of us, for he was never given to depression or despair. So far at this point, few of the facts were known, but they would come out.

The Air Force flew my parents, along with me and my sister, Cindy, to Vandenberg Air Base, where we met with senior officers. We were treated with courtesy and patience despite my father's embarrassing verbal abuses and open disrespect. At a meeting that day, we were told that my brother was recently passed over for promotion for the third time, meaning he could not renew his contract when it expired in a year. My brother requested to be allowed to serve out the remainder of his contract in Bittburg, Germany, where he was stationed earlier. The Air Force initially approved his transfer request, but three days later, it was rescinded with no explanation. Upon receiving this news, my brother left the base early in the day, went to his apartment and shot himself. His phone records and the upstairs neighbor who heard the shot revealed he shot himself immediately after speaking with his mother for three minutes. My mother was defensive when asked about what she said in that final conversation with my brother. She never answered the question, and to this day we don't know.

We were taken to my brother's apartment. The moment I entered, I understood that the premonitions I had weeks earlier were the Lord forewarning me and urging me to pray because it was my brother who was going to die, not me, for he was in deep spiritual darkness. We were shocked to see a large quantity of hardcore pornography of the most perverse kind was everywhere, especially in his bedroom. Oddly, all of the women in the photographs were Asian, and a large Japanese flag was pinned to his bedroom wall. Almost three dozen rifles, pistols, and shotguns, most of them in their original boxes and never fired, were stashed everywhere in his apartment. This was a side of my brother that none of us knew existed.

The investigating Riverside Police detective who met us there was especially helpful when he learned I was a fellow officer. I knew that my brother had been robbed of his firearms at gunpoint in his apartment a year ago, so I wanted to see scene photographs and other evidence to satisfy myself that this wasn't a second home invasion robbery that had gone bad. My parents were desperate for any reason to believe Buzz was a crime victim, that the cause was anything other than suicide. But it was not to be. The second I saw photographs of my brother, the position of his body on the bed, the handgun that his hand had released after pulling the trigger, his bloody head wound, and that his apartment was locked from the inside and nothing was taken, I was satisfied that his death was suicide, but seeing those images of him lying in his own blood would haunt me for years afterward.

That night my father and I were in twin beds in our room on the base. It had been a hard day, and the shock was just setting in.

"I don't know how you do what you do, son," my dad said.

"What do you mean?" I asked.

"All the death and dead bodies you deal with. I can't handle even this. I don't know how you do it and then sleep at night," my father said.

"It's the nature of my work, that's all, Dad. You can adjust to anything if you see it enough," I replied.

"Can you tell me why couldn't Buzz have been more like you were?" my father said. I asked him what he meant.

"I mean you were in and out of love with this girl and that one, someone new almost every month. You won and you lost over and over and it made you strong, able to handle tough times, and letdowns. You always moved forward. But your mother never let loose of Buzz, and I never was there for him. He was thirty-two and had never had a girlfriend and few friends, all because of his mother wanting to control him. Buzz tried hard to be his own man, but he was never strong enough. I feel your mother and I are both responsible for this," my father said.

My dad was right about us: my brother and I were total opposites. I was the oldest, and he the youngest. In terms of health, I was the strongest of the four kids; he the sickliest. Growing up, we were both targets of our father's verbal and physical abuses, especially when he was drinking. Our mother instinctively tried to overprotect and make her boys into sheltered, overly refined, emasculated "gentlemen." I rejected her efforts; my brother accepted. Buzz was the quiet type, a serious student; I was kicked out of several schools for picking fistfights, bad grades, skipping class, smoking, and gambling.

Whereas I worked after school every day as a box boy and apprentice mechanic, held summer and weekend jobs working construction labor, worked out and practiced boxing constantly, fought, drank, and chased girls, my brother was only allowed to work a few hours a month during the summer as a grocery store box boy but never if was too hot. That way he would always be clean and comfortable. Mother never allowed Buzz to date, not even for his senior prom, and my sisters and I thought it odd that he went along with this. Mom always gave Buzz cloth napkins at all meals, while my sisters and I were given paper. Paper was too scratchy for his hands, he said. I voluntarily enlisted at age nineteen, itching to go to Vietnam, and I did two tours of duty there; Mother made sure that my brother went in as an officer in the Air Force. My father's assessment was right; both parents shared some blame for my brother taking his own life, but it was he who made that choice.

There was a memorial service at McChord Air Base in Washington, followed by a funeral in Bellevue that exploded when the so-called Christian Science Practitioner, who was there at my mother's request, stood coldly staring at my family in silent contempt as we all wept and grieved heavily at my brother's closed casket. My father flew into a rage at the Practitioner's behavior, and he wasn't the only one who was upset. At this my parents openly fought with each other again, and everyone else, my dad blaming my mother and her insistence on the Christian Science church for ruining my brother. My dysfunctional family disintegrated even further, the fragile peace we had known was shattered. My mother cut off the rest of her kids for not being more attentive to her during the funeral, saying it was for her, and my father went on a two-month drunk in his sailboat, drifting around Puget Sound, and my sisters and I fell out of contact with each other. At my mother's house on the day of the funeral, Kristene assumed a servant's role to my family, cooking and serving food and keeping a low profile out of respect. Except for when I was at work, Kristene never left my side, and I withdrew from everyone except her. It meant a lot to me that each of Kristene's brothers called me to see how I was. Seeing the deep despair we all felt, Kristene on her own initiative supported my mother, who lived alone, by calling her often and taking flowers to her.

Death is so final; all chances of correcting mistakes, of asking for and granting forgiveness are gone forever. For the next few months, every day was a chore for me to get through, and I dreaded going to work. I tried not to show it, but having to respond to routine suicide and natural death scenes rattled my composure, for every one reminded me of the photographs of my brother's death scene; clear thinking left me, leaving only emotional turbulence. I went home at the end of each day seeking solace from Kristene. I was greatly weakened by this chain of events: my brother's sudden and violent death by his own hand, that he could be so involved in such darkness, and the shameful response of my family to such a tragic loss grieved and sickened me. For months afterward I was unable to take the lead in things as I normally would.

What strength I did have I drew from reading and meditating on the Word of God, especially the Psalms, and from seeing Kristene step up to the plate in my stead. Because of our oneness, Kristene always knew what to do; discussion wasn't necessary. She knew exactly when I was grieving; no matter how far apart we were physically. One afternoon when I was feeling down, Kristene called me at work.

"Hi Honey, are you too busy to come up to the house for a minute? I have something here for you."

"You do? What is it?" I asked.

"Just come up and you'll see," she said.

Kristene was dressed in only a bathrobe when I came through the door. She took me by the hand, led me down the hall to the bedroom, and began undressing me.

"We're gonna rebuild your family, Darling. Let's make a baby!" she said, smiling. I was speechless as she completely undressed me, slipped out of her robe, and pulled me onto the bed.

"C'mon, make me pregnant. I want to rebuild the Hansen family! New life! I want your baby, Baby!"

Thereafter Kristene launched an aggressive campaign to bring new life into my family. She had me every morning before I went to work. I had to skip going to lunch with the guys and instead come home every day, where she was always ready and waiting for me; I wasn't allowed to even eat until we were done. She gave me no rest. If I said I was starting to "run on empty" in the evening, she invented new ways to arouse me. She was always on and always ready, and she kept this going for over two weeks, up until her period was due again. When it didn't come, we crossed our fingers. We waited a week to see her gynecologist, and then we got the news: Kristene was pregnant.

There were immediate changes. She put in her two weeks' notice that she was quitting her job. (We agreed she would not work again once we started having children). She devoured books on natural child birthing and parenting, completely gave up alcohol, and switched to eating only organic foods.

"I'm going to breastfeed our baby and make the baby food here at home," she announced, "and we're going to adopt the family bed concept."

"Family bed? What's that?" I asked her.

"I just finished this book about it. The baby sleeps not in a crib but between the parents in their bed until he or she is ready to move to his or her own bed. It's an ancient custom in Middle East cultures and is even mentioned in the Bible. The child is emotionally stronger and mentally more stable if the nurturing continues until the child decides it's time to move," Kristene told me.

As the holidays approached, the signs that new life was on the way were showing. Kristene's tummy began rounding out, and in our daily prayers, I would lay my hands on her there and pray the Blood of Christ over our baby. The very promise of new life brought rejuvenation, healing, and joy all around. My parents were elated when we broke the news just before Christmas, and Kristene's side of the family was especially happy for us. Kristene's appearance was changing: her facial features rounded, and her skin and hair took on a lustrous radiance, a glow from within that I had never seen on her before. She was more beautiful in pregnancy than ever. Always a fan of Starbucks coffee, Kristene switched to herbal teas instead; a lover of pastry and pasta, she ate a carefully balanced diet of only vegetables and lean meats and fish. She experienced a strange craving for lemon meringue pie, and she and my sister Cindy met often at a restaurant called Charlie's for pie and tea.

Christmas that year was more meaningful than any previous year; Kristene's being with child produced an atmosphere of eager anticipation for the future throughout her family and mine. For my parents it eased the pain of their first Christmas without their youngest child as they looked forward to the birth of a new grandchild.

Right after New Year's, an ultrasound test determined our first baby would be a girl and the due date would be the first week of March. Kristene began buying furniture for the baby's bedroom. From my mother she collected all the cards that my mother received when I was born, assembled them into a collage, and framed them for the baby's room. We bought an oak rocking chair from an unfinished furniture store that I stained and lacquered for her to use when nursing our baby.

In February we began natural childbirth classes at Overlake Hospital, sitting on cushioned mats on the floor in a circle with other expecting couples, practicing breathing, timing, and coaching techniques. It was all great fun, and one of the best rewards was that we met and became lifelong friends with Ron and Brenda Egge, a Christian couple several years younger than us. By now Kristene's tummy was getting bigger almost by the day. When the baby moved, she would put my hand on her belly to feel the movements, and we laughed and prayed together. Every night I rubbed olive oil on her abdomen to prevent stretch marks from becoming permanent after delivery; such was how our intimacy was deepening.

On the night of March 5, the day after my birthday, contractions began and increased in frequency all through the night. At 2:00 a.m., I drove Kristene to the hospital, and she immediately went into labor. The hospital called our doctor and family friend, Jim Van Ostrand, known to the nurses as Dr. V. O. For hours we worked together applying the breathing and pushing methods we thought we had mastered in class. But now it was the real thing, and none of it was easy. Kristene was gripped with fear at first and nearly broke my hand in hers with every major effort to push the baby out. By noon we were no closer to delivery, and we were both exhausted from lack of sleep and the drama. Kristene's yells and screams could be heard all over that wing of the hospital every time she pushed. When Dr. Van Ostrand finally arrived and took over, he ordered Kristene to stop yelling and just push. I was mad at him for speaking to my wife in the tone that he used, but he was known for his abrupt style, and what was really important were Kristene and our baby, so I let it go.

After a grueling fourteen-hour labor, our firstborn, Kristena Rose, was born, a healthy eight-pound girl with eyes wide open. We were so excited that we forgot how tired we were. There are no words to describe how I felt holding Kristene's baby, our baby, in my arms. I went home to grab a few hours' sleep and to allow Kristene and our baby to rest and nurse. I got a brief second wind as soon as I got home, so I called everyone in the family to announce the family newest arrival. Then I slept.

My mother was the first person in the family to visit us at the hospital the very next day. The change I saw in Mom was nothing short of miraculous; she was totally enthralled with the arrival of new life in the family. There was joy in her face as she held her granddaughter in her arms. Not a trace of her former grief was there.

Through the arrival of new life did Kristene initiate the rebuilding of my shattered family. Mourning and lamentations were put aside, for there was life anew. All because of Kristene's love. She was a living fulfillment of Isaiah 58:11-12:

"You will be like a well-watered garden, like a spring whose waters never fail.

Your people will rebuild the ancient ruins and will raise up the age-old foundations; you will be called Repairer of Broken Walls, Restorer of Streets with Dwellings."

Such was Kristene; such was her love, like a spring whose waters never fail. And yet there would be more to come.

Rebuilding our family with new life. Baby shower, 1987

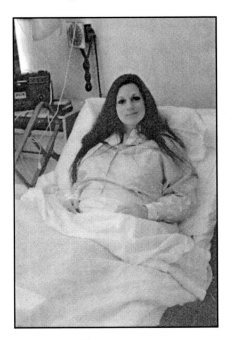

The new mom

The proud father

Shirley Hansen - A Joyful End to Grief and Mourning

Ray Hansen – Grief and Lamentations Set Aside.

CHAPTER EIGHTEEN

The arrival of a newborn can pacify even the most strained family relations. It was no less true with us: grudges, frictions and factions were forgotten as waves of amazed well-wishers visited Kristene and her first baby at the hospital – amazed, for no one had ever associated Kristene with motherhood. In six years, Kristene had transitioned from being defiantly single to happily married, to glowing motherhood. The family beauty who didn't want to ruin her figure with child-bearing was now the poster child of motherhood, wifehood, peace, and happiness.

New life brought new beginnings. Our six-year honeymoon had shifted into a new season the day we brought our newborn daughter home. Our romance, the chemistry we had always had for each other, had changed as we had changed through Kristene's pregnancy and birthing, but it was still in play. No more were we two freewheeling, adventuring, married lovers; now we were a family of three, and the demands of parenting were already refining and honing us: sleeplessness as baby nursed at the breast day and night, three of us in the family bed, never-ending exhaustion from interrupted sleep, irregular hours, responding to baby's cries, and yet this is what we wanted. We had great joy as we entered a new season of life.

Overnight our thinking changed. "Self" as our core perspective on how we viewed life was replaced by "us" instead. When I wasn't too tired to think about it, I understood the biblical term "joy unspeakable" because how we felt now was simply indefinable; all I could find to do was give God thanks for everything. Pregnancy and parenthood gave a new dimension to life now; it even enhanced our physical attraction to each other. We were more desirous for each other than ever before, but ironically, most of the time we were also too tired to do much about it. As good as life had been for us already, these would be our Golden Years.

Motherhood utterly transformed Kristene. In her new role as mom, she became like a she-bear in her protective love. For several weeks she stayed home and allowed no visitors until the baby had time to develop strength and immunities. Doctor visits were the only reason mother and daughter left the house. I only left home for work, groceries, and church. Sequestered by choice, Kristene stayed inside and devoured books on mothering and parenting and read her Bible voraciously when she wasn't nursing or otherwise tending to her baby. She had collected tapes of nursery rhymes and songs during her pregnancy and played these during the day, singing along with them, and read Scripture verses and sang songs and worship choruses to our baby. She cordoned off our wood-burning stove to prevent any chance our baby would fall against it when she reached the toddler stage, and we stopped using it for home heating. She had stockpiled organic flour, grains, legumes, and rice, and game meats and birds from my hunting were in the freezer. Kristene always had a fresh pot of organic soup or stew on the stove and bread in the oven. Every time I came home from work in those days, the aroma of food on the stove, the sound of children's music, and the loving warmth of my family and my home embraced me and pulled me across the threshold. My wish for a home like I saw Ron and Kay had the first time I visited there years ago had been fulfilled. *Could life be any better than this?* I wondered.

I was alarmed when a young family was injured in a wreck near our home in the same make and model of Korean sub-compact sedan as ours. With Kristene's bargain-driving abilities we quickly got all our money back from the dealer and replaced it with a recent model, full-size Oldsmobile with low miles. It was a good-looking car that met our needs: metallic dark blue with matching vinyl roof, blue velour cloth seats, and power everything. It was heavy and sturdy enough to be safe in a wreck. After we secured the baby seat on the back seat, I felt better about my wife and daughter being on the road. It was the perfect family car, and for many years it gave us trouble-free service and cost little to maintain. Roomy and comfortable, we could ride in it for hours without tiring, and the trunk space was huge enough for all our baby supplies. We traveled often that first summer to visit relatives and friends, attend church, and go on picnics at local parks, keeping the stroller, toys, change of clothes, diaper supplies, and picnic basket conveniently in the trunk.

We kept in touch with couples from our Lamaze classes too, especially Ron and Brenda Egge. Between Halloween and Thanksgiving, Kristene hosted a dessert and coffee party for the parents and the babies, having a playpen in the living room for the little ones and the oak rocker in a spare bedroom for moms to use when nursing. During these early days, we bonded with the Egge family, and a deep friendship developed that continues to this day.

After the New Year, Kristene sensed the Holy Spirit urging her to again visit her parents in California. There was no negative news about George's health, yet she sensed the Lord was prompting her to go. She took a video camera with her to record our baby with her grandparents and came back in three days. Two weeks later, we received word that George had gone back into the hospital. Kristene was on the phone constantly with each of her parents and hospital staff. George sounded weak and groggy on the phone and seemed to understand that he was passing away. Kristene and Ron and Kay talked to George about spiritual things and led him in the sinner's prayer on the phone.

We were relieved that George was Heaven-bound, therefore we knew we would see him again, but I had to smile when I thought of George and spiritual things. I still remembered Kristene's story that years ago

George once told her that because he believed in reincarnation, he believed that his marriage to Matilda was punishment for his bad deeds in a previous life. He was enduring Matilda without leaving her, he said, so he could pay his debt and be free of her in the next life!

Ron and Richard flew to California to arrange to have their father's body shipped home, and brought their mother back with them. George Kinssies was buried on a grassy slope along the treed edge of the Aberdeen Cemetery, overlooking the harbor. The day was bitter cold, but the rain stopped, as if out of respect for our service. Kristene and Richard held their emotions in check, but it was Ron who was openly grieving for his father. Ron, a true man's man, found me in the crowd of relatives and wept and grieved as he hugged me. More than blood kin, Ron and I were brothers in the Holy Spirit. Ron was the eldest brother of my wife; he held the honor of being my best man when I married his only sister, and he was my closest friend. We had spent years meeting together for Bible study and entering God's throne room in prayer together, and our two families worshiped, ate, played, and worked together. In all that time, we had bonded as men do. A sacred trust grew out of years of spiritual and family bonding, a trust that enabled deepest confidences to be shared, a trust that was an unuttered oath of mutual accountability between us.

The family split began at George's funeral. Bob stood next to his mother at the burial site, posturing as the one son she could lean on, his arm around her, making a show of assuring her in a loud voice that he was taking charge of her, that she could count on him alone.

"Don't you worry, I'll take care of you, Mom," Bob said. Matilda was crying and shaking during the funeral and burial.

After the burial service, Bob and Angela created a stir by not showing up at the family reception immediately afterward, and Bob later refused to pay his share of the funeral costs, which resulted in heated arguments between Ron and Bob. Ultimately Bob's share of his father's funeral expenses and his mother's airfare costs were paid equally by Ron, Richard, and us. Bearing the extra cost because of Bob's refusal to keep his word wasn't easy for any of us, and triggered a widening social and emotional gulf between Bob and the rest of us.

For Kristene's sake, I set aside my disappointment with Bob and did my best to stay neutral as the split between Bob and Ron deepened. But neutrality wasn't possible with Bob. To be in keeping with the directive in Romans 12:18, "If it is possible, as far as it depends on you, live at peace with everyone," Ron wrote a letter to Bob that he read to me before mailing. It was a plea for peace, written in humility; but Bob remained obdurate, and the result was the shredding of the family unity we had known. Out of respect that Bob was Kristene's brother I attempted neutrality and distanced us from Bob and Angela as quietly and as peaceably as possible and focused instead on my own family. Kristene was already talking about having another baby, and I wanted a different house for us before we did that. Kristene seemed content with our little house, but for me, my two prior failed marriages there made it impossible for it to be *ours*.

I wanted to move out of Bellevue. All my life I had lived and worked there except for four years of military service, and I had had enough of the stifling sterility and plasticity the town was locally known for. Our next home had to be bigger, not in Bellevue, and on more land. The time was right for a move, for the Seattle housing market was white-hot, with property appreciation reaching unheard-of heights, beyond anyone's expectations. People everywhere were speculating in ever-increasing real estate values, some became overnight millionaires on paper, and others acted as if they were. Banks, lending institutions and private financiers all jumped into the game by lowering lending requirements and shortening the time it took for loan approval. Houses, commercial property and raw land alike were turning over with rapid speed, and the sudden equity increase for established homeowners gave many a false sense of prosperity, for the land and home rush lacked a viable basis such as new industrial contracts at companies like Boeing that would support a true demand for more housing.

Hardly anyone paid attention to the fact that wages and job growth weren't keeping up with the increased cost of real estate, so the "boom" as some called it, was an illusion of prosperity fueled by wild speculation and a lowering of lending standards that would eventually result in the average person and the first-time buyer being unable to buy a home. "Buy land—they're not making any more of it" or words to that effect was a slogan heard everywhere.

A risk-taker by nature, I knew the inflationary trend could better my financial position *if* I timed my moves just right. I assessed my financial situation and outlook: the grim truth was that I was a glorified clock-puncher, living payday to payday like nearly everybody else, except that we had started a new family later in life than most, and I would be facing college for our kids and retirement for us at a later point in life than most others. When I reached police retirement age, our children would be still at home, facing college; that was the downrange perspective. I needed another way to feather our financial bed; I decided to risk jumping in while the real estate game was still hot. There was a tight time window in which to make that move.

It was a gamble for a family on one income, but I considered it worth the risk: I took out a second mortgage on our home, an adjustable rate mortgage that had a ridiculously low interest rate, a 'teaser' rate that gave me three years of low payments before I had to face the music. I took out enough cash for both a down payment on our next home and any changes to it we needed to make before we moved in. I also obtained pre-approval for our next mortgage so that we could close quickly when we found the right place. The ink was barely dry on the loan documents when Kristene called me from a pay phone.

"Honey I'm in Issaquah and I found a place you've *got* to see," she said.

As I pulled up to the gas station parking lot where she was standing outside the car waiting for me, I was again impressed with Kristene's striking good looks. Her beauty was bone-deep, through and through, no makeup needed; pregnancy and motherhood had actually enhanced her physical perfection so that even a loose burlap bag couldn't hide her voluptuous figure, glowing skin, and lustrous hair. *I couldn't have done better if I had designed her myself,* I mentally remarked.

Issaquah was a historic turn-of-the-century coal mining and timber town located about fifteen miles east of Bellevue. Nestled amid lush green hillsides and with three creeks flowing through it, its quaint town core had been lovingly preserved by caring citizens; it was and still is one of the most picturesque small town settings anywhere in America. Driving there eastbound on Interstate 90 from Seattle or Bellevue, one is greeted by soothingly lush green mountains and hills straight ahead and on the right, and huge, blue Lake Sammamish to the left.

Kristene was with Jeanette, our real estate agent, and we got in the agent's car and went to see the home we would live in next.

CHAPTER NINETEEN

could live here for the rest of my life, was my thought the first time I walked around the outside of what would become our next home, for never had I seen such an idyllic setting for a home right in town, so suitably situated in historic Issaquah. Like the proverbial pearl of great price, it was tucked onto a one-third acre lot at the end of a dead-end street, the property was a small peninsula formed by Issaquah Creek wrapping itself around three sides of the lot in a hairpin turn. The seclusion was near-perfect, for the entire bank across the creek was at least twelve feet high, thick with brush and tree-lined, giving the house such privacy that one could literally walk all around the outside and not be seen from across the creek. At the tip of the property, where the creek made its 180-degree bend, the lawn sloped gently from the house down to the water to a sandy beach that was perfect for wading and fishing. I walked down to the little beach and stood in the sand at the water's edge. It was late spring, and the creek channel was broad, and wooded on both sides; its waters were clear and shallow, the sounds of their muted murmuring muffling the noise of the town and the freeway, just enough to override it with peace and calm. In my mind's eye I visualized our kids happily playing here with their friends on hot summer days.

Four fruit-bearing apple and cherry trees in leafy bloom lined the southern bank of the property, affording even more seclusion to the side of the house where the family room and kitchen were. Near the edge of the lawn near the kitchen patio a huge weeping willow with a wooden swing under it graced the upper lawn, close to the house, and a few yards from the willow, a hammock was stretched between an elm tree and a maple. Across the creek, blackberry bushes cascaded down the higher bank in wild green tangles, hanging over the water, berries ripening for the coming summer for anyone willing to make the easy wade through ankle-deep water. Rainbow trout were in the creek year-round, and salmon by the thousands would fight their way upstream every fall to spawn and die. The setting made everything else we had looked at seem sterile and cold and made us feel dissatisfied with our present home in Bellevue. It appealed to me so much that I resolved to buy it before I even entered the house.

This was no cookie-cutter tract house in a housing development. It was built in 1958, a time when even modest homes were well-built, of good materials and craftsmanship. It exuded character and a sense of history. It was twenty-seven hundred square feet of old fashioned individuality; an L-shaped four-bedroom rambler built the old way, before plywood and chip-board were in use. Every window was wood framed, no metal or plastic; the exterior siding was all number-one grade clear cedar shiplap with red brick trim; and the subflooring was the best: hand-milled, hand-fitted, tongue-in-groove two-by-six planks over four-by-ten beams on twenty-inch centers. With one-inch-thick red oak plank flooring on top of the subfloor, the floors were as rigid and strong as if they were reinforced concrete instead of wood. The roof, too, was best-quality, hand-split, thick-butt cedar shakes, not the thin shingles that became common in homes built later. In many ways the house and its woodsy setting reminded me of the home I grew up in, before my parents divorced, and it made me long to live here, in this place; to me it was a chance to recover a lost time in my life, to do better for my family than my father had done for his.

The house and the working-class neighborhood it was in were a step back in time, to a more stable era of working middle-class families that stayed together, neighbors who knew and watched out for each other, town identity and pride. *We can build our family and live out our lives right here, no need to ever move again,* was my thought.

The historic charm of the town awakened in us what we really wanted in a home: community with a sense of pride and history, and Old Issaquah had it all. The neighborhood was part of the historic downtown where mom-and-pop businesses that had been handed down through the generations still flourished. Within walking distance of the house were the butcher's shop, hardware store, supermarket, grain and feed store, ice cream parlor, stage theater; a city park, railroad museum, and city hall were all in one adjacent space, and old-time taverns, diners, and a barber shop lined both sides of Front Street.

The deal closed quickly, for our loan was pre-approved. A week into the buying process I learned by sheer chance that downtown Issaquah had a history of flooding, and the house we were buying was in what was called the hundred-year flood plain thus lenders required flood insurance before a mortgage would be issued. Our real estate agent never mentioned flooding to us and acted dismissive when I asked her about it. I paid for a second inspection of the crawlspace under the house and talked with residents and city officials. There had been a significant flood two years before, and ground water nearly filled the crawlspace beneath, but didn't enter the house itself. I was concerned that the current owner didn't disclose this and that our "experienced" agent seemed to be ignorant of the flooding issue. But by then our desire to live there was so strong that it overrode my nagging doubts. We went ahead with the purchase and hired contractors to remodel the interior, including removing an interior wall, painting, new carpeting and updating the electrical wiring to current code requirements, all of which delayed our move-in even more.

Already there were signs that life in Old Issaquah would be worth waiting for; far better than we expected. While we were still working on the house before moving in, neighbors bringing refreshments came by to introduce themselves and welcome us. On moving day, several neighbors walked over and helped us unload furniture into the house.

Two months after the purchase, we finally moved in to a new home and a new life. As we unpacked boxes and set up cupboards and cabinets in the summer heat, there was a knock at the kitchen door from a smiling man in his sixties, holding a tray of lemonade and paper cups. He introduced himself as Lou, a widower and a devout Christian who lived directly across the creek from us. Lou had waded across the creek in his rubber boots to welcome us, and thus began a long friendship.

The traditional style of our Issaquah home lent itself to Kristene's decorating tastes better than our old place in Bellevue did, for its style was northwest contemporary. But this home was traditional in style, in a gracious, serene setting that matched Kristene's beauty, style and personality perfectly. Kristene was very traditional, a Renaissance woman; a lady in the classical sense. More often than not, she wore dresses and skirts, rarely pants or jeans, and feminine blouses, shirts and tops, her hair was long, dark and heavy and she wore it in traditional styles, mostly down but sometimes pinned up, so that in every way she radiated beauty and sensuality in the classic European tradition.

And now here at last, in the lovely pastoral Eden of our new home, itself an expression of tradition and beauty, Kristene's strong artistic flair had an avenue of expression. Italian watercolors of plant life, framed in oil-rubbed wood frames were everywhere, fine color prints depicting English hunting scenes, of dogs, horses, game animals and mounted men adorned master bedroom walls, throughout the house were Middle Eastern pattern wool rugs and long runners down the hallways, white plaster niches holding flower vases were inset into the entry and hallway walls, beautiful custom tiles in pastel colors and floral patterns graced the bathrooms and kitchen backsplash, invitingly deep, overstuffed sofa, chairs and ottoman covered with heavy white brocade broadcloth, a crystal chandelier hung over the gleaming 1940's dining room table that was burnished to a high sheen, so that in all, our new home exuded both old-time elegance and down-home warmth that made visitors put their feet up and overstay, for this home gave one the feel of going back to a more comfortable time.

We bonded immediately with Terry and Sallie Cowgill, neighbors who lived a stone's throw down Birch Place from us. Terry and Sallie were our age and had three daughters and a son. The two oldest Cowgill kids were Callie and Annie, followed by Russell and Lindsay. This beautiful family looked as if a Hollywood film producer had selected them each for a weekly family television show. Terry was handsome, having thick, dark bushy hair, a trim mustache, a baritone voice, and stoutly built. Sallie was a beautiful, tall, willowy blonde, radiating a constant smile that emanated from her sweet spirit. All four of their kids were blue-eyed, tow-head blondes; tall, slim, bright, and well-mannered.

Contented as we were to be here, nights for me were difficult. Deep down, something was very wrong, somewhere, somehow. For weeks after we moved in, my sleep was disrupted by a sense of alarm. Was it the Holy Spirit? To no avail, I wracked my brain and prayed to understand it, but it eventually subsided, and I dismissed it as the stress of a major change in life.

We now owned two houses with three mortgages between them. We could easily sell the Bellevue house; the Seattle housing market was still white hot; bidding wars among buyers for even undesirable properties were commonplace. Our old home in Bellevue had quickly appreciated well beyond the new second mortgage valuation even before we moved out, and I concluded that there was more money to be made by keeping it for at least another year. It rented quickly. Our first tenants were a nice couple with two teenagers who were relocating from Oregon after their business failed. They chanced moving to Seattle with bad credit and no job to look for work because the Seattle job market was much better than it was in Oregon.

Renting out our former home was my first serious business transaction. Negotiating terms, signing the lease agreement, and receiving initial rent deposits were a turning point for me, a step forward as a provider, and I felt deeply satisfied that I was doing more than just punching a clock to provide for my family. Now I was a landlord. I had income other than my job. All those years of hanging on to the Bellevue house, of Kristene and I pouring our love, sweat, and treasure into it had paid off. At least some of our money was working for us now, instead of us working for it, and that gave me immense satisfaction. As I drove the twenty-minute drive to the police station every morning, I felt like I was on top of the world, with too many blessings to count.

Parenting was changing us. We volunteered for the church nursery for the first service every other week and joined a Sunday school class for young marrieds, even though we were the oldest couple in the class. Kristene devoured books on motherhood and child rearing, secular and Christian alike. Every night I read children's books on Bible stories to our daughter, re-enacting some of Jesus' parables to her, and helped her memorize Psalm 1, Psalm 23, and the Lord's Prayer.

"Honey, it's time to make another baby," Kristene whispered in my ear one night as I was drifting off to sleep.

"Huh? Wha-what? What was that?" I said.

"Yes! Get me pregnant right now!" she said, on her knees in the bed now, throwing the sheets aside and pulling off my bedclothes.

"I want a summer baby so we can be outside when it's warm. Let's make a boy this time!"

And so began our second baby campaign. For three weeks, we engaged intimately at least twice a day, morning and evening, in every room at home, in the car, wherever and whenever Kristene's sense of romance and adventure took over. We were excited when her very next period was a no-show. We waited. Two weeks later, the doctor confirmed Kristene was pregnant with a probable due date in late July.

"All you have to do is look at me and I'm pregnant!" Kristene beamed at me.

Christmas was weeks away now, and it was typically cold and gray outside – indoor weather. Little Kristena, called 'Dih-Tih' by her mother, was walking and talking and helped us decorate the tree as rain pelted the windows, the logs in the fireplace crackled, and Christmas music filled the house. The things Kristena told Santa she wanted were wrapped and hidden away, and she was bursting with excitement that Santa would come down the chimney a few nights from now.

Life was better now than it had ever been; everything around us was rich with new beginnings and great promise. We had each other and our first child, so young, healthy and strong; we had another child on the way, a new home that we loved, with new friends and neighbors. We enjoyed the support and involvement of a large extended family, deep friendships, and strong ties to an even larger church family. All of the usual rounds of holiday family dinners and parties were enlivened by the news of another baby on the way. In all this, Kristene was my greatest joy. No one had ever loved me as much as she did. She was the gift that kept on giving, more and more, with no end in sight. Glowingly beautiful with or without cosmetics, selfless, utterly devoted, stunning, maternal, amorous, devout, sensual, loving, and a faithful wife, mother, and daughter. Kristene stood out among other American women of our time, her social refinements and conduct, and her views of gender roles were from an earlier era, another century. In addition to her traditional style of hair and dress, her manners and social graces were the old style, unfailingly polite and courteous. She was a home-body, a capable home manager, a creative cook, and she set a beautiful table for every meal. She was a man's woman, having three older brothers and a father who were good to her, and because of the discrimination against her by her mother and aunts, she preferred the company of men, she thought it proper to defer to men, so that men liked her and were comfortable with her because they sensed that she liked them, and expected them to be what they were: men. With her I was a blessed man.

By late spring, Kristene's tummy was so big she looked as though she could go into labor at any time, even though she was only six months along. The baby was shifting around inside her, and she was carrying high. Every night in bed I talked to the baby as I rubbed her belly with vitamin E oil to prevent permanent stretch marks. Kristene was so huge that the manager of a furniture store asked her if she was about to deliver. When Kristene said no, the manager said he thought otherwise and asked her to leave. We went in for an ultrasound, and I watched as the technician smeared clear ointment over Kristene's huge mounded belly and ran an instrument over it that looked like a microphone. On the screen we could see the outline of a head, hands and feet.

"It's a boy," the technician said as we watched. Kristene began sobbing.

"I asked the Lord for a son, and He told me that's what we would have," she said through her tears.

By late July, there were no labor pains. Kristene was bigger than ever and I teased her, as her walk had become a waddle. One afternoon she called me at home minutes after she had left in the car. She was at a pay phone, and she was crying, saying she had been in an accident and the man in the other car was being rude to her. I raced over to where she was, just four blocks from home. Kristene was fine; she had rear-ended a car driven by a man who was with his equally pregnant wife, and their four little kids who were in the back seat. When he saw me, he was polite and civil. No one appeared to be hurt, and the damage to his car was minimal. When we exchanged information, I learned from reading his business card that he was a personal injury attorney. He told me he would have his wife and kids checked by a doctor. I almost died on the spot. I drove Kristene and Kristena home and walked back to get my detective car. I took Kristene's car keys away and told her there would be no more driving for her until after the baby came. I prayed that everything would be okay (a lawsuit like this I *didn't* need), and thankfully, we never heard anything more about the accident.

By the evening of the last day of July, Kristene began labor pains. *Oh no! Tomorrow is our anniversary. He can't come on our anniversary!* I thought. But the contractions grew stronger all night.

"Happy anniversary, Sweetheart, is there any way we can put this off until tomorrow? Tie your legs together, maybe?" I joked. Kristene smiled and tried to laugh, but another contraction shut her off.

"Doesn't look that way, Baby," she gasped, smiling through her pain and sweat. It was hospital time. I got Kristena dressed and put her in her car seat and helped Kristene into the car. We took Kristena to Ron and Kay's on the way to the hospital. The contractions were stronger and more frequent. I worried that we might not make it to the hospital.

Kristene's contractions were building in frequency and force when we arrived at Group Health hospital in Redmond. Orderlies scrambled to get her into a wheelchair, as I half-carried her inside, and we reached the maternity ward just as she began the Lamaze method of breathing through the contractions, saying, "Pahhh!" with each exhale. This labor was much shorter and easier than Kristena's was. We entered the hospital at 9:00 a.m., and our son John was born by noon as the nurse handed him to me. God's word to Kristene was fulfilled. We now had the two children God told her we would have on the night of our first date eight years earlier.

"For great is His love toward us, and the faithfulness of the Lord endures forever. Praise the Lord." Psalm 117:2

Maternal grandmother Gladys 'Mom' Gardner as a young woman in about 1910. A rock of unconditional love, her legacy of civility and loving kindness continues to impact her descendants to this day.

A family symbol of safety and refuge. The Kirkland home of Ray and
Gladys Gardner, maternal grandparents of the Hansen kids.

1957. John's refuge from his father was his grandparents and his horse.

CHAPTER TWENTY

Kristene was always right about things concerning family and home life, for such was her life focus, and her desire to have a summer baby was no exception. Warm weather permitted her on an afternoon to sit on the swing under the willow tree, and sing to Johnny as she rocked him to sleep in the shade, and neighbors would walk down the street or wade across the creek to visit and see our newest little one. Summer is a basking, tranquil time of year, when doors and windows could be left open all day, filling the house with fresh air, the scent of green grass and trees, the sounds of the creek tumbling gently over rocks, logs and tree branches, and the occasional splash of a large trout breaking up out of the water to catch a flying insect. Early on some mornings, deer would be on our lawn when we awoke, having walked up the creek and stopping to feed on our flowers and shrubs. On such mornings, I would awaken Kristena to see them before they left, heading further upstream, and we would share in her excitement. On other mornings, fishermen in hip waders worked their way upstream past the house, working the deep holes in the creek, pulling big rainbow trout out of the water. On the hottest afternoons, neighborhood kids came over to play on our sandy beach with Kristena, all shepherded and guarded by our dog Kaiser. Sunday school classmates and neighbors came over with home-cooked meals, and to spend time relaxing on our patio over lemonade and iced tea.

Of course, my parents were elated that we had produced a son who would carry on the family name, and my father was especially pleased that we had named him after him and me. Like his sister, Johnny never knew his crib, only the family bed. At first, Kristena was mad at us for bringing home another baby. "Take Johnny back to the hosipal" she demanded. But she soon got over it, and became "the little mother" who took charge of her baby brother, spoon feeding him, talking constantly to him, and speaking on his behalf to other people.

My hunting car in those days was an old metallic blue VW Super Beetle with a sunroof and snow traction tires, its rear-engine design perfect for a man and his dog to travel muddy mountain roads and cross ditches to reach out-of-the-way hunting grounds. In it, Kaiser and I hunted the local mountains and foothills for blue grouse and the lowlands for ruffed grouse during the cooler nights and foggy mornings of September. Kristena would come out to talk with me while I skinned and cleaned the birds on the outside patio before I left for work. It was a memorable setting for father-daughter chats. The days were warm and sunny after the fog lifted, and all around us were the sounds of gently babbling waters and salmon splashing and struggling mightily upstream. The birds thus prepared, I would hang them in the cool of the tool room for proper aging. After two days I would smoke the birds in a small metal smoker, using apple or alder wood chips dampened with water until the skins were sealed golden brown and give them to Kristene for oven roasting, with garden vegetables purchased from the roadside stands of local farmers. Dinnertime was story time when fresh wild game was on the table, and I became a skilled storyteller, recounting the details and deeds of the hunt that had produced our fare, that included the field exploits of our dog Kaiser, who was known for his keen nose and hunting drive.

Not all of Kaiser's exploits were on planned hunting trips. There was the time Kristene and I were on a countryside drive, daylight was fading into twilight when we spotted a big ruffed grouse perched on a branch of a fallen tree at the edge of a brush-choked pond.

"John, look there – that's dinner!" Kristene exclaimed.

I pulled onto the shoulder and stopped, hit the trunk release button below the dash and got my shotgun out of its case in the trunk. The grouse stayed put while I assembled and loaded the shotgun. It took to wing as I shouldered the gun. Bang. It went down into the brush, dead. I could not find it in the fading light. We went home. Early the next morning I returned to the spot in my hunting rig with Kaiser. I walked him to the edge of the heavy brush and pointed at it.

"Kaiser – Dead Bird!" I commanded, to which he zipped beneath and through the brush with his nose to the ground in the direction I pointed, he disappeared in seconds. Less than a minute later he reappeared with the grouse in his mouth. I cleaned it on the spot and we went home. After allowing it to age a day we oven-roasted it with butter, salt and herbs, with white wine and wild rice. A sumptuous meal it was, that of course we shared with Kaiser.

Aspects of actual hunts were shared at these dinners: the freezing pre-dawn cold while sitting hidden in duck blinds, calling in flocks of ducks and geese, the long licks of flame as shotguns pierced pre-dawn darkness, the dogs swimming through broken ice to retrieve downed birds, the hot afternoons hunting pheasants in cornfields rustling in the wind, dogs encountering skunks and having to be doused completely in tomato juice to remedy the smell. All of it was enthralling to listen to, and fun to relive in the telling.

Thus tale-telling transformed meals into feasts, and became a tradition, woven into family lore as much as Grampa George's sea stories were in times past.

It was always Kristene's tradition to decorate our home with flowers and produce of each season. For our first fall in Issaquah, our home was bedecked with ears of red Indian corn, yellow and orange gourds of squash, and plumes of game bird feathers she had tastefully set upon house walls inside and out, giving the place inviting eye appeal and warmth from an earlier time. As a result of Kristene's touch, our home environment was one where guests felt they were in a simpler time, where they wanted to stay and not leave, so comforting was it.

Every year in the fall, when salmon by the thousands complete their return from the ocean and rivers to spawn and die in Issaquah Creek, giving their life for the next generation, throngs of people from near and far crowd the town for three days, as it holds its annual Salmon Days celebration, kicked off with the town mayor leading the parade in the back of an open convertible, followed by many floats and marching bands. Front Street is blocked off for the parade and everywhere vendors are hawking everything from cotton candy to corn on the cob. The town park is filled with pony rides for little ones, a miniature merry-go-round, dancing to live music on the park lawn. High school kids dressed in military Junior ROTC uniforms direct traffic. The state salmon hatchery, only a couple hundred yards upstream from our home, attracts huge crowds. We invited relatives and friends to leave their cars at our place and walk the block and a half to see the parade, enjoy the festival and then rest and visit with us before going home. When visitors had gone and the kids were asleep, Kristene and I would sit on the patio talking and listening to the last of the live music in the park, and the sounds of the creek, until it was time to turn in. We loved our home, and we loved Issaquah.

Such a strong sense of community prevailed in the historic part of Issaquah that was fading away in much of America that it really was like living in a Norman Rockwell painting. Families knew and looked out for each other. We all knew each other's kids. If one of our kids were where they shouldn't be or getting into trouble, a neighbor would call us and step in to protect our child or even our family pet until we got there.

One night the phone woke me up.

"Is this John?" asked a male caller.

"Yes, it is. Who are you?" I asked as I looked at the nightstand clock. Twelve-thirty.

"Hi. This is Bill down here at the Union Tavern on Front Street. Do you have a German Shorthair dog?"

I sat up in bed immediately, now fully awake. "Yes, I do," I said, alarmed.

"No problem. Your dog walked right into the tavern here, and the guys and gals here began feeding him and we just read your name and number on his tag. Thought you might want to come get him," Bill said.

I dressed quickly and went to the Union, where Kaiser was amusing the five or six patrons by catching tossed chunks of hamburger mid-air. I thanked the bartender and the patrons as I took Kaiser home. Female dogs everywhere were in heat just then, and Kaiser had taken to wandering for days at a time to fulfill the mating urge. I moved his bed to the outdoor tool room and locked him in for the night.

Like the Union Tavern, Fischer's Meats is a family-owned Front Street business that had been there many years. It was a small shop with a rock-solid reputation and a repeat customer base made up entirely of neighbors and local hunters who brought in their annual take of deer and elk for butchering. The front of the shop and red neon sign outside were reminiscent of the 1940's era, and Kristene loved the fact that she could call in an order and the employees recognized her voice right away and always asked about the kids by name. At the shop, customers often exchanged greetings and bits of gossip as they waited for their orders, something that Kristene also loved. A tall, strapping teenager named Nate usually waited on us. We liked his polite and decisive ways; it was "sir" to the men and "ma'am" to the ladies, and he knew the customers by name and remembered their preferences in cuts of meat, fish, and whether they liked the special house-made sausage.

Down the block a bit from Fischer's was another adventure in time: Lewis Hardware, an ancient place of high ceilings and red brick walls covered with shelves of galvanized buckets and brackets; rubber, plastic, and copper tubing; hammers, pliers, screwdrivers, and pry bars; old oak hand-laid, wide-plank floors, scuffed and scarred from decades of use, on which stood three revolving bins of nails of every size, shape, and finish. Long-handled shovels, rakes, and garden hoes stood in racks along one wall, along with rows of rubber work boots, hip waders, and rain ponchos. There was lumber stacked vertically in the back to save space and boxes of rifle cartridges in hard-to-find calibers and shotgun shells, and reels, lures, rods, and hooks were sold at the front counter. I always bought my hunting and fishing licenses there and took every occasion to play hooky from Saturday chores by going there for some 'needed' item, so I could linger at the sales counter to visit with the friendly, flannel-shirted old timers who owned and ran the store.

An aerial photograph of our house surrounded by water in the 1986 flood appeared on the front page of *The Issaquah Press*, the town weekly. Of course I had already been told about the flood before we bought the house, but seeing it was still a shock. The photograph was published again to draw attention to the next town council meeting that would address the flooding issue. The rainy season was approaching, and I went to the meeting.

The Issaquah City Hall, and the police and fire departments were lodged together in a one-story complex on the edge of the park that was the scene of pony rides and music bands during Salmon Days. The council chambers were packed for this meeting. Mayor Rowan Hinds was a friendly, balding man in his mid fifties of Norwegian descent who possessed typical Scandinavian features: tall and lean, muscular, broad shouldered, and ruddy. Rowan led everyone in the Pledge of Allegiance, all standing, hands over hearts, followed by prayer for the meeting led by a local pastor who didn't mince words about ending the prayer with "in the Name of our Lord Jesus Christ." There were several "amens" uttered by the council and the crowd as we all sat down.

I had been savoring the all-American flavor of this little town for the year we had been there, but the color and the family atmosphere of the town council meetings was icing on the cake. *It doesn't get any more Americana than this,* I thought. But I was wrong. An array of colorful male and female local characters, some of them looking like they had been camping in the woods for months, took their turn to speak at the podium before the main agenda was discussed. Each read from notes on scrap paper and ranted vehemently about one obscure topic or another. Jeers and groans and mutterings like, "Give it up, Jackie" or "Get a life Harold!" came from the crowd. One old woodsman refused to stop speaking when his time was up.

"The speaker will give up the podium, his five minutes are up," Mayor Hinds said, slamming down his gavel.

"I won't do it!" the man said, gripping the podium as the police chief stepped up to escort him away.

The amusement I felt was displaced by the agenda: flooding. Angry residents and business owners whose property had been damaged by the "hundred-year flood" of 1986 spoke up. After three years, they still had not recovered from their losses, and nothing had been done to reduce the risk of another flood. I went home with a knot in my stomach, for I realized that by buying this home, I had made a mistake I may not be able to correct. It would be hard to tell Kristene the truth about our situation.

When the Indian Summer of mid-October ended, the rains returned in force, and the creek began rising. The change in weather forced a move to the indoors, but otherwise life went on as usual, except that we kept a nervous eye on the water level in the creek and the weather reports. We remained active at Neighborhood Church, attending Sundays and Wednesday nights. We had many family dinners, with everyone dressed up and glad to see each other, dining on the pheasants I took in the fall and the ducks in early winter. We had wonderful Thanksgiving and Christmas holidays too, but still the creek rose higher with each heavy rain and subsided only slightly when it was over, becoming progressively higher after each heavy rain. This was an ominous sign that the ground was becoming saturated. I wondered if the 1986 flood being called a hundred-year event meant there wouldn't be another that severe for another hundred years.

Our first year in our new home had passed so blissfully that for the time we forgot about flooding. But three days after New Year's Day of 1990, the weather report said a new storm they called a "Pineapple Express," so-called because it is created by cold Arctic air colliding with warm tropical winds from Hawaii and resulting in heavy precipitation, was headed toward Seattle from the Pacific. At least two to four inches of rain in less than twenty-four hours were predicted if the storm reached Seattle. It had been raining lightly and steadily all night, and the creek had risen to the point that it covered the beach the kids had played on during the summer. I hammered a three-foot-long surveyor's stake in the tip of the lawn just above the water's edge so it was more than two feet above the ground and visible from the house. I prayed fervently for protection before I went to work, instructing Kristene to keep me posted on developments. I prayed in the car all the way to the station.

I had a knot in my stomach that I couldn't shake, and my hands were cold as I sat at my desk. I had been there an hour when Kristene called, saying the storm had hit, the police were going door to door warning neighbors of an impending flood. I told my supervisor I had an emergency at home and left without waiting for approval. It was raining so hard that it was necessary to have the wipers on high speed in order to drive home. When I got home I checked the stake I had posted earlier: only a foot was now above water. The once clear creek water was now a muddy brown torrent with white foam flecks, created by its churning action. I had never seen anything like it. I changed clothes and went outside, not knowing what to do next. Mayor Hinds came by and said he would order the city street department to deliver sand and sandbags.

Moments later a city dump truck dropped off two hundred sandbags and three yards of sand where the street and our gravel driveway met. Terry Cowgill and other neighbors helped me get started filling sandbags and wheel-barrowing them to the house. Terry showed me how and where to stack them so as to create a barrier. We labored in the driving rain together for hours without letup, our only talk being the task before us, our heavy sweat chilling our bodies beneath the rubber rain suits as the damp cold that is peculiar to the Northwest permeated our rainproof apparel, sucking heat from our bodies. The deep-seated fear I felt caused me to go into my house to defecate two or more times in less than two hours. About noon, the city brought by more sandbags and dumped more sand just as two pickup trucks full of high school kids in raingear and boots arrived. Without a word, they hopped out and began filling sandbags, asking where we wanted them. I was bewildered. Terry saw my confusion and explained that Issaquah High School, also located right downtown, let out early so the students could help save homes and businesses. This was so new to me I didn't know what to say; I had never seen such a thing and I was deeply impressed. As we labored together, Kristene swung open the kitchen windows and handed everybody hot cocoa or coffee and grilled cheese sandwiches.

Within several hours, we had completed a solid wall of sandbags three feet high between the house and the creek. The increased momentum of the water was terrifying to see the first time. Mayor Hinds, an engineer by profession, told me the water pressure at this stage was moving at 32,000 cubic feet per second and could easily push a house off its foundation. Water at the back of our house now completely covered the lawn and crested the opposite bank, flooding several of the homes right across from us, including Lou's place. Daylight was fading fast, and the rain was still beating down. The ground was so saturated it might as well have been concrete; the water was rising above the creek banks because it had no place else to go but up and over its channels in ever-increasing force. I checked the crawlspace under the house and was greatly alarmed to see that water had come up out of the ground to within inches of the subfloor. It was time to abandon. I helped Kristene pack up things for the kids and us and told her to go to my mother's place in Bellevue. Water was coming up through the heat ducts everywhere in the house as she left. I put Kaiser in my car and moved it up the street. Grabbing flashlights, I shut off the power as brown water breached the sandbags and poured into the house, filling the interior. We had lost the fight. Everything we owned in there, our furniture and appliances, clothing—all of it was standing in over a foot of filthy water. Tons of moving water was now pressing against the house, and I wondered if the pressure would push it off the foundation. In the dark, I sloshed through the living room in water that was over the tops of my rubber boots and was startled by a salmon that darted between my legs.

As one man, neighbors and volunteers shifted their efforts away from my place to the next home we would try to save. We worked for hours more in silence, too tired to talk except in short sentences that were barely more than grunts: "need about six more bags here," or "water's comin' through that wall there." We were cold, wet, tired and hungry; our numb bodies and hands working robotically through back pain and joint stiffness, our minds nearly blank. Eventually the rain subsided and winds blew, rapidly lowering the water levels. Some homes we were able to save by erecting walls of sandbags and installing gas-powered pumps, but even with that many were overcome by the raging flood.

Before it began to recede, the creek had flooded Terry and Sallie's basement. It was an even more nightmarish sight across the creek, as fast-moving logs and debris torpedoed homes and storage sheds already engulfed by raging torrents of filthy water and darkened by the loss of electrical power. It was a terrifying sight. These were the homes of my neighbors, neighbors who only months before had waded across ankle-deep water to honor our son's arrival and bring us trays of good eats. Now we stared at each other from across the angry flood, mere outlines in the dark, dressed in raingear, too far away to speak, too numb to even wave goodbye. I noticed that the high school volunteers were gone; the crisis over, they seemed to have vanished as quickly as they appeared. Driving out of town, I saw that many homes and businesses close to any of the three creeks that flowed through town were sitting in the dark, power shut off, partly submerged in floodwater. Many streets were blocked off. I drove to Bellevue, where a hamburger and two coffees with brandy at the Yankee Diner warmed my insides before going on to my mother's.

It was nearly midnight when I got to my mother's home. I was comforted to see our blue Oldsmobile in the driveway, for that meant Kristene and the kids were safe. I put Kaiser in an enclosed kennel with a large fenced run and went inside. Everyone was in bed. Only the hall nightlights were on, and the house was completely quiet. Mom had left the door unlocked for me, and had graciously moved down the hall to give us her bed. Kristene was in bed with Johnny, and Kristena was asleep in another room across the hall.

"Hi, Honey. You okay?" she asked softly.

I kissed her, undressed, and stepped into the shower; the hot water felt good, warming my chilled skin and rinsing away layers of nervous sweat. When I slipped under the sheets, exhausted from long hours of cold, exertion and shock, Kristene put her arms around me and pressed against me, crying softly. We talked in whispers for what must have been a long time, holding each other.

"Don't worry, Darling. Somehow everything will work out fine," I assured her. I was in the same state of shock that she was, but I wouldn't let on: she needed me to be strong.

Tomorrow we would face staggering new challenges. I drifted into sleep, pondering the oft-quoted Scripture in Romans 8 that assures us that in all things God works for the good of those who love Him and are fitting into His plans. How this promise would work out in our present crisis, I did not know, I was too tired for thinking.

CHAPTER TWENTY-ONE

When I returned the next morning, the creek had receded to almost normal levels for winter. The extent to which the flood transformed our property was stupefying; vast quantities of sand blanketed the entire property, so that it resembled an ocean beach. Gone without a trace was the green, pastoral setting of so much peace and happiness that had been our private Eden. Seeing it this way, trying to comprehend the scope of the destruction, for which I could find no adequate words, I was truly speechless. I walked around the outside of the house, then went in. Fortunately, the structural sturdiness of the house enabled it to withstand hours of tons of muddy water rushing against it without buckling or warping or moving the frame off the foundation. Inside was the real ruination, for here our appliances, carpet, oak flooring, furniture, and personal belongings were utterly destroyed. It was so overwhelming I didn't know at first where to start, but it soon came to me that the first thing to be done was to dry out the house to save the structure from rotting.

Without flood insurance, we could never recover; without it, bankruptcy and walking away from everything, to the destruction of our financial credibility would be the only logical option. We were impressed by how promptly government adjusters came out from Washington DC to survey the damage and immediately advance emergency funds to us to live on and start the salvage work. We plunged into salvaging the house and preparing our insurance claim; Kristene itemized and I photographed ruined or damaged property. I was grateful now that Kristene was a thorough record keeper, for she had receipts for everything we ever bought in file folders, and her organized documentation of purchases and my photographic proof of loss sped the payment process.

I worked almost around the clock in a race against time. The flood had set us back to beyond zero. Our home equity was wiped out, and our accumulated possessions were destroyed, and so were we, yet this was no time to rest. Our days were brutally long; neither of us slept much, for with the unseasonally warm weather now we were desperate to dry out and chemically treat the house before mold and rot set in. Every hour I wasn't working at the police department I was laboring with workers I hired from a downtown mission to shovel and scrape away yards of sand and debris and truck it to an approved dumpsite. These men were homeless; in an earlier time men such as these were called hoboes. I not only hired them, I worked right alongside them to keep the work going. Kristene brought us plenty of hot coffee and food and I listened to their personal stories during these breaks in the work. By the end of each day when I paid them cash for their work, I knew each man by name and something of his background. Most of them were always grateful for the work and the kindness and wanted me to ask for them by name if I needed help again, and I did.

There was lots of work to do that didn't require special tools or skill. Carpet was ripped out and hauled to the dump with water-logged upholstered furniture, while hardwood furniture, tables, chairs, dressers, and cabinets were sent out to be refinished. The bottom two feet of sheetrock and pine paneling of the interior walls and wet insulation were removed and industrial-grade blowers were rented to facilitate complete drying to protect against damp rot. The original oak plank flooring was buckled and warped beyond repair by standing water and had to be ripped out. Insulation under the floor was removed to allow the subfloor to dry completely. For weeks on end I hardly slept; coffee, junk food, and nervous energy kept me going. Even in all this upheaval and bleakness, Kristene was loving, loyal, uncomplaining, cheerful and kind; always available and always wanting physical intimacy with me. I was a blessed man.

She was too selfless and noble to show it, but the stress was worse for Kristene than it was for me, for there was no way for her to get a break. Displaced from her home and caring for two little ones all day in the home of a mother-in-law who clearly didn't like her, Kristene partnered with me to recover our losses and rebuild our home without breathing a word of complaint. Her days were a juggling act of tending to a toddler and a young child and working with insurance adjusters while keeping a low profile at my mother's house.

To not interfere with my mother's social life, Kristene withdrew with the kids every day to the basement, where she homeschooled Kristena on the alphabet and numbers and read to Johnny. Mom's behavior added to Kristene's stress load, for Mom was openly scornful of Kristene's working-class roots, her lack of a college education, her parenting skills, and her voluptuous figure. Although I offered to pay rent and bought groceries for the house every week, my mother openly complained to her friends and family that we were a financial burden to her and how heroic she was for taking us in. I tried to discuss with Mom that her comments were hurtful, but rather than talk, she turned tables.

"After all I've done for you kids, the years of sacrifices, this is what I get. Only your brother was grateful," she would say.

There was no way to win with Mom, and to move again before our house was ready would be too much stress for Kristene, so I let it go.

One morning Kristene's stress reached the breaking point when her lower back gave out while showering. She yelled for me, and I found her collapsed on the shower stall floor, loudly sobbing in great pain and unable to move. It was slow process moving her to the bed. I carefully half-carried, half-dragged her out of the bathroom, across the floor, and onto the bed, as she shrieked in pain at every move. My mother came in and stood at the foot of the bed, coldly staring at Kristene, who was naked, crying, and unable to move. Twice Mom ignored my requests for her to leave and close the door, continuing her cold stare until I finally escorted her out by the elbow and shut the door.

Kristene's back trouble stemmed from a work-related injury that happened years before we met, when she slipped on greasy concrete steps in the kitchen of a restaurant where she was a waitress, fracturing her tailbone. Back pain haunted her ever afterward, pain that never went away completely; sometimes it immobilized her for several hours, always unexpectedly. This time, with the help of a chiropractor, Kristene was back to normal in a few days.

I made a point of taking Kristene out on evening dates once a week or more, and when Mom was out of the house during the day, I often brought in Chinese takeout and red roses and we lunched while the kids napped.

To anyone who questions the goodness and generosity of the American people, I say keep reading. A man from the Red Cross walked to our house one day while I was laboring with a crew of workers, and before he left, he had written us a generous check toward replacing our washer, dryer, and refrigerator. The police officers' guild gave us a check for $3,000 to assist us in recovering. My supervisor gave me as much free time off as often as he could to deal with the recovery of my home. Members of our church came by on Saturdays to help with the cleanup and rebuilding, and even Mayor Hinds came by in person to ask what he and the City of Issaquah could do to help us recover and update us on flood prevention proposals. Our mortgage company gave us a free month off from monthly payments and offered us more time if we needed it.

That so many people stepped forward to help us when we were down was humbling; that we mattered to the community produced a profound change in us. The change was a new awareness that *our lives are not our own.* Our lives belonged first to the Lord, Who sent people to us and spoke to us through them. We belonged to each other, to our children, to our extended family and our community, town, and church. Of course, this runs contrary to the "me-first" thinking of contemporary society, but as we worked our way out of devastation, we had new desire to be more giving of ourselves than before, and the knowledge that we mattered to others became the secure platform for our new readiness to serve without worry about rejection.

As the repair and rebuilding of our home progressed, I met often with Mayor Hinds at the Issaquah Café for breakfast. I attended town council meetings and befriended neighbors who were also flood victims and worked with them to find solutions that would prevent or minimize the risk of future flooding. Kristene's friendships with neighborhood women became stronger as a result of the flood, with Sallie Cowgill especially. At church we took our turn serving in the nursery, we served as door greeters, I was an usher, and we fellowshipped during the week with our adult Sunday School classmates.

Although we were already a strong couple before this happened to us, the furnace of catastrophe, personal loss, and the struggle for recovery welded us together stronger than ever before. Our intimacy and trust became deeper, sweeter, and satisfying beyond the power of words to describe. Even though we were displaced, we continued our custom of praying together every morning, and discussing the business of the day over coffee and toast. We were one in heart, and our chemistry and desire for each other remained in high gear. No matter what circumstances we faced, we lived in eager anticipation of each other.

Six months of dealing with insurance adjusters and various contractors had elapsed by the time we could move back home. By then it was early summer. Warmer weather and sunshine made the moving and resettling process that much more pleasant. While we were away, I had taken the time to start a vegetable garden on one side of the backyard overlooking the creek. I planted in the spring so that we would have fresh produce ready for the picking by the time we moved home in the summer. The garden was large, eight feet by sixteen feet, framed with treated posts and a seven-foot tall trellis along the south-facing side. In the early spring, I filled it with yards of rich black topsoil atop sand for drainage and planted rows of carrots, radishes, cucumbers, red potatoes, romaine and bib lettuce, zucchini, and squash. To climb up the trellis I planted tomatoes and two varieties of green beans. Between the far end of the garden frame and the creek, pumpkins were growing, the seeds of which had been washed downstream during the flood. Symbolically, our garden was already yielding fresh produce as we moved back home.

Our home was even better now than before the flood. There was new paint on the walls, new carpet everywhere, new oak flooring in the kitchen, a new carved white wood mantle and green marble graced the living room fireplace, new appliances were in the kitchen and laundry room, and everywhere our restored, refinished wood furniture gleamed. Custom new tile, sinks, tub, and toilets set the bathrooms off as showcase rooms. The bedrooms featured new wallpaper, mattresses, sheets, and pillows, and the kids snuggled into their beds excitedly. The first few nights we slept with our French windows and doors cracked open, listening to the soothing sounds of the creek once again. It was so good to be home. As we had done in our previous home, we resumed here: intimately re-christening every room, tip-toeing through the house while the kids were asleep. Such was our intimacy; still undiminished after two children and a disaster. It was great to be home again.

Life on the creek resumed, as neighbor kids came over to see Kristena and Johnny, and played all day in the water and sand of our private beach. A little girl named Adrienne who lived across the creek from us had a crush on Johnny, and every day during the summer she would stand at the edge of the bank facing our place and call out to him, "Joooohhhnnny!" and Johnny would call back "Aaaaadrienne!" and she would come over in her swimsuit and play for hours, throwing rocks in the water, making sand castles, and wading in the shallow water with our son. Kristene would bring the kids lunch and snacks throughout the day.

A childhood crush developed between young Russell Cowgill and Kristena; the two alternately argued and played intensely. After having a nose-to-nose disagreement, "It is too!" followed by "It is not!" they found things to do together. Russell often rode his bike to our place, dismounted, and knocked on the door.

"Yes, what is it, Russell?" I would knowingly ask him. Blushing, looking down, and scuffing the toe of his shoe on the patio, Russell would stammer, "Uh, well, uhhhh, is Kristena here?" If Kristena was napping, I would close the wooden gate to discourage Russell, but he was not to be deterred. The young suitor would heave his bicycle over the gate, it would land in a crash; he would then scramble over it himself and boldly knock at our door. Always the young gentleman, Russell would put her helmet on her head, mount his bike, put her on the back, and together they would ride in endless circles around our driveway. I took videos of these priceless scenes at our little beach and in our driveway that are preserved to this day.

Life for us now was the happiest we had ever known. Kristene was completely content. Her life was at home as wife, mother, and homemaker. She regained her figure by working out at a local gym three times every week. She was involved in women's ministries at the church, and she devoted herself to taking care of me and the kids. She indulged her skills as a creative and imaginative cook; every meal, even the simplest soup or sandwich was a new culinary experience that would have rated five stars in any contest. Neighbors along the creek came by to have coffee and visit. As a woman who grew up being avoided or shunned by other women, Kristene was guarded and selective in her female associations, but she and Sallie Cowgill bonded immediately as close friends. They met often for early morning walks around town together, except when the weather was bad, and the roots of a lasting friendship grew from sharing their lives as they brisked along, shoulder to shoulder through town during the waking hours. My friendship with Terry developed too, though we were each busy with our occupations. In such a special time as this was, an equally special bond between our families developed that continues to this very day.

Summers were especially great times, for then neighbors walked through the creek to visit and share lemonade and ice tea. In the backyard we set up a tent and a long strip of yellow plastic for the kids to turn the garden hose on and run and slide down into the creek. I bought a full-size wood smoker, the kind that had the fire going in the bottom, a water pan for steam on the rack above that, and then two racks for the food. With a little practice, I was turning out gourmet memories: whole smoked turkey brined for a full day in salt and brown sugar water, then stuffed with celery, carrot, apple, and pear chunks, and coated with pure maple syrup. Slowly smoke-cooked for six hours, the meat was kept moist by the steam. I made whole chickens that were smoked with hickory wood that had been seasoned with whole bay leaves slipped under the skin and rubbed with coarse salt, fresh ground pepper, and Old Bay Rub, the cavities stuffed with apple and pear chunks from our own trees. My sister Cindy and her husband, Chuck, came over with their two little ones, and so did Ron and Kay, Richard and Barbara, my father and his wife, and couples from our Sunday school class. Our home was so much its own world that there was no need to go to a state park; everything was right there and with privacy.

Our garden was bursting with so much fresh produce in the warm summer sun that we gave away much of it. All our salads and vegetables at lunch and dinner were from our garden, homegrown, and completely organic, and the rich flavor made store-bought produce seem plastic by comparison. Our trees produced apples and Bing cherries, and flowers, especially red roses, bloomed in brick planter boxes along the south and west-facing sides of the house.

Kristena set up a lemonade stand down by the mailboxes where the pavement of Birch Place met with the gravel road to our house. She made her own sign, selling lemonade at five cents a glass, and set up a table and two chairs from the family room to do business from. Johnny helped his sister make the lemonade and bring it in plastic pitchers with paper cups to the kids' very first business venture. Neighborhood adults and some of the older kids became Kristena's customers.

I was the first to get up every morning, whereupon I would get the coffee started, and go to the family room to have a quiet hour of prayer and Bible reading until Kristene joined me, greeting me with a hug and a kiss. I say an hour, but in truth it was less than that, for it typically takes me awhile to focus on prayer, to pull my mind in from mental wood-gathering, and focus on God. But after I settled in and entered God's presence in prayer, I spent most of that time giving Him thanks. Everything was so good for us now, yet in these early prayer times, I sensed that something was missing. Another change was coming, and whatever it was, I knew I wasn't ready and had no idea how to get ready.

At work I had begun to feel desiccated, frozen to the spot; the cases I was working on were repetitive, I felt I had nowhere to go in the department, for a promotion would mean reduced income due to loss of overtime pay and transfer back to working nights and weekends in patrol; not acceptable. It was the same angst I had just before I went into detectives. I remembered how I was back then: feeling there was nowhere to go, frustrated with the thought of being forever stuck in patrol, and my drive to be not a church benchwarmer but a doer. The answer was to be proactive again. Over the years I had gradually slipped into being reactive as a Christian. Again the answer was in actively reaching out and helping others – but how? Pastor Rozelle suggested I join a new ministry to street people that was starting. I remembered that my obedience to His call to service opened the door to a new season of great change: promotion to detectives and meeting Kristene, the right woman for me, and a bright future.

Recalling that prior experience and the answers it wrought, I joined a Monday night outreach ministry at the King County Jail in Seattle. Including me, there were five men on the team. Kristene, ever possessive of my time with her and the kids, was resistant at first. But I went, and once more the heart of God for the lost did I see, the desperate and the destitute. In going my eyes were opened to the perpetual plight, constant turmoil, agony, and self-deception that marked these men's lives.

Our "hymnals" were copies of old hymns and worship choruses on sheets of paper stapled together. We put an emphasis on singing the old hymns for the benefit of our congregation of inmates in laying a spiritual foundation; for the hymns possess a sense of history and great depth in their lyrics not found in modern choruses. Knowing them forged a bridge with earlier generations of Christians, that have passed on ahead of us. None of us played a musical instrument, so we did our best to carry the tunes as we sang together. The result was crude, out-of-tune music, but it was from the heart, and God was pleased. The most popular hymns among the inmates were "Amazing Grace" and hymns about the blood of Christ, such as "There is Power in the Blood", "Nothing but the Blood" and "The Old Rugged Cross", hymns with strong themes of forgiveness and redemption.

Most of these men were from broken homes, few even knew or remembered their fathers, and were either raised by relatives other than their parents, or in a series of foster homes. Very few of them had any exposure to the Gospel while growing up. Instead of absolute truths, the shifting sands of situational standards were the only basis they knew regarding right and wrong. With such men we were starting from scratch, teaching the fundamentals of the Christian faith and biblical truths.

As we met with these men week by week, I came to understand that knowledge of right and wrong, of good and evil is written on men's hearts, and from this platform we taught them. We worked to show a personal interest in them by asking about their families and friends, their court dates, actively listening to them and sharing the

Gospel with them through the telling of our personal testimonies of how God changed our lives and then praying with them for their individual needs. We rotated the Bible teaching each week, so I had to prepare a Bible lesson and give a sermon about once a month. Doing the preparation and the teaching and answering questions afterward had a strengthening effect on me and increased my desire to see men turn to Christ. But more than that, I came to understand the human side of pastors; why so many burn out so early; for I discovered a drain, a letdown that occurs after preparing and delivering a lesson, a sermon, and counseling those who respond to it.

As time went on, I came to treasure those weekly outings as the highlight of my week, for we were leading men to Christ almost every week, and ministering to those we had already led to Him. Some of the conversions were dramatic, with men falling to the floor, confessing their sins to God. We would meet at the church and carpool together to the jail in Seattle; we spent an hour and a half visiting and ministering to and praying for each man until it was time to go. We fellowshipped together afterward, usually over cheap, sumptuous dinners at one of the out-of-the-way, hole-in-the wall eateries that stayed open late in Chinatown. Those were great times of bonding, camaraderie, fellowship, and growth; rich memories that I carry with me still.

Our prosperity seemed unstoppable at the time, but it was an illusion. We sold our rental house in Bellevue at exactly the right time, while the housing market was still hot but ready to cool off. We came away with a healthy profit and banked the cash, giving ourselves a cushion that let me sleep better at night. Kristena was doing well in private Christian school and often had friends stay overnight on weekends. We read Bible stories and prayed with the kids at bedtime and led each of them in asking Christ into their hearts. Our family tradition of Sunday night spaghetti dinners featuring Kristene's homemade marinara sauce continued, often with guests. I added another wing to the garden in the spring and planted eight rows of corn, and in the fall we harvested fresh corn on the cob, along with red potatoes, radishes, carrots, squash, and pumpkins. I hunted with Kaiser and provided pheasants, quail, grouse, and ducks for the table. Family and friends loved coming to our place for big dinners, laughter, and conversation. At church, some of the men who had been part of our jail outreach came by after their release to see us and attend church with us, and our jail team and the church welcomed them. Our Sunday school class had picnics and barbecues together, and couples and little ones came to know each other better.

During the day when she was home by herself, Kristene secretly practiced playing her father's musical saw. I only know this because I heard her playing it once when she thought I wasn't home. I happened to see her from behind, sitting on a stool, the saw handle held between her knees and the blade slightly bent with one hand, as the other hand held the bow as she drew it across the blade, making once again the most beautiful sound this side of Heaven, and I thought of Grampa George. In Heaven now, he must know that his only daughter was honoring him by following in his footsteps. Ever loyal, ever honoring, ever faithful was Kristene. Surely God broke the mold after He made her.

Off and on, I would hear Kristene singing as she worked around the house, and the beauty of her voice never failed to stop me in my tracks. She was once the featured soloist at a denominational women's conference where she sang the great old hymn Amazing Grace without instrumental accompaniment. Her performance was the talk of the church.

"You should have seen Kristene Hansen sing! What a voice! Not a dry eye in the place – she had us all in tears - wow!" the church ladies exclaimed.

While their compliments had me beaming with pride, I was also humbled that she had chosen being my wife over anything else in this life, for with a voice such as hers, she could have made music her career.

I came home for lunch one day while Kristena was in school and Johnny was taking a nap, and I sensed right away that something was on her mind. We were in the kitchen and she was making me a cheese sandwich. I kept silent, waiting for her to speak.

Kristene sat down at the table and made eye contact with me before she spoke. Her countenance was long with a serious look. I began to eat as I waited for her to speak.

"All you have to do is look at me and I'm pregnant," she announced.

I put my sandwich down. "What's that supposed to mean? Are you pregnant again?" I asked.

"No, Honey. But Bill and Judy are expecting their fourth baby now because Bill didn't get a vasectomy. I can't physically do another pregnancy at my age, two is enough," Kristene said. "Please get cut. Do it for us."

Two weeks later, we all went to the Seattle clinic for the procedure. I let myself out and went inside while Kristene parked the car. Dr. Lilledahl was the very picture of what you would want your family doctor to be like: fatherly, late sixties, trim, and silver haired, with a warm and kindly manner. I shed my trousers, climbed onto the table, and put my feet in the stirrups. The nurse began prepping me, swabbing me with a cold brown antiseptic solution and the doc felt my abdomen for abnormalities when Kristene burst into the room, Johnny on her shoulder, burping up his last meal into her long, thick hair. Kristena was hanging onto her skirt with one hand, with a pacifier in her mouth, and Kristene was sobbing.

"Oh please, doctor, don't do it! Not yet! We might want to have another baby!"

The doctor nearly fell over from roaring with laughter, and the nurse was laughing with him.

"Go home, you two! Make more babies!" he told us.

After the kids were asleep and we had gone to bed, that night, I asked Kristene, "Do you really want another baby, Baby?

She smiled and said softly, "Try me."

The Lord had brought me so far since the days when I first came to Him, to look back on those early years and compare them to life now was too much to grasp. Then, I was lonely and often felt isolated; now, the blessings were beyond count. I was married to one of the most beautiful women I had ever seen, one God picked for me and we had strong, healthy children, a beautiful and harmonious home, many friends, and meaningful work. The words of Psalm 23 were being fulfilled in my life: *"He makes me lie down in green pastures; He leads me beside the still waters, He restores my soul."* Now I understood that what I had was God's green pasture for me, and He had indeed restored my soul, my mind and emotions, along the way. Saying that I knew this and was grateful to God for it would be understating it. God had given me all this just for choosing to give up my ways and follow Him, and I was amazed by His grace, favor I did not deserve. My prayers consisted more and more of praise to Him and thankfulness and less and less of personal petitions. In the stillness of the early mornings, when I had my prayer and worship time, I took to heart a Bible verse that is set to music in the Pentecostal churches: "Thy Loving Kindness Is Better Than Life".

Winter in our Issaquah home

218

At the hospital with newborn son John, 1989

Kids playing on our private beach – Issaquah, 1992

Kristena and Johnny set up their lemonade stand at the edge of our driveway, 1994

Ready for guests to arrive. Issaquah, 1993

Happy & Content, Issaquah, 1994

CHAPTER TWENTY-TWO

As good as life was now, we still lived in fear of another flood. I took to reading *The Farmer's Almanac* after I noticed that it had predicted the first flood down to the month and forecast that yet another season of heavy precipitation and flooding was one year away for the Pacific Northwest. What we had learned about preparation from the first flood could have prevented the damage had we known what to do. The key was to be ready and able to quickly erect a wall of sandbags between the house and the rising water, then to seal the house exterior with plastic sheeting, duct tape and sandbags, and then employ a gas-powered pump to keep the crawlspace dry. To be ready for the next flood, I stacked sandbags from the first flood along the fence inside our driveway by the carport and at other key places on the property. I stored several rolls of heavy plastic sheeting, duct tape, and a staple gun in the tool room. I made arrangements with two different tool rental shops to be at the top of their list to rent a pump if and when another flood came. When I had done all this, I walked around the property, satisfied with my preparations but not liking the sight of it. Similar in purpose and presence to lifeboats that line the deck of a luxury ocean liner, the stacks of sandbags around our property were stern, unsightly reminders of the menace we lived with each fall and winter.

I sensed that another major change was on its way, one that had to do not with home, but with work. It was in the early morning that it was strongest, a foreknowledge that the time was coming for me to move on, to leave police service. It wasn't a premonition, as in other times; there was no foreboding or portent of evil, only the knowledge that a major life transition was imminent. Even so, I panicked at the thought, for I had a family to support, and I knew no other way to earn a living. I was filled with constant anxiety and became irritated with Kristene for not joining me in my nighttime fretting.

"Trust the Lord. It'll be okay," she would say and go back to sleep. Hah! How dare her! Didn't she understand *anything* after all these years?

What was worse was that I was losing interest in my work, something I thought would never happen. Rather than ask God about it, I resisted the coming change by trying to mentally rally myself to crack cases like I always had. But my best efforts were futile; within a few weeks, I had to face the truth. The anointing that had been on my investigative work was gone, and it was time to go, but to where or what? In desperation, I sought the counsel of Milt Sessions, one of the elders at my church. Milt prayed with me on the phone one morning after I explained everything to him, and as he prayed, he suddenly fell silent. I waited.

"John, God's trying to bless you and you're fighting it. Let go, and let God have His way."

The next day I felt led to call Roger Dunn, a former police academy classmate who had left the King County Sheriff's Office after only eight years and had since become highly successful as a private investigator. Roger and I had stayed loosely in touch over the years since the academy. As a result of our conversation we agreed that I would get my private investigator's license and work at his firm as an independent subcontractor at an hourly rate more than twice what I was getting at the police department.

"Turn in those papers and come on over here," Roger told me. "There's life after government."

I promptly turned in my resignation letter, to be effective in sixty days to allow time to train my replacement and handle cases for my partners, all of whom were in trials at the time.

I called Kristene at home to tell her the news – I had taken the leap. She was overjoyed, shouting, "Hallelujah! Thank You, Lord," over and over, tears in her voice. This was the right move, I was still nervous, but not like before; there was no more turmoil within.

I had been with the department for twenty-one years; I was forty-four years old and would have to wait until age fifty before I could receive my pension. My last day was November 4. At the small ceremony in my honor, I stood before my senior officers who were now the top brass and said, "First of all, I want to thank you guys for not firing me during my first year when you should have." They all laughed and nodded in agreement, for they remembered what a wild kid I was back then. "Thank you all for believing in me. It's been a great ride," I told them. Kristene and my parents were there, beaming with pride as everyone applauded.

The rest of the year, which consisted of eight weeks, I took off to be with Kristene and the kids, to set up my first business, and to rest. I was out on my own now, and it felt great. To my surprise, I slept very well at night; the anxiety of a new adventure, of boldly striking out on my own was there, but it didn't bother me. Again, Kristene had been right (she always was) when she told me to trust the Lord in leaving the department; the inner peace I had was so complete, it confirmed her words.

Roger Dunn's office was on the ninth floor of a prestigious office building in the core of downtown Seattle. It was spacious and had the classic feel of the 1940s. Including himself, Roger had six private investigators in his firm, mostly subcontractors. Roger was about my age, a handsome, former college football player turned cop who afterward became an astute suit-and-tie businessman. Were it not for Roger Dunn, I would never have survived my first year in business. He taught me the basics of estimating costs, budgeting a new case, invoicing, record keeping, taxes, following up with clients, and much more. Roger was one of the most gracious men I ever met in the business world; he helped me get started in business knowing I would be out on my own within a short time.

To return Roger's kindness, I worked hard on all the cases he gave me, and they literally fell open for me, one after another. The first was an embezzlement case that involved a trusted employee at a major car dealership. As I used my interrogation skills, the employee confessed to years of skimming funds amounting to hundreds of thousands of dollars to maintain a high lifestyle. As a result of my work, the police were called, the employee was arrested, her assets were seized, and she ultimately went to prison.

For three mornings in a row that winter, the Lord impressed upon me to tithe twenty percent of my income. Not ten percent, but twenty. I was hesitant, but I obeyed. Within a very short time, clients of my own were referred to me by attorneys I had worked with as a cop. I set up a home office, using a guest bedroom adjacent to the family room, and Kristene recorded the announcement on my business phone. Business poured in so fast that hiring help was necessary to keep up. My first employee was a colorful young woman who had worked for me as an informant when I was a cop. She had been a prostitute and an exotic dancer, but had never been arrested and her life was transformed when she accepted Christ. She excelled at research of public records and undercover assignments. Next I brought in a CPA to handle business fraud investigations. Then I began networking with other PIs on surveillance and armed protection details. I had never seen as much money as I was making now; we weren't rich, but we were stable and comfortable enough that Kristene could continue to stay home and take care of me and the kids.

The following spring, my father repossessed the Hadlock property where we had honeymooned years before. Before he sold it, Dad developed the property into a destination resort, complete with marina, restaurant, and a twenty-five room hotel. The people he had sold it to on a private contract that included monthly payments to him, had failed to run it profitably. The marina was destroyed in a storm and the owners pocketed the insurance money instead of rebuilding the dock. After the storm, they eventually abandoned the building, letting everything fall into a terrible state of disrepair, and filed for bankruptcy. I went with Dad when he appeared as a secured creditor at the bankruptcy court, and the court awarded the property back to him. Weeks later I received a call from one of my father's friends.

"John, your dad had an apparent heart attack while working to get the resort at Hadlock reopened and was taken by ambulance to the local hospital," was his report. At seventy-seven years of age, he was desperate to rescue the fruit of his labor, for it was all he had. I learned that when he woke up at the local hospital, Dad threw off the sheets and forced his way past the doctor and nurses, and had a friend drive him back to the hotel, where he went back to work.

It was a call to duty. I put our business on hold, arranged for the people who worked with us to take care of our clients, and told Roger Dunn that I would be taking a leave of absence for the summer to assist my father. For the entire summer of 1993 and into the early fall, Kristene and I worked with my father and his wife and a handful of employees to get the restaurant and hotel up and running again. The place had changed substantially since we honeymooned there years ago: Dominic and Rita, their trailer and garden were gone, and the building shell had been filled in to become a hotel and restaurant, but it had been closed for more than a year. Utilities had been shut off for non-payment, and it required long hours to restore it to the point that it could pass health department inspection and be open for business again. While we worked, my father paid for someone to babysit the kids for us.

This was my first and only experience in the restaurant and hotel business, and it was an eye opener. It was sixteen hours a day, seven days a week of promoting the reopening in town, booking reservations, waiting on tables, cleaning hotel rooms, weeding the outside grounds, and much more. Friday and Saturday nights at The Plant were colorful, for there was live music and dancing in the dining room and the liquor flowed and the restaurant was busy all night; people from all over came to eat, drink, and dance.

In the middle of every week, when it was the quietest at The Plant, we went home to do our laundry, pick up mail, and check on the progress of my open cases. When the tourist season ended in mid-October, we went home, dead broke. I had no money in the bank, no receivables coming in, no open cases, and my employees were gone due to lack of work. From rock bottom I faced utility bills and a mortgage payment. I had loaned my father money at the start of the summer, but it was too soon to ask him if he could repay me; I waited. On our first night back at home, when everyone was asleep, I slipped out of bed, went into the living room, and sought the Lord for help.

It was a quick prayer. I prayed, "Lord, Your Word says it will go well for us if we honor our father and mother. Lord, we have gone out of our way to obey You by helping and honoring my dad. I have no money now to pay my bills. I ask You to help me with that, and I ask in the Name of Jesus. Thank You." I went to bed then, figuring "what will be, will be."

The very next morning, an employee theft case came in from a new industrial client that had been referred to us by a Seattle law firm. Over the next three weeks, my investigation exposed a ring of several employees who were stealing from the company, the first three of whom confessed their crimes to me in writing and were prosecuted. Other members of the ring, for whom there was insufficient evidence for an arrest, were fired. The client paid me every Friday, regardless of the volume of hours I put in, thus immediately solving my cash flow problems. As this case was winding down, the same client had an even bigger case at another of their facilities. I worked this next case right through the Christmas season, closing it out by early January, so that all our bills were paid on time, and there was enough left over to provide for one of the best Christmas seasons we ever had.

Work is cyclical in the private investigation business, with the post-holiday season being typically the slowest. By now I had learned to coast through slow periods on receivables and savings and use them as a time to tend to business housekeeping, and to rest. But rest I did not get that winter, for the flood we dreaded did arrive. This time, our preparations saved the day. Working through the day and long into the night with neighbors and volunteers from our church, we saved the house by building a three-foot high wall of sandbags several yards away from the house, then wrapping the lower half of the house in sheeted plastic, sealing the bottom of the sheets with sandbags, and continually pumping out the crawl space with a rented pump. It was an all-night ordeal, and Kristene sent the kids to Ron and Kay's and stayed to labor all night with me, but we saved our home. By morning the waters had receded to within the normal creek channel. The yard was a mess and the garden was gone, but the house was fine. So now we had a second so-called hundred-year flood in three years. Fearing another flood, I left the house-wrap on until spring.

Seeing our home wrapped in plastic and surrounded by filthy sandbags forced me to recognize that our move here was a mistake that the Lord cautioned me not to do, but I had stubbornly plunged ahead. I was just beginning to realize the gravity of my mistake in terms of loss of home equity, and difficulty of being able to sell the house, but I had no idea how to correct it; I was stuck.

By the spring of 1994, business was booming to the point that I could no longer afford to work at the rates Roger Dunn was paying. I worked entirely out of the tiny spare room in our home, next to the family room, and I loved being there. One morning I was on a three-way phone conference with a client in New York and their attorney's office in Seattle; all of us were on speaker phone. It was about ten minutes into the conference when Johnny came into the office, in his pajamas, binky in his mouth, carrying his stuffed toy bunny and Kristena was trying to grab him. Just as Kristena yelled, "Dad, make Johnny give that back!" the toy rabbit went off, "Here comes Peter Cottontail , a-hoppin' down the bunny trail! Hippity-hopping all the way!"

"Mr. Hansen?" New York asked. "Is that you, Mr. Hansen?" I could have died right there and then. It was time to get a real office.

CHAPTER TWENTY-THREE

Two little ones, Peter Cottontail, and overflowing business volume compelled us to look for a new place to headquarter our business that had room for expansion. We found it in the Pioneer Building, in the colorful, often-rowdy Pioneer Square district of downtown Seattle, barely a block from the busy waterfront. Perfectly preserved since the nineteenth century, it boasts a classic exterior of original red brick, grey granite blocks and wood-framed windows, and an interior that features heavy dark mahogany floor trim and door and window moldings, old-style translucent glass interior door windows, brass fittings, and exposed cables in the brass-framed elevator shaft, all beautifully polished and maintained, ever attune with the atmosphere of salt air and frequent tooting of state ferryboats that sally in and out of the waterfront docks. The Pioneer Building is one of the grandest icons of Seattle history in a setting that oozes waterfront character and a sense of constant adventure.

Our first little office there lacked an exterior window and was so narrow it was a squeeze to fit two desks and two people in it. But for me, having an office downtown was a thrill, a sign that I was moving up in the world, and I looked forward to driving in to work every day. My oldest daughter, Sara, then eighteen, came to work with me full time to help with secretarial and administrative tasks. We hadn't seen much of Sara during her teen years, and for me this was a golden opportunity to regain lost time and ground with her.

As we worked side by side every day, our relationship mended, and we became closer over the months. There was the feeling that, as father and daughter, we were making up for lost time as much as possible. When I shared our story with inmates on jail ministry nights, it clearly had a powerful effect on men who had reached the end of their rope, and were finally open to true change if only they knew how. My personal story of loss and redemption won several inmates to Christ who had been either hostile or indifferent to the Gospel but now began showing signs of transformation as they came to meetings week by week, smiling now, and packing their Bibles with them, often telling me that it was hearing the details of my restored relationship with my daughter that flipped the inner switch for them. Knowing and hearing this was rewarding for me, for my work in the jail had resulted in a compassion for the less fortunate that I did not have before, and now I wanted only the best for each of them. And there was something else that I knew now: that God was pleased.

What I didn't share with inmates were the negatives that came with trying to restore Sara to our family circle, for the consequences of divorce these men already knew, they themselves being victims of domestic discord, abandonment and dysfunction. Sara struggled at seeing how happy everyone was in my new family. Once upon a time she was my one and only; now she felt like an outsider when she visited us, like someone pressing her nose against a store window at the display on the other side of the glass. At first she visited us at home, but after it tapered off, she confided that she felt jealous of Kristena and Johnny for having the childhood with me that she didn't have. Hearing her say that broke my heart, for Sara had been left behind and she was now an adult, her childhood over, the damage done. Healing and forgiveness were needed all around.

It was what I *didn't* know that contributed to my failure to integrate Sara into our family. Unbeknownst to me, my mother demonized Kristene as the evil stepmother to Sara and to many others, poisoning my family well without my knowing it. Kristene quietly withdrew from association with Mom when she caught on to this and focused instead on shielding our kids from my family's legacy of turmoil.

I was learning the importance of accepting the things in life that cannot be changed or undone, but still I tried to make the best of the situation by treasuring the time I had with Sara working with me, hoping that things might work themselves out over time; but they didn't.

Certain conclusions about life came to me from the work I enjoyed growing vegetables in my garden. The main one being that I could only expect to reap what I had sown. Of course I already knew this, but learning it anew, from nature itself, somehow clarified my understanding. So it goes, then, if I sow seeds for, say, carrots, I can expect a harvest of what I had sown, that and only that; its quality being dependent on the care I took to weed and tend the soil during the growth process. The most salient point of all is that everything in life requires care and maintenance. Failure to tend, to maintain the soil of our relationships, occupations and possessions, to weed and water those things in our lives will inevitably produce undesirable results, the weeds and thistles of life, choking and poisoning our most important relationships. Our words and deeds, whether good or bad, are the seeds of that which we will harvest later, for ourselves and those around us, and the soil represents the climate in which our seeds grow.

The turmoil around my oldest daughter was a case in point. Sara's entire life was impacted by the seeds of domestic strife and divorce sown by her parents and grandparents, while what *she* wanted was harmony and unity in her home, not strife. She was caught in a cycle of ugliness not of her desire or making; others before her had produced and perpetuated it. My parents were still fighting and reliving their divorce more than thirty years after it was over, selfishly ravaging everyone around them, while Shelly's parents had stayed married but their union too was stormy and strife-ridden at best. Too few of us really comprehend how our actions and words affect others around us, especially our children, even our unborn.

Yet more had I learned: Two failed marriages, betrayal by my parents, and estrangement from my firstborn taught me two more life principles concerning relationships: the first is that you can't unscramble eggs. Relationships are like raw eggs that have delicate separate parts; once they are scrambled, restoration to their original state is impossible. So it is with human relationships: breaking trust through continual deception, neglect, discord, abuse, and betrayal scramble and traumatize a relationship to the point of no return. The damage cannot be undone; the fragile wholeness that once was is gone. Sometimes a relationship can be restarted after the passage of time, hence the saying, "Time heals all wounds," but what has really happened is the relationship didn't resume in its original state of being; rather a 'reset', called by some a 'new beginning', has occurred, but even then the scars from the scrambling of the first will always remain.

The second life principle is that not everyone can be won over; not by love, persuasion, reason or even self-interest. There are times when it is in everyone's best interest to stop striving for peace, unity, or healing, leave the matter with God, and walk away, for God calls us to peace. There are many times in the Bible where even God reached a point when He stepped back from certain persons or groups of people He just couldn't reach. A case in point is Saul, Israel's first king, who continually disobeyed God's commands until He finally stepped back from Saul and removed him as Israel's king, replacing him with David, who was "a man after God's own heart." In teaching the new church about marriage, Paul instructed in I Corinthians 7:15 to let the unbeliever go who wants to go, the believing partner is free to begin anew, for God calls us to peace. It is important to know when to let go, stop striving and step back. God does not expect or want us to be like crash test dummies in car safety tests by subjecting ourselves to endless abuse and rejection. God calls us to peace.

For Kristene and me, we were able to resume our relationship after being separated four months because there had been no damage, no discord, no betrayal, and no trauma when we separated. We had known only love for each other, so our "eggs" were never scrambled, for we were careful about that. Over the years, we discussed this many times and resolved to protect our marriage by never doing anything to break trust, to never allow anger and bitter words or neglect to scramble the eggs of our marriage. We agreed to obey the Scriptures about honoring each other above all others, even our kids, and to get rid of anger before evening. Kristene was better at taking the initiative on this than I was, even though hers was the more volatile personality.

Another principle we applied was that we were always careful to *never take our love for granted*. For twenty-eight years I never stopped courting, wooing, and pursuing Kristene; she never felt unwanted or unnoticed by me. I constantly looked for new ways to surprise and please her. Even during the hardest of times I took her out on a date at least once a week, and I often brought her flowers, racy lingerie, and expensive perfume. I consistently complimented and praised her on everything: her beauty, her voice and smile, her lovemaking, her cooking, her home decorating, and her care of the children.

I kept our physical intimacy alive and vibrant with creative surprises and flirting that had no end; all these things and more I did that kept our romance not only alive, but also as passionate as when we first met and married. I went even further than this: at every opportunity I got, I praised Kristene to everyone I met; I bragged about her whether they knew her or not. I carried pictures of her with me everywhere and always looked for an excuse to show them to people I met. And of course, it filtered back to Kristene how crazy I was about her, and this in turn deepened her love for me, and all this strengthened the foundation for a legacy of love, trust, and harmony to pass on to our kids.

Of course, Kristene was not one to be outdone. She showered me with unending loving attention and affection. She hunted all the time for unique gifts she knew I would like. She shopped men's stores for bargains on suits, jackets, shirts, and ties, so I was the best-dressed detective in my unit. No king who ever lived had it as good as I did with her; Kristene was my crown.

Our marriage is best understood as the real-life adventure it really was;
it wasn't a surreal, sugar-sweet bed of roses. We were real people, fault-ridden
folk who fought almost as passionately as we loved and lusted for each other.
After all, we were each street tough, bold, aggressive, and intense, and we
brought those traits with us into our Christian walk, our marriage, and our
parenting. Even after a dozen years of marriage, we each had residues of
carnality, namely pride, still in us, but it was steadily dying. We understood
that we were in a life-long maturation process, and we had rules for fighting
so every fight had a good outcome and made us stronger as a couple, and
into better people. Our rules were unspoken, unwritten and simple: no
name calling, no personal insults, and no physical violence, not even mere
touching, and always make up before the day ended.

I knew when to back off, apologize for my part in it and let Kristene
vent and have her space. Then I would ask the Lord to intervene. Typically
my prayer consisted of reminding God that He declared us to be one flesh
and one spirit in His sight; that He had put us together and His will for us
was that we would be together. Sometimes I reminded Him of the vision
He gave me of the Philippian jail years ago when He declared we were one
in His sight. When we fought, I *always* repented of my anger and asked
God to bring us back together. I *always* told Kristene I was sorry and then
let it alone and went about my business, leaving it in God's hands, and
always sooner than later, she came around.

It was my experience that God always answers prayers like these, and
quickly. Usually it was only minutes before Kristene would reach
out to me and we would make up. There were times when the roles were
reversed: Kristene would be the one to apologize and then step back,
pray for me, and wait for me to cool down. This was the most important
key: neither of us tried to 'make' or push the other into reconciling,
but instead did our part in apologizing and then giving the other the
dignity of personal space and time, allowing God to work unhindered.
Applying this biblical technique always worked, no matter how bad the
argument was; this way we both 'won'.

So we were living life in this manner, that is, to the fullest, when the dream case came in. A case that fulfilled unrealized dreams and unspoken desires, the stuff of romance novels, it was. In the year following the second flood, we unwittingly made ourselves ready, for the weather had been peaceable, home life was richly rewarding, and we were on the fourteenth year of our honeymoon, now with kids. During that time I built up my detective business while keeping my hand in the work, personally interrogating criminals, doing surveillance and going undercover with my team of detectives that now numbered five. I got Kristene licensed so she could work surveillance and undercover cases with me, and in this she was especially effective, so that when the call came from a cruise ship company to work undercover as tourists to crack the case of ongoing thefts from passengers' cabins, we were prepared. Because Kristene was also a licensed investigator with me, the company agreed to send us and the kids on a ten-day cruise aboard the troubled ship while it was in the Caribbean.

We were now a family of four undercover agents. Understanding that her role would be to bait the thieves, Kristene borrowed expensive jewelry to flaunt and gain the attention of the thieves, and I had video cameras built into some of my luggage, to leave on whenever we left our cabin. Our passports were issued just in time to fly to Florida to catch our ship, and the client even provided us first class seating.

"Thank You, Jesus," Kristene cried softly through tears as she walked the gangplank ahead of the kids and me onto the ship, the Caribbean sun gleaming down on a sparkling white ship and aqua green waters. I fell in love with Kristene all over again as I walked behind her and the kids. She was dressed in a simple, loose, off-white summer dress, and her long dark brown tresses cascaded down her back and shoulders beneath a broad-brimmed white straw hat with our two kids in shorts and T-shirts, at ages eight and six, close behind her. Kristene was so beautiful to behold, that for a moment as I videotaped the scene, I forgot where I was.

As soon as the ship left port, I was invited to a secret meeting with the ship's captain and top officers to discuss the case and explain the investigative plan. No time was wasted implementing it. Every time we left the cabin, I purposely left a few cash bills, coins, and jewelry items on the cabin dresser in front of the camera that was built into a suitcase lying on a bed. Evening meals required formal attire, providing a daily opportunity for Kristene to dress provocatively and flash the borrowed jewelry she wore at every chance. She was so stunning and statuesque that all eyes were drawn to her at every meal, men and women alike. Dinner time was a parade of male passengers and table waiters repeatedly walking past our table to get a closer look at Kristene, and wives stared and whispered from their tables across the dining room.

Afternoons at sea we spent poolside, sunbathing and swimming while the hidden camera was on inside our cabin. People came by where Kristene was sunning on a chaise lounge in her bathing suit, obviously to get a closer look at her tattoo. By now I had adjusted to the fact that people can't help but look at Kristene. Now in her mid-forties, she had become even better looking with time, a rare thing indeed, and I was a blessed man.

We were sunbathing side by side on chaise lounge chairs one afternoon, the kids were playing in their children's pool, the sun was hot but cooled by the gentle sea breeze, and a live band on deck was playing Calypso music. I looked over at Kristene, smiling serenely into the sun.

"Look at us now, Baby. Here we are with the kids on a cruise ship, on the Caribbean, all paid for, and we're being paid to be here. Does it get any better than this?"

Her eyes were closed, and the sun was glistening on her face. She reached for my hand.

"No my love, it doesn't get better than this. Take me to your cabin, sir - now."

Before we got to the first port of call, Kristene almost caught one of the thieves by accident when she was putting on her robe after an early shower, and one of the crew came in unexpectedly. The man quickly backed out in a panic, apologizing, calling her "Mrs. Hansen." We reported this to the captain. The man was wearing the uniform of the ship's plumbers; there was no reason for him to enter our cabin, but it had happened too fast for Kristene to positively identify him from a photo lineup.

The theft ring must have decided to lay low after such a close call, for there were no theft incidents during that entire cruise. We couldn't have known this, of course, so we went about enjoying the rest of the cruise as if we were regular passengers. We gave the thieves ample opportunity to steal from us by going ashore at every port of call, including a guided tour of a Jamaica coffee plantation and the beach waterfall that was one of the scenes in the first James Bond movie, *Dr. No*, the Cayman Islands, the Bahamas, Cozumel, and the home of famed novelist Ernest Hemingway in Key West, but the theft ring had pulled back until another cruise. We came home tanned and relaxed with the best part of the summer still ahead of us.

Thefts from passenger cabins on the ship predictably resumed right after we left, and the company sent me back aboard alone with instructions to stay with the ship until I caught everyone in the theft ring. It took me two weeks of interviews and interrogations, but by the time the ship had sailed up the East Coast, stopped at New York City, and went from there to Quebec, I had identified all members of the theft ring and obtained confessions from several of them. All those involved were terminated and removed from the ship. Kristene's description had been accurate: the man who entered our cabin was a senior member of the ship's plumbers, and he confessed to a systematic theft scheme involving other crew members to loot passenger cabins.

We enjoyed the best Christmas that year, selecting and cutting down our Christmas tree at a local tree farm, train rides between North Bend and Snoqualmie Falls where I first kissed Kristene, horse-drawn carriage rides in downtown Seattle, Christmas plays, the kids with Santa, and much visiting and dinners with friends and relatives. The little kid in Kristene came out every Christmas in the way she wrapped presents and hid them until Christmas Eve. That year we left an apple, orange, cookies, and some walnuts on a plate on the living room coffee table by the fireplace for Santa. The kids were determined to stay awake and greet Santa when he came. Kristena even camped out on the living room floor in a sleeping bag. By 2:00 a.m. they were both asleep and we put presents under the tree and bits of orange peel and apple core on the plate for Santa. Then we went back to bed.

"Oh noooo! He was here again and I missed him!" we heard Kristena exclaim in the early morning. Kristena woke up Johnny, and we watched as together they opened present after present.

The reverie of that Christmas was short-lived; the New Year would bring unwelcome change as another so-called Pineapple Express came in from across the Pacific, bringing day after day of torrential rains that left behind swollen rivers and creeks in western Washington and saturated ground. Yet another storm after this one was expected in a few days. The cold terror we had come to know so well gripped us again, for we now had a keen nose for approaching disaster. I immediately prepared for the worst before the next storm; working alone I encased the house with plastic sheeting and walls of sandbags and reserved a pump. The rains returned while I was at work. It was early afternoon when Kristene called me.

"Honey, I think you should come home now, this looks really bad. The creek has already covered the lawn and reached the sandbag wall."

Neighborhood side streets near our house were already covered with several inches of water as I drove home. Kristene looked at me as I came in the house. She was calm, ready for the worst.

"Kay has taken the kids, and I can't find help just yet. It's just you and me now," she told me.

The government TV channel announced the creek would reach stage four, the highest level in about an hour, and more rain was on the way.

With the ground already saturated and unable to absorb more water, the already-high Issaquah Creek rose above flood stage very quickly, and water was pressing against our defenses in no time. It was a weekday, and getting volunteer help was harder than before. In spite of having a pump in the crawlspace and our other precautions, our home flooded again, worse this time than the first flood. We labored together all through the night, just the two of us, desperate to save our home, until at last the power went out and incoming water overwhelmed the pump, and we waded in the dark through knee-deep water out of our beloved home, and drove to a motel, wherein we held each other, cold, defeated, exhausted, and a heartsick Kristene clung to me as she wept bitterly.

'Remarriage ceremony on a cruise in the Caribbean Sea. June 1995

Christmas, downtown Seattle, 1995, just before the final flood

CHAPTER TWENTY-FOUR

We never returned to Issaquah again. It was a modern-day case of Paradise Lost. Our idyllic life was destroyed, and the bitter reality for me was that moving there had been my mistake, and my family was suffering for it. Not only had I failed to heed the Lord's warnings, but I also failed to fully look at the facts before I bought. I should have seen that unrestricted development had paved over too much permeable soil that formerly absorbed heavy rains, combined with environmental restrictions on dredging the creek beds had resulted in more frequent and severe flooding because rain waters had nowhere to go but over creek and river banks, victimizing homes and businesses alike.

Each flood brought ugly consequences with it: years of environmental and economic damage. The increase of silt in the creek channels greatly impaired the salmon spawning beds that require clear water and gravelly bottoms. Increased silt also set the stage for more frequent flooding, which translated into diminishing property values and destruction of years of home equity for homeowners.

The increasingly frequent and severe flooding was bad for business and hence the city's tax base was adversely affected. It damaged stores, restaurants and shops, causing them to lose revenue by having to close for repairs. Town council meetings degenerated into heated shouting as homeowners and business owners demanded action from the city fathers and the county council, who also faced protests from environmental groups and Indian tribes who opposed dredging the creek because they wrongly believed it would further harm salmon spawning beds, and they also faced greedy, well-heeled developers, bandits who wanted the right to continue ravaging the land by paving over more open spaces for even more housing (and more profits for themselves). Issaquah's small-town all-American charm was being supplanted by the ugliness of competing interests warring against each other over a charming gift of nature that was the crown jewel of the town's many assets. It was a sickening mess.

Our situation was overwhelming. We were stuck with property we could no longer live in and no one would buy, for its market value had evaporated. The three floods totally wiped out our home equity, and we were still responsible for the mortgage payments, which meant that wherever we moved to next would mean doubling or even tripling our monthly overhead. We were financially ruined. The third flood and evacuation traumatized Kristene and the kids. Our children had been torn away from their friends; Kristena's competition swimming and Johnny's baseball and boxing were over, and guilt tore at my insides when Johnny cried himself to sleep and Kristena suffered bad dreams. For six years Kristene poured herself into making this our ultimate home, *ours*, as it was our hope to live out our lives there, to see our kids married on the lawn by the creek and our grandchildren coming over to visit us, but now six years of sacrifice and the sweetest memories we had ever known were gone, gone overnight, and Kristene's heart would always bear the scars of this loss.

Lesser women have left their men for much less than this, but to her credit, Kristene never once complained, blamed, accused, or chastised me, nor did she consider for a moment leaving me, for she knew the anguish I felt about the way it had turned out. Loyal to the core, Kristene knew my heart and lovingly supported my efforts to correct my mistake, to strengthen the things that remained and work toward finding the best possible way out of a nightmare.

Just one week of living at my mother's again, with her inevitable and unkind "I told you so" comments was all we could stand. When my dad invited us to come out to Hadlock for the weekend, we jumped at the chance. Dad's resort business there was thriving, and he let us stay in a model home he had built on the upper property where Dominic and Rita's trailer had been years before. After that weekend, we decided to stay a week, and when the week was over, we enrolled the kids in school, knowing my dad had a pending sale of the property that might close inside of sixty days.

Having honeymooned there years ago, Hadlock became in our minds a safe haven after the trouble we had been through, because it is located in the heart of Washington's "banana belt," so-called because of a weather phenomenon created by the geography of the Olympic and Cascade mountain ranges that results in less annual rainfall, more sunshine, cooler summers, and warmer winters than the rest of the state, aspects that now held much appeal to us. Here would be our place of rest: dry, on high ground, room to roam, privacy, and a slower pace of life. For a time it would be our nest where we could recover, regroup, and plan our next move.

Healing began for us when we resumed our tradition of Sunday night spaghetti dinners. The aroma of fresh garlic, olive oil, and noodles in a boiling pot permeated our little two-bedroom house. Resuming bedtime Bible stories, prayer-time, and other family traditions nourished our souls, and the clear skies and salt air refreshed Kristene's frayed nerves.

To a very limited extent, we now experienced the plight, the displacement mentality of the homeless, of being on the outside looking in. It was sobering for me to see the gravity of my mistakes that got us here and made me realize even more the value of my family. Our home was destroyed, and we couldn't go back. We were in Hadlock this time not as honeymooners or tourists, but as refugees. The same people who were so nice to us when we were vacationers contributing to the local economy now treated us as invaders from the city. Churches here are typically small; about forty members seemed to be the average. We needed friends and a church home, so on Sundays we visited different churches and eventually chose to put down roots in a nearby church, where our future landlord and his son and grandchildren all attended. It wasn't, it would turn out, a wise choice, but it would be one from which we were to learn much about turning the other cheek.

We took refuge in Hadlock thinking we knew it as a community because of our many visits there, but we quickly learned how depthless our understanding was. As visitors we only saw it as a rural region of improved climate and natural beauty, sparsely populated by mostly working-class people and retirees; of its culture, history, commonly held values and crippling economic struggles we were ignorant. That was about to change. As only full-time residents can, we would understand through personal experience the dynamics and true character of the community, and what the forces of history had made of its people.

"An environmentalist," the locals bitterly observe, "is a hippy that has his cabin built." Due to outside political influences from well-financed leftists purporting to be environmentalists defending the 'Spotted Owl' as an endangered species, Hadlock and the surrounding communities that make up the Olympic Peninsula had been losing their economic base that had been their pride and defining identity for which they were known, upon which their culture was built: commercial fishing and logging. For decades, due to political pressure, extraction industries like mining as well as fishing and logging have been disappearing until little is left, leaving the populace to scrape by on seasonal service work as cooks, waiters, bartenders and clerks, jobs made possible by Seattle tourists. When the tourist season ended there was little else to do but squeak by on meager state unemployment benefits until the next tourist season. It became a cruel cycle of humiliating unemployment, underemployment, followed by drug and alcohol abuse, and long-established families in the sparsely populated region developed a siege mentality toward the outside world, and they intermarried, leading to an ingrown community that felt alienation toward outsiders and was inclined to shun newcomers. Our friend, Jimmy Katsikapas, told us that he had been an employer and a member of the community for thirty-two years, yet most locals still regarded him as an outsider because he wasn't born there.

Even in the church, it was difficult for us to find friends in Hadlock. The pastor, who knew our situation, made no effort whatsoever to get to know us or ask how he could help us. Instead all we got from him was no-eye-contact, a limp handshake and a curt, "Nice-to-see-you-goodbye," at the door after the service ended. I thought it odd that church members we would chat with on Sunday after service acted like they didn't know us when saw them at the supermarket. They would look away and hustle off in the other direction. One day it dawned on me: they had booze in their shopping carts! Aha! Hiding our vices, are we? What's next – tobacco? Heaven forbid! So much for church piety! Nevertheless, we determined to make the best of our time there, and involved ourselves in the community through our kids' sports and music activities.

Hadlock and its environs still had its original country charm. Little had changed since our honeymoon there fifteen years earlier. It still had just the one four-way flashing red light, and Port Townsend remained the only incorporated town in Jefferson County. We were grateful to my father for giving us a free place to rest and mend. We decided we would stay at least until the school year ended. If we decided to stay permanently, we would somehow buy a place of our own.

I commuted to my Seattle office daily, a trip of over an hour of driving to wait in line to catch the half-hour ferry ride to Seattle. I continued to participate in Monday night jail ministry, but this brought me home after midnight and feeling exhausted on Tuesday. The combined costs of commuting, in terms of gas, ferry tickets and vehicle wear, were heavy, and the pace wore on me: the daily commute into town, a full day at the office, then commute back home, plus Monday nights. The six hours of traveling plus an eight-hour workday every day allowed little sleep, and I treasured each minute of my weekends at home.

In sixty days, the sale of my father's resort and marina went through, and in the nick of time we found a new place just a few hundred yards away. We signed a one-year lease with option to buy on a house Jimmy Katsikapas owned. It was a gorgeous setting: a never-occupied unsold beachfront house overlooking Oak Bay, around the corner from Port Townsend Bay, truly spectacular view property on a level acre lot on the edge of a low bluff. Below the embankment was a sand spit that was a park and a prime public clam and oyster beach. The house was a beautiful new four bedroom rambler with enormous picture windows facing the bay, fourteen-foot ceilings, beautiful white oak floors and cabinets, a grey slate fireplace, red tile roof, cedar deck, and a Jacuzzi for two in the master bath. The scenery was breathtaking at any time of day.

Back in Issaquah we took our morning coffee sitting by the creek (weather permitting); now our morning cup was on our deck, overlooking marine traffic in Oak Bay. It was out of the rain and in the sun, out of the city and on the beach. Trees and open fields were all around. There was room for the kids to ride their bikes, for Johnny to hunt robins, squirrels, and crows with his BB gun, and of course, the beach below us.

There's a catch, a downside to every upside, and according to folk wisdom, he who is wise will always know 'what's the catch' before acting on a decision. In Issaquah it was the threat of flooding; here the catch was the lease payment being more than the mortgage payment in Issaquah, (which I was still paying) and the additional time and expense of commuting to Seattle made both family time and money in short supply; another new hardship for us.

Our deliverance was the beach right below us; a public prime clam and oyster beach, capable of feeding us all for free. The legal limit for digging clams was forty clams per person per day for certain months, and within certain months could oysters be taken there also. I bought the required permits and drove the four of us to the beach every other day with clam shovel, rubber boots, and bucket, where we worked together in the cold and the wet, our hands numb from digging in wet, frigid sand as we harvested clams, oysters, and mussels for the table.

It was fresh, high quality food free for the taking in a time of crippling double house payments, when every little bit helped. Luckily for us, Kristene knew from her childhood just how well a family can live on clams and oysters and a few vegetables. At lunch and dinnertime the air in our new home was filled with the salivating aroma of Kristene's stews and chowders, oysters grilled, fried, or smoked on our old smoker, clam omelets, and fresh French bread for dipping in the broth; there was never a time before or since that we ate so much fresh seafood for free.

Even in the depths of financial devastation and displacement, I courted and wooed Kristene, bringing her flowers, leaving her notes, and taking her out for a bite or a cup at a café or bakery somewhere while the kids were in school, soaking together in the Jacuzzi, waking her up for lovemaking in the deep of the night, and bringing her coffee and toast in the morning. Kristene's lower back pain persisted, and we tried a variety of specialty mattresses until we settled on a very expensive one made in Sweden that helped the most.

Small lumps showed up in her left breast that worried me. We made an appointment with a doctor that would be a couple of weeks away. On my drive home from the office one night, I was listening to *Focus on the Family* on the local Christian radio station. Dr. Dobson was interviewing a man who said that when his wife was diagnosed with early stage breast cancer, he fasted and prayed for her one day a week for six months and the lumps disappeared and her doctors pronounced her cancer-free. I immediately embarked on a program of fasting and praying for Kristene's health all day on Wednesdays.

We were waiting for the final flood insurance check to come in, and I wanted to save it toward our next home. Our overhead costs were higher now than ever before, and our finances became disorganized and wasteful in the mayhem that followed the flood. Now that business volume and cash flow were up sharply, it was time to review and reorganize. I was burnt out on the long days and the commute to Seattle. The type of cases that were coming in now had shifted away from field interviews and surveillance to research investigations I could do myself from a computer at home. This was surely the Lord enabling me to be home more.

I checked out videos about small business management from the public library, and wrote out a business plan to downsize and streamline business operations. I replaced paid employees with independent subcontractors, closed the physical Seattle office, opened a virtual office downtown that would give me downtown presence, and moved my work home. Regrettably I stepped down from the jail ministry too; I needed to be home. Restructuring my business eliminated thousands of dollars in monthly overhead, reduced my stress load, and increased my family time. Kristene was isolated socially by the women in the area and didn't mind a bit when I set up a computer work station, office phone setup, and fax machine in our bedroom because it gave us that which we craved most: time together. God blessed my return to the home office in unexpected ways.

With more disposable income, we were able to pay cash for a fine used boat and trailer without touching the insurance money I had set aside for a down payment on our next house. I was home enough now to enjoy taking Kristene and the kids on daytrips around the islands in our boat. It was a quality fiberglass offshore cruiser type, its hull shape the deep-water 'V' design, twenty-two feet from bow to stern, sleeping berths for four, an inboard V-8 engine, and rigged for open water fishing. Kristene named it *Meant to Be*, after us. We found moorage within a minute of the house and went on frequent weekend trips all around Port Townsend Bay, Oak Bay, and Point-No-Point, fishing and crabbing, learning to handle breakdowns, replace broken propellers when we ran over sunken logs, and bettering our docking and navigating abilities.

By early summer our sea-skills were sufficient for us to take the kids on an extended adventure exploring the San Juan Islands of north Puget Sound that extended into Canadian waters. We planned and stowed our provisions, extra clothing and emergency gear and cast off our lines from the dock, venturing north on a sunlit morning through Port Townsend Bay into the upper San Juan Islands with no destination in mind, just wherever chance would take us, sleeping in the boat when we docked in various island towns for a meal and a visit. Our boat was smaller than most of the boats that roamed these waters, but its deep-v hull design and structural strength lent it uncommon stability even in choppy whitecaps.

We wandered into an island cove on the final night, and docked below a small, rustic hotel and restaurant set into a hillside. The island was the last before Canadian islands and waters. Perhaps it was the Canadian influence, but this restaurant had the atmosphere of an English pub, crammed with bustling waitresses and boisterous, suntanned voyagers roughened by outdoor living, many of whom were boaters who had sailed, kayaked, or motored into port with their women and children, thirsty for hearty drink, table fare and beds, high-spiritedly sharing stories of inter-island seafaring.

The few rooms of the hotel were already filled, leaving us to sleep aboard *Meant To Be*. Kristene and Kristena slept beneath the starry sky on the open rear deck atop piled-up seat cushions and pillows, snuggled warmly into blankets and sleeping bags. Johnny and I burrowed into sleeping bags in the forward berths, and I lay listening to my wife and daughter chatting and chuckling above the fading din of rowdy revelers in the pub. For all our hard times of late, I knew I was a very, very blessed man.

Our voyage home was unique. It began before we even left the dock. We were up with the sun, having breakfasted at a dockside diner, and were stowing our gear when certain incoming boaters caught our attention. It was an ethereal scene, mystical, reminiscent of Norse mythology, and my attention immediately locked on to the mesmerizing, fixating moment. On two sailboats were several teenage girls, not city girls on vacation but country girls, tanned, lean, Nordic looking, barefoot in long homemade dresses made of burlap-like rough brown cloth, alluring and beautiful in their rusticity. That they seemed to be from neighboring islands was indicated by their dress, hairstyle and appearance. I wondered if they were possibly from a religious island camp, as I watched them standing on the bows and gunnels of their boats that were skippered by similarly dressed adults. The girls squinted into the golden morning sun that highlighted their pulled-back long blonde and red hair, their profiles creating a total head-to-toe halo effect that was reminiscent of a scene from a religious film, as their graceful vessels skimmed slowly across glassy water past us to the docks beyond us. We cast off our lines as they passed by and shoved away from the dock, filling their space in the channel as we motored slowly out of the small bay toward open water.

We waved goodbye to the kayakers and boaters we met the night before as we passed them into the open waters of Puget Sound, headed for home. Except for the island we were leaving, land on either side of us was miles away, and the water was calm and slow-rolling, oil-like. I opened the throttle to three-quarter speed, and we set to cruising, leaving a beautiful white wake behind us as the bow lifted under the thrust of the throbbing engine. Thus we cruised for some time, Kristene and the kids relaxing on the rear deck, happily smiling, talking, lifejacketed, until a loud bump broke our reverie, and suddenly we were dead in the water with the drive shaft emitting a high-pitched whine.

The prop shattered when it hit a submerged object, possibly a log. I had a spare in my tool box, but the cotter key holding the busted prop to the drive shaft broke as I removed it, leaving me with nothing with which to secure the new prop to the drive shaft. We were adrift on open water; the nearest island on the horizon was miles away and there was no one in sight. I had only a wooden oar; hardly adequate to get us to the nearest island before nightfall. I rummaged through my toolbox and spare parts kit for anything I could use: nothing. We were bobbing helplessly in the water. This could quickly become a desperate situation; I had to come up with something fast.

I stood staring at my drive shaft, wracking my brain for a solution when a lone boater appeared on the horizon, headed right for us. He was fiftyish and tanned, with salt-and-pepper hair and mustache, wearing only a red swimsuit. He pulled up alongside us, and I told him what the trouble was. Without a word, he searched around in his toolbox until he found a used cotter key that was the right size. He stayed with us until I had the new prop on and fired up the motor. We waved goodbye to him as he headed off into the sun, and I throttled the engine to two-thirds speed for the last leg of our journey home.

The way our rescuer appeared, assisted us, and left caused me to wonder: Could he have been an angel of the Lord? What had happened and the way it happened was consistent with Hebrews 1:14 which says: *"Are they (angels) not all ministering spirits sent forth to minister for those who will inherit salvation?"* Even if he was a man and not an angel, there could be no doubt that God sent him to us by divine appointment.

The water remained calm and flat, a huge sheet of dark blue glass, and the afternoon sun's golden rays reflecting off the surface were blinding at some angles. A moment after the bow lifted out of the water, creating a new white wake behind us, dolphins appeared on either side and in front of us, rolling partly up out of the surface and back down under again, playfully, in unison, as if they were there to escort us the rest of the way home. For more than two hours, the dolphins accompanied us until we entered Port Townsend Bay, when they vanished as mysteriously as they had appeared. Again, the timing of the appearance of the dolphins to escort us home was clear evidence that God was demonstrating His care over us. We were a blessed family.

As summer wore on, Kristene and I went for a boat ride by ourselves. The kids were visiting friends, the day was hot and windless, and it was ours. We wore only swimsuits, even though the water was always too cold for swimming. We cruised between Port Townsend Bay and Oak Bay and around Indian Island, passing as close as we could to a rock jutting out of the water that was covered with sea otters, and then we passed friends' beach homes, Kristene waving to them as we went by, her statuesque figure glowing under the sun's radiance and tanning oil, long, dark hair glistening, moving with her body. We dropped anchor in a calm cove called Mystery Bay, shared coffee from a thermos, and sunbathed for awhile. I tried to lure her into the cuddy cabin, but she saw through my ploy and told me to wait until we got home.

She laid on her back on the rear seat of the boat as we motored our way toward home, she in a pink one-piece swimsuit, soaking the sun into her body, eyes closed, unconscious of how powerfully she was radiating sensuality, her lustrous dark hair formed a halo round her head, as the boat glided effortlessly through glassy waters and the sun bathed her in warmth and golden light. From the steering wheel, I looked over my shoulder at her heart-stopping pose that would have made a great photograph if I had brought a camera. In another week I would have been married to her sixteen years now, and my eyes had never stopped drinking in her beauty as my necessary nourishment. At forty five years old, she radiated sensuality; stunning and intensely feminine, hers a classic profile that commanded attention wherever she went.

She could have been a success in films or magazines or music were it not for marrying me. She was beautiful head-to-toe, everything in the right place. She was spiritual, loving and faithful, gracious, kind and forgiving, and a devoted lover, wife, mother, daughter, and homemaker. She was the heart of our family, my crown, and the symbol of God's favor upon me. Kristene was the sum of all womanhood.

"You're the best wife I've ever had, Baby," I would tell her teasingly.

"Hah! That's saying a lot! And you're the best husband I've *ever* had," she would laughingly respond.

"Only because of a lack of competition," was my comeback.

Our passion and desire for each other was undiminished after all these years. With Kristene I was a blessed man.

Of rest and peace there had not been enough, as summer neared its end. We found we lacked the energy to move back to Seattle – we were still too exhausted to even decide if we should move or stay. We agreed to stay in Hadlock through the coming school year and give serious consideration to the idea of settling there permanently. We enrolled the kids in Cedarbrook Adventist, the only Christian school in the area. Set at the edge of a large hayfield with bales of harvested hay in the old-fashioned round style awaiting final pick up, and surrounded by a thick forest of fir trees, the school setting could just as well been in the nineteenth century as we met the new principal, Brad Booth, to fill out enrollment papers.

Cedarbrook consisted of two small two-story buildings, a playground, and a sports field set in a gravel parking lot; it held classes for kindergarten through eighth grade. We felt welcome here, and we quickly became friends with Brad and his wife, Ruthie.

Small lumps reappeared in Kristene's left breast. I fasted and prayed again for her healing again every Wednesday through the fall months up to the beginning of the holidays when the lumps again disappeared. The doctors reported that they were benign fatty cysts, but they couldn't explain why they disappeared, although we knew it was the Lord. I breathed a sigh of relief and thanked God for healing her, and that her back trouble had also cleared up. We focused now on contributing to the community through our kids' activities. Kristena began piano lessons at a private home, and we signed John up to play basketball after the holidays.

Anonymous handwritten letters came every week in the mail. The letters stopped just short of being hate mail. The writer scolded us about what the Bible teaches about pride and arrogance and the importance of humility. I considered going to the pastor about this, but for all I knew the letters could have been from him, for many of the phrases and topics in the letters were nearly direct quotes from his sermons, and he continued to be unfriendly toward us, his face often flushing beet red and his neck veins bulging whenever Kristene greeted him. I was all for finding another church, but the kids had formed friendships there by then, so we stayed and put up with the unfriendliness. Our landlord was very anxious to let us have the house we were in at very favorable terms that were hard to turn down, so we kept our minds open to the possibility of becoming permanent residents. We kicked back and went with the flow of where we were. We would know soon enough. In the meantime all we wanted was time to rest.

CHAPTER TWENTY-FIVE

Gradually we concluded that it would not benefit our kids if we settled permanently in Hadlock; doing so would severely limit their opportunities for growth and the likelihood that they would go to college and find career fulfillment. We were there only for a season of rest and finding new direction, and our season would end soon enough.

Knowing that, we delved into making the most of our remaining months there by being active in the community. We stayed on at the unfriendly church for our kids' sake, continuing to tithe and treating those who were unfriendly to us as we wanted to be treated. I volunteered as assistant coach of Johnny's basketball team (which was never my game or my son's), and Kristene contributed to the team by supplying post-game snacks for the boys, and thus we built relationships with other parents. My dad and his wife came often to Kristena's piano recitals and both kids' ball games, and we became friends with our landlord and his wife, their son, and his family. We did these things to push past social ostracism and do the right thing; we were applying the principle of turning the other cheek and ignoring rudeness and rejection. And life for us became better and better as a result. We discovered it was less stressful and more rewarding to keep our focus on pleasing Christ, Who in turn enabled us to see people and situations through His eyes; indeed, we discovered that His burden is light, and His yoke is easy, just as He said.

Our friendship with Brad and Ruthie Booth was another expression of God's care; their company was refreshing to us, and our time with them was a soothing balm, calming and restorative, like sitting beside a cool pond on a hot day, dangling our feet in the water. We met other Adventists through school functions and learned about the Adventist way of life. I never did agree with basic Adventist teachings, but I came to deeply respect and admire them as true Christians and a credit to our faith. Since Adventists are vegetarians, Kristene prepared completely meatless meals when the Booth family came over for dinner. Kristene lost her taste for red meat during her pregnancy with Johnny, but for me, I never could adjust to a steady regimen of no red meat or shellfish, though I tried. Out of respect for Brad and Ruthie, I was a vegetarian for an evening when they came over, and Kristene worked magic with eggplant, cauliflower, kale, and potatoes and a variety of sauces that wrought compliments from our beloved guests. Even so, I went to bed with an objecting stomach every time.

As I look back at that time now, I realize that God put Brad Booth into my life and Ruthie into Kristene's life in the places that Ron and Kay had held while we were away. Brad became like Ron Kinssies to me: a best friend and confidant with whom I could discuss deep things about faith, theology, politics, and personal philosophy, as men do. Brad, a man of medium height and build with black, wavy hair parted on the side, dark eyes and brows, and a thick mustache, bore a distinct resemblance to his ancestor, John Wilkes Booth, the man who shot Abraham Lincoln; Brad was descended also of William Booth, the founder of the Salvation Army. A living letter from Christ was Brad; principled and learned, with advanced degrees in education and psychology, a Bible student, a deep thinker. The pleasant memories of our families bonding are with me still.

Assistant coaching Johnny's basketball team that winter taught me what I would need to know for the coming baseball season: the kids from the three rural communities of Hadlock, Chimacum, and Irondale were clean-cut, rough-and-tumble country kids whose working-class families had deep roots in the region, and many were poor. At eight and nine years old, they were quick to put up their dukes and punch it out with each other on the basketball court and thought themselves too tough to cry or whine if they got hurt. I broke up more than one fistfight on the court. Some involved my own son and others didn't.

Port Townsend kids were the very opposite, and that is what made the mix so interesting. The parents of the Port Townsend kids were generally former hippies who dropped out of society during or after the '60s. As adults, they lived on the edge and dominated Port Townsend politics, so most chain stores and restaurants were kept out. These boys showed up to play ball with spiked blue or green hair and nose and earrings, reflections of counter-culture parents who were prone to whining and protesting, often crying foul, making for some contentious games. It was my opinion that these kids were sitting in the back row when parents were being handed out, and I felt sorry for them.

I coached my own girls' softball team that spring, to ensure that our daughter and Aubynn Booth could play on the same team. I strongly felt this was important because they were the only girls on the team who were attending private school, and the bias against them from the public school kids would be less severe if they had each other. Little did I know the education about the community I was in for, beginning with the player draft.

We coaches met, introduced each other, shook hands and wasted no time getting down to choosing players as each player briefly demonstrated her ball-handling skills. After my daughter and Aubynn, I picked a skinny ten-year-old girl with braces and long, light brown hair whose excellent coordination and speed made her an obvious asset to our team. Right after I drafted her on, she came up to me.

"Coach, you have to pick my twin sister too or I won't play," she said.

Not knowing what to say, I looked to the coach sitting next to me, a young father, athletic looking, probably in his 30's.

"Yep," he said with a nod, "the twins always play together. Pick the other one too. They're both great players."

I took his advice and got the other twin on the team. I soon had a team of sixteen girls between ten and twelve years old, and one of the moms as assistant coach. The league issued me two aluminum bats, three batting helmets, and a set of protective catcher's gear contained in a heavy-duty black plastic lawn and leaf bag.

Practice began at a county park the next day after school. Volunteer parents brought the team in carloads and stayed to help. I divided the girls into pairs and had them play catch while I began the process of finding out who my pitchers would be. I saw one of the girls remove a foil tobacco pouch from her hip pocket, pack her jaw full of whatever was in the pouch, and return it to her pocket. I walked over to her.

"Okay, let's have it," I said.

"Honest, coach, it's just gum. Got the pouch from my uncle—he chews when he's workin' in the woods 'cause he can't smoke there, and he loans me his mitt every season 'cause we can't afford one," she said, spitting on the ground ballplayer style. The pouch was filled with pink bubble gum; I smiled and handed it back to her.

When we practiced again the next day, I established a warm-up routine of jumping jacks, toe touches, and running twice around the outfield to reduce the risk of sprains and injuries. The girls groaned and whined, but they did it. I placed our most promising pitcher on the mound and filled the other positions and set the remaining girls to playing catch until they could be rotated in. I had the pitcher throw to me, and I batted grounders and line drives to infield and outfield. Then I hit a line drive that hit my pitcher on her thigh so hard it knocked her to the ground, crying. Parents and I ran to her, but she quickly got to her feet, refusing to leave the field. Within minutes a golf ball–size lump appeared on her leg, red and blue with swelling. I was about to call an ambulance, but her mother refused.

"Nah, she'll be okay," she said as she helped her daughter hobble to the bench, refusing to leave practice.

One of the twins came up to me (I could never tell them apart), her braces a tin-grin smile.

"Coach," she said, "playing catch is okay, but when are we gonna work on forced plays?"

I stared my caught-off-guard stare, my mouth open. "Excuse me?" was all I could say.

"Yeah," she said, "last year my sister and I went all the way to the all stars, and that was because our coach had us practicing forced plays all the time. We should get going on it soon."

"Uh, well, sure, that will come later, maybe next week. But for now I need to see which players will do best in which positions," I replied. I looked at my watch. "As a matter of fact, right now would be a good time to stop for today. Everybody go home, work on your homework, get some sleep. See you all here same time tomorrow." I gathered all the issued gear into the black plastic garbage bag, dropped off Kristena and Aubynn, and headed to the public library, where I checked out videos on coaching youth baseball. *Dang! I'm in trouble! These darn kids know more about baseball than I do!* I silently remarked to myself.

The injured girl was back at practice the next day. I watched in amazement as she ran with a hobble to favor her injured leg as she moved around the infield, ably catching and throwing with determination, through her pain, her mom cheering her on from the sidelines. These girls have real grit, I concluded. This one was still hurting from the day before yet she uttered not a word of complaint; it was as if the injury never happened. We practiced until dinnertime every afternoon that week, always beginning with warm-up exercises. At the end of our last practice before our first game, I called out "Time to turn in, ladies, got a game tomorrow."

"We're not ladies!" one of them called back.

My girls were tough and aggressive; they won most of their games that season as much by intimidating and taunting the other team as by skill and plain old-fashioned pluckiness. Before each game they intimidated the other team by doing jumping jacks while reciting jeering chants in front of their dugout. They booed, hissed, cat-called and jeered the other team's batters, slid head-first onto stolen bases, including home plate, and licked their palms wet when they had to pass by and high-five the other players at the end of each game, which often started arguments, name-calling, and even fights. Baseball was the pastime of the region, a region where there wasn't much else to do, and these kids lived to play, eagerly playing two or three games and two practices a week. Every time I canceled a practice to give everyone a breather, I got calls at home from my players begging for a practice, literally crying and sobbing until I gave in. They even fought with each other in the dugout waiting their turn at bat, one accusing the other of having head lice.

The season was made even more memorable by Aubynn Booth. Her Adventist upbringing strongly emphasized honoring the Sabbath on Saturday, a day our team played every week. Brad and Ruthie wisely let the decision to play or not be hers. Aubynn carefully considered what to do: consulted with her parents, me, and Kristena. In the end, she chose not to play Saturdays, winning the respect of even the most begrudging of her teammates and their parents for her commitment to her convictions.

I was so busy coaching girls' softball, commuting and working cases that Kristene had to fill in for me at most of our son's games. Baseball was such a big part of the cultural fabric here that even my son's team of seven and eight year-old boys was playing full-on hardball with hard-throwing real pitchers, not parents gently tossing softballs underhand across the plate, like they do in the Seattle suburbs we were from. These younger boys were no less hard core than the older girls on my team, for every week, John's team also played two games and had two practices. During games John and his teammates did jumping jacks and pushups in the dugout while waiting their turn at bat. Our boy John, a southpaw like his mom, distinguished himself playing centerfield and first base, the power of his throwing arm able to throw clear to the catcher from centerfield without the ball once touching the ground, wowing players and parents alike again and again. John's batting power was no less substantial. On the last game of the season, with the bases loaded, on the last inning, he hit a grand slam home run, clearing the bases and winning the game, jubilant teammates carrying him off the field on their shoulders.

By the time baseball season and the school year ended in June, we had made arrangements to move to Mercer Island, a prestigious suburb of Seattle. Located in the southern half of Lake Washington between Seattle and the suburbs collectively known as the East Side, having a Mercer Island address was a status symbol. Mercer Island students at all grade levels consistently scored among the top ten school districts in the nation, and dominated in certain sports year after year. Mercer Island has its own police and fire departments, its own school district, phone prefixes, and zip codes, and bridges connect it to either lake shore, affording an easy commute for its residents. Palatial homes with private docks line its shores, and its neighborhoods are not cookie-cutter, suburban shoebox variety tract houses. No two homes are the same, they are individual and eclectic in their variety, owned by doctors, lawyers, well-paid professionals and CEOs. Property values and taxes on the Island are higher than elsewhere in the county, and all of these factors combined to create and perhaps justify an elitist mentality in the minds of its residents, a certain arrogance that Mercer Islanders were locally known for.

We were able to buy a home there while still carrying the Issaquah house payments because my payments were always on time, and the City of Issaquah had sent us a letter, stating their intent to buy our property on the creek within sixty days. Our new home was a three-story, three-bedroom house of the late '60s vintage on the south side of the Island, a solidly built structure it was, that backed onto a forested greenbelt and had three wood decks and separate living quarters in the daylight basement that became my new home office, for it had an exterior door, bathroom, and fireplace and was large enough for three computer workstations plus file and storage cabinets.

Moving in went smoothly, and both kids made new friends in the neighborhood right away. It was summertime, and we often went to the beach to picnic, swim in the lake, and just lay on the beach. It felt great to be back, and we quickly resumed the social life we knew before the flood: seeing Ron and Kay and Richard and Barbara, renewing old friendships, and revisiting old haunts. It was bittersweet to visit Terry and Sallie Cowgill, to again be in our old neighborhood, for our old house was still standing, empty, rotting, and haunting, stripped of anything useful or valuable, weeds and brush overtaking lawn, driveway, and garden. Kristene was unable to even look at it. To get us off the hook, I had sold the city on the idea of using the property as a "passive use" park, which meant the house would be torn down and the land allowed to return to its natural state to allow floodwaters to collect there, thus taking pressure off neighboring creek-side properties. After the purchase went through, and the old home was torn down, we found that the emotional hooks of Paradise Lost were still embedded in us, precious memories forever in our souls; ever would there be a sad, wistful longing that we could not have remained there for the rest of our days.

The kids had started school by the time the deal closed. Life was moving on, but not without more pain, for after the bank loan was paid off, all we had left was a mere $25,000 to show for years of building home equity, much of it with our own sweat. We were set back to nearly zero at a time that I was fifty years of age, and it hurt. I felt embarrassed and angry with myself for my poor judgment, and I was bitter at the greedy real estate agent, the developers, the short-sighted county and city officials for granting building permits for the sake of revenue, and I was bitter also with the city for low-balling us when we were down, just because they could.

The city's offer was the only way out of a bad deal, and I had no choice but to accept it. I was hurt, yes, but counted myself lucky to be out from under a bad deal that had seemed impossible. Lesson learned; at least we had a little cash left over. It could have been far worse; my former neighbors were stuck, still victims of reduced property values and living with the dread of the rainy seasons every year.

Once more God rescued me from my own folly, and in my private prayer time, I thanked Him for His mercy and grace. Had I listened to Him in the first place, we would not have gone through this suffering, and I vowed that from now on I would consult Him before making any major decision and not act without the Lord's peace on the matter.

That Kristene's love for me was so strong that she understood the situation and my pain and that she thanked and praised me for getting us out of a hopeless mess without a word of complaint or resentment was healing balm to my wounds, and I gave the Lord praise and thanks for giving her to me.

Mercer Island was a new start for us, and we welcomed it by pouring our energy into it without looking back. The kids were behind Mercer Island school standards and needed private tutoring to catch up. It was refreshing to be in a community that placed so much value on academic excellence. Both of them joined soccer teams and brought home friends after school, and through the schools and the kids' sports activities, we socialized with other parents, and the fullness of life resumed.

Finding a church home was our next step, and we visited nearly every church on the Island, including all the mainline denominations, Lutheran, Methodist, Presbyterian, Catholic, and others, and met with the pastors of several of them, only to be disappointed. Sermons were tepid commentaries on news or current events with a Scripture verse thrown in. The pure Gospel, of repentance of sins, living for Christ and dying to self, was never preached. The congregants were like the pastors, smug, stuffy and complacent, satisfied with canned religion, with 'churchianity', in which the sermon topic for five years in advance was pre-determined by the denomination head office, irrespective of situation or needs, unspiritual but still thinking themselves right and good and in need of nothing, yet knowing nothing of the Bible or how spiritually wretched they really were, like the Laodicean church in the Book of Revelation. We met personally with different pastors, and not one would say he had been born again. One pastor who came to our home told us, "Homosexuality is sin in the eyes of the church *for now*."

"'For now'?" I echoed. "Does that mean the church believes right and wrong are subject to change?"

"Yes, times change," he said.

I was genuinely shocked to hear a clergyman say this. "What about the Biblical teaching on this? The Bible clearly condemns this behavior in both the Old and New Testaments," I asked.

I had unintentionally cornered him; I really only wanted to know his views, but his stark reply took me off guard.

"Biblical interpretations change with the times," he gulped.

He was lying, and he knew it; he was wrong and he knew it. Somewhere in his past he had exchanged the truth he knew and principle for comfort and acceptance, and he knew it. The look on his face and his nervously shifting eyes betrayed him and his words; it was the look of a rabbit caught in a snare, unable to wriggle free as the hunter closes in. To spare him further shame, I thanked him for coming.

When he left, Kristene and I looked at each other. "There's a new Foursquare church right over the bridge in Bellevue," I said.

CHAPTER TWENTY-SIX

Church meant more to us than a cultural accessory to our lifestyle, a mere place to dress up and be seen at on Sundays. Rather than compliance with lifeless religious rituals and rules, it was our *personal relationship* to the Lord Jesus Christ that defined us as Christians; it was the fulcrum of everything in our lives, the meat-on-the-bones of who we were, and active participation in the church that God planted us in was an outward expression that we belonged to the body of Christ, that obedience to Him was our first priority. Thus church was our identity, lifestyle, our society and our value system, of which we partook throughout the week, year round. We had lacked a church family since we left Issaquah.

Returning to our roots at Neighborhood Church was unworkable because it had suffered a split after Pastor Rozell retired to enter the mission field in Asia. Controversy swirled around the new pastor until he finally left under a cloud about the time we lost our home and moved to Hadlock. The trouble over the new pastor ultimately led to severe membership decline and endless internal turmoil that reduced it to a mere shadow of the powerhouse it once was.

Now we especially needed a church that had a strong youth ministry, for our kids were now preteens, a crucial time for final grounding in the faith to prepare them for the challenges ahead, changing hormones, peer pressure, and skepticism that are inevitable aspects of the teens and early twenties.

My sister Cindy, who had been a widow for the past three years, followed us with her two kids, Matt and Molly, onto Mercer Island and began attending Bellevue Foursquare Church with us. It was a small church, its growth potential severely limited by the fact that its small building was inset into a steep hillside, but the worship, the preaching, and the music were so rich and powerful that none the physical limitations mattered. People who attended there experienced God personally, week after week. The worship team was a handful of young musicians and singers led by Cindy Gosk, a tall, guitar-strumming young woman with short blonde hair who looked and dressed the part of a modern-day folk singer. Pastor Peter Van Breda preached simple, direct sermons that struck home time after time so that at the end, people crowded the altar in a range of emotions between weeping and rejoicing with hands upraised. The services were never particularly long but always powerful; one always left refreshed, having met with God at the personal level, and the effect of Sunday lasted all through the week.

Business began booming in unexpected ways as soon as we moved into our Mercer Island home. I originally entered private investigation expecting to build a white-collar, nine-to-five firm catering to the business community, but most of the cases coming in now were from businesses needing armed protection and surveillance on a short term basis, cases that sometimes required multiple personnel. The hours were long and irregular, but the work was highly profitable. To meet the manpower demands, I hired fellow private investigators who were former police officers like me and who were licensed to be armed.

The nature of this new work compelled immediate changes in the interests of safety and liability. I customarily maintain a fairly high level of physical fitness, but now I and my men needed to upgrade our fighting and guarding skills. I began training twice a week at the dojo of my old friend George Ledyard, an Aikido master who had developed a system of defensive tactics for police and security officers that was recognized by the state training commission. The system George developed was an early form of what later became known as mixed martial arts: blocks, punches, kicks, and takedown techniques, borrowed from judo, boxing, karate and aikido into a new system that was simple, effective and easy to learn quickly. For us who were sometimes called upon to bodyguard, George's training even included methods of protecting a client from multiple attackers.

At age fifty-one, I was training and sparring with young men half my age. One of them I recognized and hired on a full-time basis was Nathan Vance, the same kid who used to cut meat for us at Fischer's Meats in Issaquah years before. Nate was now twenty-one and stood a lean and strong six-foot-three; he was a candidate at several local police departments. His high work ethic and personal integrity were an example for other young men we later hired, and in a short time he became like a son to us. After a few months, a beautiful young woman named Heather came to work for us at Nate's recommendation.

Financially we were breathing easier because of increased business volume and because Seattle-area real estate values were on yet another upward arc with no end in sight. It was another false boom in real estate values that I meant to use to our advantage. With business cash flow in high gear, we were steadily rebounding from the loss of our original home equity. We understood, of course, we would never fully recover the lost home from Issaquah; we would always be behind where we would have been were it not for the flood situation. In order to strengthen our position this time, I applied a lesson from my parents: we avoided debt of any kind, especially a second mortgage or a home equity line of credit. If we couldn't pay cash, we didn't buy.

We received word the following April that Kristene's beloved Aunt Kate had passed away. She was eighty-four. Leo buried her in the Hoquiam cemetery, mourning the loss of the one he loved so much and for so long, for since the time of her stroke, he had faithfully cared for her twenty-four hours a day, seven days a week, for twenty-three years. Leo's humility and sacrificial love deeply imprinted my soul well ere the passing of his beloved Kate. After Kate's death, Kristene continued to remember Leo on his birthday, on all holidays, calling him and sending him cards, and made a point of it to visit him at his home every time she was in the area.

The negative influence of my parents on our kids reached the point that we could no longer look the other way and not do or say anything. My father delighted in verbally abusing his wife, Jeanne, and taking the Lord's Name in vain in front of us, even when the kids were present. Worse yet, Dad openly favored our son over our daughter, showering him with compliments, always calling him "Hansen" while ignoring and often mispronouncing Kristena's name, deliberately I thought. A severe alcoholic, Dad in his old age still went on occasional drinking binges that would kill an ordinary man, never sober for days or weeks at a time, during which he would not eat and would make personally insulting phone calls to me and Kristene; for her own safety, Jeanne would leave him during these times until he either sobered up on his own or went into a sanitarium to dry out.

Exposure to my father was having a corrupting influence on our son. He became foul mouthed and incorrigible at home and at school, often threatening his sister with remarks such as "Shut up or I'll knock your block off," after being around his grandfather. After being unsuccessful at addressing my concerns to my dad, I limited visits between us. My mother was an equally adverse influence, but being the manipulator that my father was not, she tended to be more subtly subversive. She would take our daughter on what she alleged would be a lunch outing, but that became instead a shopping trip to expensive boutiques that we never patronized, in direct violation of our instructions not to buy her anything without our permission. There were several such outings in which Mom agreed to our instructions but defied us every time, buying Kristena expensive things we could not afford, all the while making derogatory comments about her mother.

"That mother of yours, she sure knows how to spend your dad's money," Kristena would tell us she said.

Finally it reached the point that of her own accord, Kristena withdrew from being alone with her grandmother. But my mother went even further than this: some of my clients who served on a downtown development committee that my mother belonged to told me that my mother was telling other members at meetings that I could not afford to live on Mercer Island, telling them, "He's only doing it for that wife of his, and you should see her figure." I lost clients as a result of her remarks. Thus Mom was hurting my business reputation also.

There was no possible way to speak to my father about these matters, although I tried several times. Years of alcoholic binges and declining health rendered him permanently hostile and opinionated and unapproachable. At least I was able to have a private meeting with my mom at a neutral place in Bellevue, whereupon I confronted her about her remarks about our living on Mercer Island to people who were my clients, and about the crude disparagements she was making about Kristene's figure to other people in town. Mom didn't deny saying any of these things, but rather than give us the dignity of an apology, she turned the tables as she had done in the past by accusing me of ingratitude.

Then there was Kristene's mother. Matilda came up from California one summer, and as was her custom, she rotated her stay among her children and her sisters every few days. When she stayed with us, we made the mistake of letting her babysit the kids while we went out on a dinner date. Both kids were crying and upset when we came home, because Matilda had physically punished them for not cleaning up their plates. I was angry, but said nothing because Matilda was only with us for a few days, and I knew Kristene was able to handle her mother.

Exposure to domestic strife throughout my childhood influenced my behavior toward Kristene without my being aware of it. After all this time, I still had a divorce mentality. I was ashamed that I had not seen this myself, for I had become more given to self-assessment since the early years. It was to my shame that it was necessary for Kristene to point it out. She was right: I played the divorce card whenever we had a serious disagreement and I knew I was in the wrong. It was a subconscious escape mechanism that was damaging my family because I often said it in the hearing of our kids. I would say, "Let's just get a divorce, then," as a way to avoid working through the problem. I repented of the harm I had done, telling God I didn't want to be this way. Of all my prayers, these were answered the fastest, and I soon stopped this behavior and the word 'divorce' dropped out of my vocabulary.

By all outward appearances we had it made on Mercer Island. We had a nice home, our kids were doing well in school, we belonged to a nice community club and pool, and we knew people through our kids' activities. We eventually found a church on the Island that suited our kids very well: Mercer Island Covenant. Both kids became active in youth group activities, and Kristena took her first missionary trip with the youth group to the seedy part of San Francisco for a week, where the kids shared the Gospel message with street people.

For the first time, Kristene worked with me in the business during hours the kids were in school: running errands, spot checking addresses for the presence of certain vehicles, and searching and retrieving public records from the county courthouse. Kristene's best work, though, was when she worked with me undercover. These cases were fun and adventure for us to work together. I was a flop at undercover work because of my athletic build and military bearing. I always came across as a cop to people who were up to no good. But with Kristene along, people tended not to pay attention to me, and with the focus on her, the crooks we investigated often let their guard down enough so that we successfully obtained the evidence we were after.

Kristene's finest hour as an undercover agent was on a case in Florida, where we went to investigate the assets of two attorneys who had for years operated a sinister scheme of falsely representing Central American children as the illegitimate heirs, survivors, and beneficiaries of American citizens who had died in plane crashes in the region. In our case, a commercial airline return flight to Seattle from Central America went down over the Pacific Ocean due to a mechanical failure, killing everyone on board. These Florida attorneys filed claims against the estates of two Seattle men who died in the crash with their immediate families, on behalf of two Guatemalan children, that they alleged were illegitimate offspring of these men. In each case they alleged that these men had gone to Central America with the intention of meeting the children there prior to adopting them upon their return to Seattle.

Their claims were dismissed by a Seattle judge after a lengthy investigation that necessitated my making multiple trips to southern Mexico and the jungles of Guatemala to verify the alleged birth certificates of the children by viewing the records in person, which ultimately exposed the claims as the cruel fraud they were. The investigation cost the surviving families nearly six figures. Our job was to see if it was worth further expense to attempt to recover the costs from the attorneys through legal action.

I determined before we went to Florida that garbage pickup at the targets' law office was early Monday mornings, so we arranged for Ron and Kay to stay at the house with the kids for five days and booked a Sunday-evening flight. Armed with a map and written driving directions, we rented a silver minivan at the airport and drove straight to the law office. We were in luck: the office was a one-story, standalone building with an alley behind it. I gave Kristene the wheel, and we circled the block twice. There were no lights on inside and no cars were parked at the front. We drove slowly back into the back alley. A dumpster was behind the office at the rear door. Kristene parked about thirty yards from the office.

"Tap the horn once and start the motor if you see trouble and I'll come running. If you see me running toward you, start the motor and be ready to high-tail it once I get in," I told her. She nodded, and I slipped from the van into the shadows.

Heart pounding, adrenaline up, mind and body on high alert, small flashlight and soft plastic bag in hand, and surgical gloves on, I slipped light-footed like a deer hunter from shadow to shadow, stopping after each move to look, listen and assess before moving again down the alley toward my target: the dumpster at the back door. Behind me, Kristene shut off the motor and lights and sat, waiting. Inside the dumpster were sheaves of legal-size papers, none of them shredded, plus notepads of handwritten notes.

Flashlight between my teeth, I leaned over the edge into the dumpster, scooping papers out and scanning them quickly for any mention of the Seattle case. Nothing yet. I dove in again for a second scoop, and was reading those papers when a light came on inside the office and I heard a door close. I froze. Hearing a male voice inside, I slithered like a lizard along the side of the building and peered into the window, exposing just enough of my face to look with one eye. He appeared to be in his sixties, medium everything and dapper, with gray hair and khaki pants. He was puffing on a cigar while talking on the phone and pacing nervously. The outside traffic noise made it difficult to hear his words, but I thought I heard him say the word "Seattle" once, and for several long minutes, I watched him pacing around the room, talking on the phone, waving his cigar in the air as he spoke, using animated gestures.

Suddenly the office light was turned off; I heard a door open and close and a car at the front start up. Thinking the car would drive away, I pored over the second set of papers I pulled from the dumpster, flashlight in my teeth.

But the car didn't leave. Instead I heard it coming into the alley where I was. When I heard the car was close, its headlight beams about to turn into the alley, I sprinted back to Kristene in the minivan, grasping papers in one hand and the flashlight in the other. Kristene saw me coming and had already started the motor, but the door locks automatically activated when she dropped the gearshift into drive as I reached the passenger door.

I was locked out and the minivan was moving. I ran alongside it, hanging on to the door handle with one hand, spilling papers and pounding on the window with the other as she drove down the alley.

"Stop! Stop! Let me in!"

She stopped, flipped the lock button and I bailed inside, rolling onto the floor through the sliding side door and hid on the floor. The car was heading for us now. I could hear its motor, its headlights lighting up our interior through our rear window.

"Drive! Drive! We gotta get outta here!" I urged.

Kristene drove onto the nearest street, and then took a circuitous route around city streets until she was sure we weren't followed before we went to our hotel.

We had been to the right office, but the papers I scooped from the trash had nothing to do with the case at hand.

The next day we drove by each of the lawyers' residences. One was for sale, and the sign on the road read "price just reduced." It was reminiscent of a southern plantation, with groves of avocado and citrus trees, a large stable and arena for horses, and even a helicopter pad. Kristene wrote down the agent's name and phone number. We bought a prepaid cell phone from which Kristene called the agent, giving her the cover story that she was from Arizona and her son would be attending college in Florida. She was looking for a place to buy so the family could be together. Kristene told the agent she and her husband were retired, but could "pay cash as long as the price wasn't over a million" and that her husband was into horses and didn't like to be in the city. The agent took the bait, saying she had just the house for us, one which was owned by an attorney, and the price had just been reduced due to some "recent event up north that made it imperative for them to sell quickly." Arrangements were made for Kristene to see the house, and I rented a new Jaguar for her to show up in.

The agent gave Kristene strange instructions before seeing the house: she told Kristene to meet her on the sidewalk in front of a certain shop in a ritzy part of town. I got there ahead of the appointed time in the minivan and waited. A well-dressed woman wearing a business skirt and jacket arrived and waited on the sidewalk. She looked around before she acknowledged a well-dressed man with dark sunglasses standing on the sidewalk across the street, by making eye contact with him. This man so strongly resembled the man I saw in the office the night before that I was sure it was him. Kristene arrived and walked up to the woman on the sidewalk. She was wearing a dark-blue sweater dress, high heels, and a pearl necklace, with her hair in a ponytail; pure, understated class, she had the look of money, the upstanding kind, no glitz. The woman looked to the man across the street as Kristene greeted her. The man nodded his approval to the real estate agent. Kristene passed inspection, for well did she look the part, and the agent led Kristene to the attorney's residence.

I followed from a distance. I didn't see where the man went when Kristene followed the agent, but he didn't follow us. It made me nervous that Kristene was in his house and I didn't know where he had gone to. I fretted and drove up and down past the house until she finally came out after an hour, and I followed her to our hotel. Kristene hit pay dirt. The attorney's wife told Kristene her husband and his partner had had a serious reversal on a case in Seattle and the asking price of the house had been reduced again for a quick sale because it was important for them to move as soon as possible. Because Kristene used to live in Florida and we had been to the Cayman Islands on the cruise ship investigation, she was able to converse knowledgeably with the attorney's wife, who told Kristene where they had transferred their bank accounts to on the Cayman Islands and described their transfers of other assets in expectation of potential judgments.

We returned to Seattle with armloads of asset information on both attorneys and evidence that assets were being fraudulently transferred in anticipation of litigation. Attorneys for the families and the Seattle courts acted swiftly in filing claims against the attorneys that were based in large part on our information. In the weeks that followed, an out-of-court settlement was reached in which my clients were made whole and the case that lasted over six months finally closed.

As we resumed our normal life rhythm after the Florida case, there was a nagging sense that something was not right. Down deep I knew what it was: once again we had moved without first asking the Lord's guidance. We were where we didn't belong, and now our contentment with our community had run its course after moving to Mercer Island, and after six years, other than one family we were friends with from the Covenant church, it was socially barely tolerable.

By outward appearances, we had it made on Mercer Island. Our kids were doing well, business was prospering, cash flow was good, and we were established in the community. It was no one's fault, but Mercer Island was a poor fit for us. The truth and the humor of it was that we were the Beverly Hillbillies on Mercer Island. Its family-oriented but liberal, elitist culture clashed with our conservative working-class values to the point that we privately joked that we were more comfortable socializing with employees of our neighborhood grocery store and friends who did not live on the island than with our neighbors. Now I understood that being able to afford to live in a certain place doesn't necessarily mean one belongs there, or will fit in. I didn't know what to do about it except wait. I prayed.

After all these years we were painfully aware that we were still struggling with legacies of turmoil and strife in each of our families, especially mine. We resolved years ago to break that cycle with us and not allow the cycle to continue perpetuating from us into our kids' lives to corrupt them and their children. We resolved instead to build a new family heritage, a legacy of Christ-centered living and loving kindness to transcend into future generations, thus displacing the legacy of strife and dysfunction. But we felt outmatched by my parents' negative influence. We prayed, asked the Lord to lead us, and waited.

In the early spring of 2001 I awoke one morning with an out-of-the-blue burning desire to move to Arizona, a place I had never been to before, but as a boy I was drawn to stories about the Apaches, and I could still remember the names of the Apache chiefs I read about: Cochise, Geronimo, Nana, Victorio. The desire to go there dominated my mind for four days before I mentioned it to Kristene. The idea gripped her too, and she responded by checking out every travel video about the Southwest in the public library. Fascinated by what we saw— the intensely blue skies, the rugged desert and mountains, and the western culture—we watched the videos perhaps a dozen times. From the videos we couldn't get enough of the Southwest, and we began looking for a way to see it.

CHAPTER TWENTY-SEVEN

An old unsolved missing person case that was surely a murder got us our first glimpse of Arizona. The key witness I needed to talk to, who could unlock the case if I could find him was a small-time crook in Tucson named Donald McWhorter, for whom there was no phone for either him or the landlord. Our client, the missing woman's stepfather, paid our expenses, and we arranged to work under the license of a highly recommended private investigator in Tucson, a former army officer named Skip who met us at the airport. The second my feet touched the tarmac, I had the strongest sense of place in my life; I knew this was where I belonged. I was home.

Skip drove us to the last known address of the witness. It was a small, run-down old adobe hut in a depressed neighborhood. The house was abandoned, and trash littered the yard. A woman next door taking down clothes from her clothesline told us the man who used to live there, "Don," moved away about three months before. We found the landlord, who told us Don didn't have a job and moved to somewhere in California because he was behind in rent payments. We had exhausted this lead, and Skip offered to show us around Tucson before treating us to dinner at a Mexican restaurant. We were enamored with everything we saw, for Tucson's many beautiful old buildings emanated Old Mexico, and they and the mountains above the town were bathed in golden sunlight. The food and authentic atmosphere at the Mexican restaurant were beyond anything in our experience. We spent the night in a hotel and saw more of Tucson with Skip the next day before our flight home. We were hooked.

We visited Tucson with the kids right after that. Like us, they liked it there, but we quickly ruled Tucson out in favor of Scottsdale when we learned that the public schools there had the highest academic test scores in the state. Thereafter the four of us made several trips to Scottsdale, usually staying at a romantic, '40s vintage, bungalow-style one-story motel at the edge of Old Town Scottsdale called the La Hacienda Resort, where the owner, Jude, always gave us the "Camelback Suite," a spacious, two-bedroom suite with fully equipped kitchen, wet bar, fireplace, and living room for only $67 per day. We liked everything about Scottsdale, and it was there at the La Hacienda that we decided we could handle the summer heat and made the final decision to sell our house and begin the moving process.

We returned to Mercer Island, having decided to put the house up for sale straightaway as the first step toward our new adventure. The selection of a real estate agent had barely begun when Kristena suddenly decided she wanted to see what her freshman year at Mercer Island High School would be like. At first we were disappointed, but the pact we made as a family was that the decision to uproot and leave all we knew had to be unanimous. We took the house off the market, not knowing that the delay would be to our benefit, for this was the year of the terrorist attacks on September 11, 2001, that forever changed America. Business came to a halt. Except for open cases already in accounts receivable, there was no work and no cash flow. It took two weeks for it to sputter back to life. Had we been in Arizona then, the lapse in activity could have collapsed our business, for we would have been newcomers. After the 9-11 attacks, I got cold feet about relocating.

My mind became wracked with doubt: How would I be able to support my family if we relocated? Had we really heard from God about this, or was it our imagination? We had it made right where we were, so why risk everything? I slept little and prayed often throughout the day without ceasing, as the Bible says to do. "Lord, please show me *clearly* what I am to do, and may one sign be that we are all of one mind about staying or going," was my plea.

My prayers were being answered all along, yet it took slow me weeks to realize it. Looking back at that time now, I am sure the Lord was fondly amused by me worrying myself into a lather as Kristene went back to Scottsdale with Kristena for the mid-winter break and sent our daughter on a weekend campout with the youth group of an evangelical church that had an active youth ministry, at which Kristena had a great time and made new friends, with whom she stayed in touch by email. Kristene began wearing new Western-style shirts she bought in Scottsdale, they were plaid with pearl snap buttons. She bought huge cardboard boxes that she packed and stacked in the garage, marked "Arizona" in large letters in black felt pen.

It wasn't long before the entire three-car garage was so filled with cartons and crates marked "Arizona" that we couldn't get one car inside. Before the holiday season arrived, Kristena decided the kids at Mercer Island High were too mean and she wanted to go to Arizona. John was also ready to make the move. When I finally saw that the Lord had been flooding me with the very answers I asked for, I had to laugh at myself. If there had been a Christian comedy show on television, I would have been grist for the script writers. God has a great sense of humor, I mused, and my fretting surely provided amusement for those who are already in Heaven. In my mind's eye, I could just see people I knew there, smiling and chuckling at me. We were Arizona-bound.

Kristena and I continued our tradition of decorating the outside of the house and the trees in the front yard with colored Christmas lights, thinking it might be our last time to do so together, for we knew not what to expect in Arizona. She would be sixteen in March, and after the holidays, I began giving her driving lessons on Sunday afternoons in our maroon Pontiac Gran Prix, using empty school parking lots to teach driving and parking basics.

Our house sold quickly to a young family, the sale yielding a respectable profit from just six years of owning a home on Mercer Island. As we waited for the sale to close, we secured an apartment in Scottsdale as a temporary residence that the management had been holding for us since Kristene's last visit there. Knowing Kristene's knack for finding good deals, I suspected that because it was being held for us probably meant it was something special.

I normally hate moving, but this time it was exciting. This time we were on a real-life family adventure; not just a vacation, but a total life change. Like Abraham and Sarah must have felt when they left everything they knew to follow God's lead into unknown territory, we were doing the same: following God's leading into new country, trusting that He had a new and better plan for us there. With excitement and unending gusto we packed our personal things in boxes and had a professional moving company wrap and load everything in a large truck that would meet us at our new address in Scottsdale in six days. Our new Dodge Durango loaded to even the roof-rack, we headed west to the coast and then south along the US 101 scenic route, stopping at every nook, cranny, and whistle stop that interested us. Of course the kids fought and argued occasionally as teens do, but all in all, it was a fun trip.

On the sixth day Kristena's cell phone rang as we were approaching Phoenix from the desert. It was the kids from the church youth group. They said our movers were there with them at our new apartment, and they had come to help us unload. We arrived shortly, the kids and the movers awaiting us in blazing heat. When each of these kids introduced themselves to me by shaking hands and addressing me as "Mr. Hansen" and began unloading the truck, I nearly fell over from surprise. I was thankful that they came, because neither we nor the movers were used to physical work in heat like this. Every few trips back and forth required a water break for us while the youth group kids hustled along, needing little to no water, like human camels.

I had to hand it to Kristene when I saw our new place: she had scored again. Our apartment was really a *casita*, Spanish for small house. Located at the back of the apartment complex, it was a one-story cottage attached to the apartment building only at the back. No other units were above us, on the sides, or below us, and it faced a greenbelt that adjoined a golf course. It had a tan stucco exterior and red tile roof. There were three bedrooms, each with walk-in closets, high ceilings, and paddle fans, it had an alarm system, living room with fireplace, washer-dryer in the hall closet, two full baths, complete kitchen, enclosed patio, and a separate one-car garage. The complex offered a pool, hot tub, weight room, and business center with Internet service and fax machine. It was a great deal, for the rent was cheap, and it was quiet there.

We filled the casita with the furniture we would use and put everything else in the garage, filling it to the ceiling; then with delight did we settle into our new digs. Every morning Kristene and I were up early, taking our coffee on the patio by the front door, enjoying the sun, watching golfers and walkers getting their exercise before it became hot. There was an atmosphere of freedom and so much life here; every day and evening we discovered intriguing restaurants, hole-in-the-wall joints with great food, and free live entertainment was everywhere, every night of the week. New neighbors began drifting by to introduce themselves, and the kids had friends right away. The master bedroom was big enough to set up my computer and fax machine along one wall as I had done in Hadlock, and I had plenty of research work from my Seattle clients. With money in the bank from the sale of our house, we were set.

One night the same kids from the church youth group came over to take Kristena on a group date to a Diamondbacks baseball game, and I was again impressed by their manners, for each one of them introduced themselves, "Hi, Mr. Hansen, I'm so-and-so", shake my hand and extend the same courtesy to Kristene, whom they addressed as "Mrs. Hansen". But the real surprise was when they asked, "Mr. Hansen, what time would you like us to bring Kristena home?"

"Uh, ten," I stammered, for I was not used to such civility in teenagers. They were back by nine forty-five, and instead of dropping Kristena off at the door, they came in and visited with Kristene and me for an hour or so. Such were their social graces that it was hard to believe these were public school kids, but they all were.

We had followed the Lord to a new country, one where no one knew us, yet never had we experienced a sense of 'place' as strongly we did now; even more than Issaquah. The reason, I knew, was because we let God lead us, instead of us leading ourselves. We were temporarily settled, but no matter; we were where we were supposed to be, and we were confident everything would fall into place at the right time. Now it was time to seek Him about a church home. I had finally seen and corrected a critical error in my approach to life as the head of a family: I had been making my own decisions without asking the Lord first, and in so doing I was repeatedly making the mistake of fitting God into *my* plans, instead of seeking to fit into *God's* plans. This was the reason so many of my decisions resulted in turmoil; they were wrong for us and I wouldn't have made them had I sought the Lord first. Out of love for us God blessed us anyway, but we were missing the fullness that we would have had if we sought His leading first. Even Jesus said He did not act on His own, but did exactly what His Father told Him. Thus it was that the Lord planted in us the desire to go to Arizona, and after some trepidation on my part, we followed His lead, and after we arrived we sought Him for a church home ahead of buying a house. In a short time, we settled into the same church where our kids were already rooted and flourishing.

I had never experienced heat like Arizona in the summer; day after day it was 112 degrees and up, and it didn't cool to below one hundred degrees until after 1:00 a.m. "But it's a dry heat," the locals like to say. Sure it is: so dry that my wet swimsuit left outside would be stiff as a wooden board in ten minutes. I couldn't imagine cops functioning wearing body armor in such heat or firemen wearing heavy fire-retardant suits fighting fires, yet it is done every day. Still, one couldn't help but notice how the blazing brightness of the Arizona sun enriched the colors and enhanced the hues of the desert and town buildings alike, washing everything in its golden rays. Every day the sky was so intensely blue it seemed surreal, like photographs that had been doctored to make the sky appear more dramatic.

We took trips north to escape the heat. On our way to the Grand Canyon, we visited the ancient cliff dwellings of prehistoric tribes at Montezuma's Well and walked with park guides along restored ancient aqueducts that were still fully functioning, a testimony to the ingenuity of the civilization that had mysteriously vanished without a trace over a thousand years ago. We drove on until we reached what locals simply call 'the Canyon', for compared to it, there is no other. I cannot think of another view that left us as lost for words as did seeing the Grand Canyon for the first time. We stood together at the rail at the South Rim in silent awe before one of the greatest natural wonders of the world, speechlessly looking below into an entirely separate ecosystem of forests, rivers, streams, lakes, and wildlife that could be seen living a full mile straight down from where we stood. The horizon to the north, east and west was consumed with the vastness of the Canyon as far as the eye could see; its scope and majesty were too much to comprehend.

Before the school year began in August, we also visited Flagstaff, Jerome, Sedona, Prescott, and other places, each having a rich and unique history of its own.

When school began in mid August, the hours the kids were in school we balanced between physical intimacy and house hunting. Not by chance was our physical relationship as strong and playful as when we were first married. We still had the honeymoon glow because we purposely kept the fires bright by feeding it with our words and deeds. We never stopped dating and playfully seducing each other. Humor and play were vital fuel to the fire, but so were our expressions of mutual respect and honor. We continually refreshed each other with endless little courtesies and compliments that resulted in unending joy at even the thought of being together. I always opened doors for Kristene, and got to my feet when she entered or left the room. When we walked on the sidewalk, I placed myself between her and the street, and I always seated her at the table before I sat down. An unexpected benefit for me, I am sure, was that unlike most of us, time had not diminished Kristene's beauty. Instead, she was actually becoming *better* looking. Her beauty was of the rarest sort: being a natural, bone-deep comeliness that actually improves with age, such an example of God's handiwork that time was never her enemy, as it is with the rest of us mortals. She emanated exotic allure even without makeup and when her hair was a mess. I was a blessed man.

We worked together to find a permanent home. Twice before I had plunged us into the wrong home by not asking the Lord first, but that mistake I would not make a third time. Together we asked God to open the doors to the home He wanted for us and close doors on the ones we should not buy. Then we acted in faith that God would answer us; she did the research, met with agents, and looked at homes while I got preapproval for a loan, and continued working the business.

I made many trips to Seattle to work cases that fall season, and eventually drove my Ford truck and later our Pontiac down to Scottsdale for Kristena to drive. When Kristena showed me her Arizona driver's license, I saw that its expiration date was forty-nine years into the future. "Hey, what's this—a typo?" I asked.

"No, Dad, Arizona driver's licenses are lifetime. At age sixty-five they want you to have an eye test."

Kristena got a job at an ice cream shop a few blocks away from where we lived. She did so well there that the owner put her in charge of closing up the nights she worked. I was concerned for her safety because armed robberies are frequent in Arizona, so every night that she worked late, I parked in the shadows of the parking lot, armed with a pistol and a cell phone, keeping an eye on my daughter as she counted the cash at closing, put it in the safe, and locked up before going home. In a few months, the shop went out of business, and I didn't tell her about this until years later.

One could get much more house for their money in Arizona than in Seattle, and the houses were newer, but finding the right house still wasn't easy. We walked away from dozens of homes because of one flaw or another, and spent a great deal of money for home inspections that exposed flaws the sellers tried to disguise. We took a breather during the holidays and put on a Thanksgiving dinner in our new place for our single neighbors and new friends, each guest bringing something for the table. It was crowded but cozy and much fun for everyone. At Christmas time, we put up a small tree in the living room and went to plays and productions at our church and attended mass at a local Catholic church. It wasn't until May of the next year that the Lord led us to the right house.

Like other homes in the neighborhood, it was Southwest style: a stucco rambler with red tile roof. It was the ideal size for a family of four, and overnight guests; four bedrooms, three baths, two fireplaces, desert plants, eight palm trees, and a pool in the large backyard. There was nothing for us to do but paint the interior to our liking, for the seller had upgraded the underlayment of the tile roof, replaced kitchen countertops with granite, installed new tile flooring and carpet, and upgraded to new heating and cooling and pool equipment, all less than a year before. We had the perfect home in new condition in a prime location close to our church, schools, shopping and the freeway. It was from the Lord and therefore a perfect fit. Unlike previous home purchases, this time everything fell into place without a hitch. No trouble was added to it, and even our furniture pieces fit perfectly where we wanted them to be.

Our social life flourished now. We began membership classes at our church, where the kids developed strong friendships in the youth group and were active on school sports teams; Kristena in volleyball and John in football. Families came to our home for dinner and post-game parties, and the kids' friends were often at our house for Friday night sleepovers. Many a Saturday morning the smell of frying bacon drew me to the kitchen to find one of John's pals greeting me, "Good morning, Mr. Hansen, bacon is almost ready" while fixing breakfast for himself. We attended Kristena's volleyball and John's football games. Kristena became very involved in Young Life, and on one occasion there were as many as sixty kids filling our home for Bible study and prayer. John took up guitar and the boys sang and played Christian songs in the backyard on weekend nights. Our kids began babysitting the younger kids of our neighbors, Chet and Letty Andrews, and John played his guitar for them at bedtime. It seemed our lives couldn't be more complete than this, but even more was yet to come.

My son and I took to exploring the desert in our big Ford 4x4 pickup. We didn't go far at first, and each venture was a learning experience that I wrote about afterward. We always took pistols, water, and snack foods with us. Often John's buddies from church youth group came along, bringing their own firearms. The boys hunted coyotes, desert quail, and even rattlesnakes, which they sometimes found in rock crevices or lying under the sand in a wash, waiting to strike whatever happened to wander by. On our many desert ramblings we found lakes and streams and even real-life prospectors and hermits, throwbacks to an earlier time, crusty men living under primitive conditions. It was then that a passion for writing, dormant and not used since my teen years except for writing police reports and legal documents but otherwise long suppressed, was reawakened as I chronicled our excursions and compiled them into a collection of nonfiction short stories I titled *Adventures in the Desert*.

We were fascinated with Arizona. It is still a wide-open land; eighty-seven percent of it is still undeveloped and cannot be built upon or privately owned, thus the wilderness is all around. Arizona has always been and still is a state and a culture that people come to for a new start in life, whatever the reason. We noticed a definite spirit of independence there, (Arizona never uses daylight savings time, like other states), a deep respect for God; at least twenty percent of the population go to church at least once a week, and a deep respect for the law. It flows from this that Arizona is a deeply life-honoring culture that passes laws to protect both the unborn and the elderly. Its laws against drunk driving are the strongest in the nation. It is so different from anyplace we had lived before that we wanted to take it all in, the distinctively relaxed, freewheeling, slap-leather, don't-tread-on-me culture, the colorful Western history, the variety of majestic scenery. So keen was our curiosity that we constantly found new places to go on dates. My way was the several cowboy bars in town, where there was always live country music, kids dancing with grandparents, and friendly crowds. Kristene and I loved to dance in these places, partly because kids are allowed in bars with their parents, lending a family reunion atmosphere to most bars in which folks policed their own behavior.

Kristene's way of dating me was to get up before sunrise and drive east into the desert where we would pull onto the dirt shoulder on the crest of a hill, facing the famous Four Peaks of the rugged Mazatzal Mountains in the far distance, put the windows down, shut the motor off, pour hot coffee from a thermos, and sit in silence, savoring desert essences, the scent of sage and the morning sounds of the desert—birds cawing and cooing and coyote packs yowling over their last kill before bedding down for the day.

What we were there to see happens every day but we never tired of it. We would fix our gaze to the east to witness the glory of the morning sun brightening the eastern sky as it ascended the backside of the Four Peaks before it finally appeared in its full glory, a blazing golden orb, rising sharply, its rays filling the sky, evaporating the last vestiges of night, heralding its own blazing arrival over the four mountain crests, deepening the blue of the cloudless expanse as it authorized another day.

Life hummed along like this through spring and summer, but cash flow suffered from a decline of new work that wiped out our cash reserves. By September, I was becoming worried. Providentially, a woman client I had done a great deal of work for in the past unexpectedly called with another large project she wanted done. Right after discussing the case terms she personally went to my bank whereupon she deposited a five thousand dollar retainer in my business account.

About three hours later that same evening, I was in the kitchen with Kristene when she answered the house phone line. Kristene paced back and forth with the phone to her ear, not speaking. She suddenly dropped the phone and collapsed to the floor, holding her head with both hands, and sobbing.

"Oh no, please, God, no!"

I helped Kristene up and took the phone. It was Kay, calling from the hospital. Ron was unconscious after bumping his head in the barn at their daughter's place and had been taken to the hospital by ambulance. It looked serious. Kristene called Richard, and he left to be with Kay at the hospital.

I withdrew cash from the bank for Kristene and put her on the next flight from Phoenix to Seattle, where she met Kay and Pastors Curt and Julie Brunk at Harborview Hospital. Ron had suffered a subdural hematoma and never regained consciousness. Ron Kinssies, husband and father of two, beloved spiritual father of many, oldest brother to Kristene, Richard, and Bob, and my best friend, was dead at age sixty one.

I pulled the kids out of school the next day, and we flew up to Seattle to be with Kristene and Kay. Not until years later would I realize that the client's retainer was deposited in my account at the *same hour* as Ron's accident. It was God's provision for us to be able to meet this crisis, for without it, we could not have gone to Seattle, much less stayed there four days. I had a vague sense of divine appointment from the timing and amount of the deposit, but I was too numb from the shock of Ron's sudden passing to ponder any of the whys and wherefores; thoughtful reflection would have to wait. There was tragedy to cope with now.

Kristene swiftly rose to the occasion once again. Putting aside her own grief in order to put Kay's needs first, she never left Kay's side, calmly helping her with the myriad of decisions and details as a deluge of relatives and friends poured in from all over the country. For Kristene, grieving the loss of her oldest brother would come later.

CHAPTER TWENTY-EIGHT

t is no overstatement to say that to have known Ron Kinssies, to have sat and talked with him was to experience what Christ was like when He was here on this earth, for Ron was a tall, lean, and muscular man of great physical strength with thick, sinewy hands, hands like those of his father, that could crush rock, and mighty forearms like Popeye from being an ironworker for much of his adult life. For all his physical strength, he was soft spoken and gentle, a kind man of great spiritual strength and depth. Rugged and masculine yet selfless and humble, Ron Kinssies impacted the lives of many people for Christ by serving and reaching out to them; as a youth he had stepped up to the plate to be a father figure to Kristene while their father was away fishing in Alaska. It was Ron who taught Kristene snow skiing and how to drive and defended her against her mother's angry rampages, and it was Ron, with Kay, who steadfastly interceded in prayer over Kristene as she went through years of anger and hostility as a young woman. Over the years of weekly breakfast meetings for Bible study and prayer, Ron's consistent life of selflessness and service to others impacted me too, so much so that there isn't enough room in this book to describe it all.

Kristena went to work as soon as we arrived in Seattle, helping Aaron assemble a video of photographs and music selections that chronicled Ron's life, then she sat at Ron's desk for hours, writing a tribute to him that she read at the memorial service.

My seventeen year old daughter read her tribute to her Uncle Ron to the many who were gathered in his honor, and her words struck home, moving many to audible tears as she recaptured Ron's characteristics, giving us a fond look back at the things about him that we all loved him for: his ability to laugh at himself and go along with endless teasing, his extreme frugality that made him the butt of family jokes, his ability to listen and make the other person feel loved and important, and his consistency in giving of himself to others without expecting anything back. On those things Kristena wrote in part:

"I loved his lack of fashion sense. I loved how he still wore clothes from high school (despite the holes in all the wrong and funny places). I loved his laugh and smile that made everyone around him laugh and smile (even when nothing was funny), and I especially loved his exceptional tolerance of teasing he received from his family about his many quirks (he was quite the sport). I remember what a huge deal it was for my younger brother and I to go and spend the night at Uncle Ron and Auntie Kay's house ..."

But there was more about Ron Kinssies than his personal warmth and good humor, more that we all knew about, yet now we needed to hear of it again, and Kristena's apt words met this need, refreshing us and breaking us at the same time as here and there the sounds of weeping could be heard as she continued to read:

"What a warm and caring person whose whole life's goal and purpose was to know and serve his Lord and Savior. He was the type of person you could go to for just about anything. He had wisdom and compassion beyond anything or anyone I've ever seen. He was constantly serving in some way or another, and I always wondered how he did it — how he was able to pour himself completely into others, wholeheartedly. Then this summer, God revealed to me what it was. It was something that so few of us are able to achieve. He was able to completely and totally surrender his heart to the Lord. His walk with God was deeper and stronger more than we will ever know. The Lord was pouring so much into him that that was why he was

able to pour so much into others. I don't know about you, but that's how I want to be. That's how I want God to work in my life ..."

After mentioning her personal struggle with why God would take Ron from us, Kristena hit the bottom line:

"So with this new enlightenment, I decided I wasn't angry at God anymore, and now I see more than ever that God has a plan and reason for everything that happens on this earth. Even though a huge hole will be left in our lives, my uncle is home. He is in a place now where there is no more pain or death, no more sorrow, no more sin. He is walking with the Lord hand in hand, and how selfish of me to want to keep him from that any longer than he had to. And through his homecoming, I know for a fact that it would be his wish that through his death people would find life in Jesus Christ. He has touched my life as well as many others, and I am honored To call him my uncle.

"As Revelation 21:4-7 puts it:

He will wipe away every tear from their eyes. There will be no death or mourning or crying or pain, for the old order of things has passed away.

He who was seated on the throne said "I am making everything new!" Then He said, "Write this down, for these words are trustworthy and true."

He said to me: "It is done. I am the Alpha and Omega, the Beginning and the End. To him who is thirsty I will give to drink without cost from the spring of the water of life. He who overcomes will inherit all this, and I will be his God and he will be My son."

I love you, Uncle Ron."

When Ron Kinssies, oldest of four, accepted Christ at twelve years of age, he petitioned the Lord to hang onto him as he went through his teenage years, for he knew he was alone in his family with regard to anything spiritually more serious than going to mass once a week. He was already playing the role of surrogate father to his younger siblings in the absence of their father, George, who was always away commercial fishing, leaving his wife and kids rudderless, tossing upon stormy seas, so Ron instinctively stepped up to the plate to mediate the turmoil.

God honored Ron's prayer, not letting him go, but kept him in His grip, and Ron grew closer to God. By the time he met Kay, and they married quickly, Ron had become as strong in the Spirit as he was physically. Here was a rugged young outdoorsman who had worked fishing boats off the coast of Alaska and worked heavy construction who was well-read and grounded in biblical truths. Kay was the right woman for him. She was as pretty as he was handsome, and she shared his passion for the deeper things of God. Together they prayed and interceded for their siblings, and by the time of his passing, all but Richard had come to Christ, such was the fruit and the legacy of their union. And so it was that Kristene, as much as Ron's offspring, was not only of the same blood, but also of Ron's spiritual heritage.

The memorial service was well attended, and among the most notable speakers who attested to the character and integrity of Ron Kinssies were several homeless men whose lives had been influenced Christ-ward by Ron during the fourteen years he served on the board of City Team, a downtown mission. These modest men, some old beyond their years, had a certain outward shabbiness that yielded to the inward shine they possessed when with smiling words and glowing faces they spoke of how just knowing Ron Kinssies had changed their lives.

Only family members attended the graveside service, and the weather matched how we all felt as the casket was lowered: cold, numbing cold, and gray. There was a reception at the church afterward in a meeting room that to this day is named the Ron Kinssies Prayer Chapel. The only humor of the day was seeing the couple who years ago declined to attend our wedding because they said it violated God's will. They seemed both surprised and uncomfortable that Kristene and I were not only still married but also had two grown children. Time had aged the two, but not their moral religiosity: they literally wriggled in their clothes when Kristene came alongside me to greet them, trying to hide their discomfort, for to them we were an adulterous couple and to see us blessed was upsetting to their narrow-minded theology, and thus they refused our offer to meet either of our kids and left hurriedly. We were mildly amused and took no offense, for twenty-three years later, the last word was ours.

We went home worried about how Kay would manage being alone. Life was difficult for us too when we got back; we found it impossible to pick up where we left off. Ron was gone, and he wouldn't be back, his sudden passing left an enormous gap in the family circle; all of us were off balance and struggling to come to terms with the finality of death. The shock of Ron's sudden death sent Kristene into menopause and a mild depression that lasted for months. She waited until she got home to grieve, and despite the emotional numbness that came over her, she dutifully kept in touch with Kay daily by phone. I took over preparing our morning coffee routine, waiting on her every need, fixing lunch for us, and taking her out more often just to get her out, the goal being to afford her opportunities to talk.

We had been home about a week and I was bringing Kristene her morning coffee when she told me very matter-of-factly that she had just seen Ron in an open vision. She told me he was outside a huge gate in Heaven, bending down, looking at the green grass outside. She said Ron called her by name, "Kristene! I am in Heaven and I have a new body! I am not old, and I can run and leap, anything I want!" She saw a glimpse of Heaven as Ron passed through a white gate, but other than that she offered no other details and I filed it away mentally without comment or passing judgment.

Ron's passing was a double blow to Matilda, for no one wants to outlive their children, and she had been a widow for sixteen years when Ron died. When her husband died, his Social Security income ended, leaving her in even worse financial straits than before. As early as our time in Hadlock we sent her financial support, which she accepted at first and then declined out fear of losing her Social Security. We sent her cash instead of checks for a while, but eventually she declined even this, and I regretted that there was nothing I could do for her. In the aftermath of Ron's death, Bob was now her oldest son. Bob and Angela had closed their ministry and moved to Florida a few years before, and now Matilda moved from California to Florida to be near her son Bob, his wife, and their oldest son, Bobby, and their young family, a move that seemed like a good idea at the time, but later turned sour.

Ron's passing left a hole in me too. I didn't grieve in the same way that Kristene did, but I was profoundly affected. Ron was my best friend; in him was a model for Christian manhood. He was my best man at our wedding, without him I wouldn't have even met Kristene. In that sense, I too was part of Ron's spiritual legacy. Whenever I was in Seattle on business I kept a watchful eye on Kay, now a widow, taking her to dinner or lunch and attending church with her every time I could.

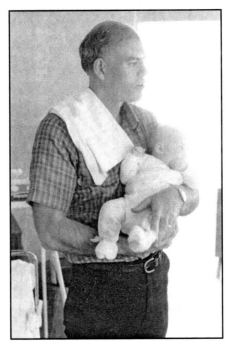

Ron Kinssies, holding Kristena, two and a half months

CHAPTER TWENTY NINE

The following winter I fell into an enormous amount of new work right at home when I was requested to be the personal bodyguard and security chief for the founder of the Minutemen, a volunteer border security movement that was within a month of exploding onto news headlines around the world. The organization was based out of Tombstone, the town where the OK Corral shootout occurred in 1881, and my work required me to travel there once a week. On one of my many trips to Tombstone, I stopped at an Old West theme park where I heard a live country band from nearby Maricopa whose female lead singer's voice sounded like Kristene, so I bought one of their CDs and played it often in my truck. I especially liked their use of the dulcimer in their rendition of "Red River Valley."

It was also Kristena's senior year in high school, and much of our time was spent going to her Lacrosse team practices and games. I was beginning to think our former life was being restored when one afternoon when we were home alone, I felt another lump in Kristene's left breast. "Hey, what's this, Darlin'?" I asked in alarm. It was small, about the size of a grape, and hard.

"Don't," Kristene said, pushing my hand away. "I'm seeing a doctor about it."

"What kind of doctor?"

"A naturopath. Dr. Crinnion," she said.

"Okay. I remember him. Keep me informed, please, that's all I ask."

"I will," she said and smiled.

When Mother's Day came, I completely surprised Kristene with a prepaid gift card for a package of ten private dance lessons tucked in a bouquet of red roses. "Honey, this is the best Mother's Day gift I have ever gotten from you!" she beamed. She couldn't wait to get started.

Twice a week for five weeks at a mirror-walled dance studio in the old part of town with a lean, silver-haired instructor named Walter, we had fun learning the country two-step, the country swing, the waltz, and the Arizona two-step. We practiced at home until we were ready to suit up in western clothes and hats and revisit the circuit of dance places we frequented the most, including Greasewood Flats, an open-air bar (no building) with a concrete pad for a dance floor, the Buffalo Chip, Harold's in Cave Creek, and other places.

The rest of the 2005 school year was a busy time as our daughter's graduation from high school was followed by her preparation to enter the mission field for a year before she would attend college. While there was the senior prom and our kids' friends were constantly in and out of our place for visits, BBQs, and sleepovers, Kristene kept a nervous eye on how her mother was doing in Florida, especially when Matilda complained to Kristene that she wasn't seeing much of Bob and Angela, that she found it difficult to get along with Angela, and that she regretted moving from California.

Kristene was ever the consummate mom: she always could accurately sense what was going on with her kids. She focused on Kristena about this time, by taking her on overnight road trips to factory outlet shopping malls in the Palm Desert area of southern California. 'Windshield time,' she called it, that provided a safe opportunity for Kristena to talk openly about whatever was on her mind, and for her mother to listen without distractions. It was a time of transition for our daughter; of leaving high school and the home nest and facing the world, and being that the world now has become more complicated than at any time in the past, Kristena's anxiety was only natural. Our home, since coming to Arizona, had always been a welcome place for our kids' friends; a second home to them in which they often slept overnight on weekends in sleeping bags and on couches, and to them Kristene had been a second mom, a confidante.

While the girls were away on their trips, John and I made deeper forays into the wilds of the Sonoran Desert in our pickup truck, equipped with water, food, emergency gear and rifles. I also took John with me on business trips to Tombstone and to the border with Mexico. When Kristene came home, we left the kids alone and went north to Sedona for the cooler weather and a change of scenery.

Months later, in the early winter months, word came from Bob and Angela that Matilda had suffered a stroke and was hospitalized. Kristene went to her mother's side at the state-run facility she was in and was distressed to find her mother completely paralyzed on the right side, helpless, and generally untended and ignored by caregivers who should have known better than to let her live in her own filth. Even more distressing for Kristene was that the news of Matilda's plight was inexplicably weeks old when Bob first informed her. Kristene extended her stay in Florida to seek a more humane facility for her mother, personally visiting each one and not finding any that would take an elderly patient on Social Security Income that was acceptably clean and provided proper care and was not a human warehouse.

When Kristene came home, she wasted no time learning what would be available for Matilda if she moved to Arizona. To our surprise, the care, benefits, and facilities Arizona offered to someone Matilda's age and of her medical and financial circumstances were far superior to what Florida offered, and Kristene, the one who had borne the brunt of Matilda's rage as a child, worked feverishly to rescue her mom by bringing her to Arizona.

CHAPTER THIRTY

The very urgency with which Kristene ran to the rescue of her mother in the eleventh hour of her life was an attestation of her integrity and depth of character, for when the scorn and abuse she had received from her mother for over fifty years is taken into account, Kristene's rescue efforts were seen for what they were: unconditional love and grace; grace, God's grace; the grace of the Gospel, the grace that is the very core of the Cross, was now being played out on the stage of human drama in real time, and I had never seen anything like it. Like Christ Himself demonstrated, Kristene forgave and forgot past hurts; she rolled up her sleeves and got her hands dirty to extend mercy and kindness to someone who desperately needed it; the Spirit of Christ was expressed in Kristene, for she loved those who hurt her as if she had never been hurt at all. I was in utter awe by what I saw her doing, yet there was more to come.

After two months of wrangling with Bob and Angela to obtain power of attorney from Bob, government officials in both states and bank managers and a nightmare of red tape, Kristene finally returned to Florida where she packed her mother into a wheelchair with her few belongings and took a cab to the airport. On the plane, she settled Matilda in a window seat in a bulkhead row and sat next to her mother, whose right side was completely flaccid and useless, her speech unintelligible, completely helpless, her mouth open and drooling; an awful sight on a grueling three-hour flight.

It was late afternoon when I met the shuttle van at Matilda's new care facility when it arrived from the Phoenix airport, and the driver wheeled Matilda inside to the admissions desk and then to her new room. Matilda's unkempt condition from months of lack of proper care in Florida was distressing to see; it was evidence of mental cruelty that was worse than how Kristene described it to me. She looked so different now, the stroke having drastically diminished her mental and physical persona. She knew where she was, and with garbled speech could answer questions at the admissions desk. Her new room was clean and spacious, with a view of the green lawn and garden and public school playground beyond it. As we left, smiling caregivers began giving Matilda a bath, shampooed her hair, cleaned and trimmed her nails, laundered her personal clothing and neatly put them away for her.

Kristene was faithful and diligent in seeing her mother morning and afternoon every day. Kristena returned from her China missions trip, and the kids and I visited Matilda on our own, but not as often as Kristene did. For me and the kids it was difficult to see Matilda, or anyone else, for that matter, functionally cut in half and made helpless by a stroke, but out of respect we did our best to not show our discomfort. I felt empathy for Matilda, a poor, helpless widow dying slowly of old age. I was ashamed of myself for being so inadequate for her in her hours of need. In the light of Kristene's selfless service I knew I looked bad, even though no one said anything about it; it wasn't necessary – I knew; and I knew also that I must change.

I resolved to become closer to Matilda, as the time was short, and to do it I had to let go of the grudge I harbored against her for her mistreatment of Kristene. If Kristene herself had already done this long ago, who was I to bear a grudge or sit in judgment? But doing this was more difficult than I thought it would be. I was surprised that my judgmental attitude was so hardened and wouldn't go away in the flash of a single prayer. Repentance and action coupled with prayer were required and there was no time to lose; the breakthrough came quickly when I repented of being judgmental and asked God for forgiveness and a new heart for Matilda, and then visited Matilda with Kristene more often. Even though I didn't feel like it, I also went to see her by myself. We would run out of things to say rather soon, but surprisingly the silence wasn't awkward, and I stayed with her until a caregiver came in to give her a bath, or take her to get her hair done, and then I would kiss her on the cheek or forehead and tell her "I love you, Mom Kinssies" before I left. How much Matilda comprehended my actions I never knew, but I was certain she understood and was strengthened that I had come on my own initiative to see her, and I knew God was pleased, not satisfied, but pleased.

Matilda was in an agitated state when I arrived to visit her one afternoon. Her speech had become less intelligible during the past two weeks so I pressed the button for a caregiver, but she wanted nothing to do with the caregiver. Without knowing that Kristene would arrive soon, Matilda fussed with her bed-sheets with her left hand and leg, shouting "Krishtheeen! Krishtheeen!" over and over through the one side of her mouth and tongue still capable of speech, shaking her head violently side to side. I tried holding her hand but she would have none of it. Kristene entered the room as I was dialing her cell phone and came to her mother's side.

"I am here, Mom," Kristene lovingly announced, taking Matilda's hands in hers. "I am here, and it's alright, everything is alright, Mom. I love you, Mom."

Matilda lifted her head off the pillow as she broke into tears at the sight and touch of her only daughter, her countenance desperate, needy and longing. As Kristene leaned down into her mother's face, touching her lovingly, smiling, her hair hanging down, Matilda gushed out broken words of love, a mighty torrent of love, long repressed, but now pouring forth like a major river breaking at long last through a dam, her words being the very words of God, immediately erasing a lifetime of heartache and pain for both mother and daughter. In perfect harmony with her mother's pleadings, Kristene began pouring forth softly spoken words; words of love and acceptance and assurance that everything was forgiven, healing words that flowed gently and surely like a rising ocean tide: strong and steady, foreordained and unstoppable, affirming and fulfilling, comforting and nurturing, refreshing and renewing; the heart of God was beating right in front of me, I was witnessing firsthand a miracle of healing, grace and forgiveness unlike anything I had ever seen.

The Bible teaches that "we see through a glass darkly," meaning that we see only glimpses into the spirit realm from the physical realm while we are here on earth. Knowing what little I do of such matters, I believe my repentance of judging her somehow freed Matilda to seek Kristene's forgiveness as she neared eternity; forgiveness that Kristene had long ago freely given, and thus did healing and reunion flow between mother and daughter, the release like a mighty dam being broken up.

The caregiver and I tiptoed out, for a miracle was unfolding, and privacy was needed. I went home and waited for Kristene; when she arrived hours later, there was a peace, a settlement about her that was new, and she told me she had led her mother to ask Christ into her life.

Right after this, Matilda's overall condition began to decline noticeably; not rapidly, but steadily, and Kristene began looking for a homier, less institutionalized place for her mother to spend her last days. She quickly found a place that had been a private residence near our home, a small hospice consisting of only eight patients that was run by a gentle Croatian couple, Christian immigrants who could speak the Croatian language with Matilda.

As Matilda settled in to her new environs we changed our plans for our Silver Anniversary. It was difficult to believe that twenty five years, a quarter century, had elapsed since we took our vows. We were to go to either San Diego for a few days, or even Rocky Point, a Sea of Cortez resort town in Baja, Mexico but decided to remain in the Phoenix Valley because Matilda was experiencing numbness and loss of use of her left leg and foot, strong indications she could pass away any time soon. We booked rooms at four different local resorts on consecutive days, and crossed our fingers as we let the kids have the house to themselves for four days and nights. We told the kids and the hospice where we were and our cell phone numbers if needed.

The first night we dined at the hotel, then went to one of our favorite places, Greasewood Flat, a bar-and-grill without a building in the open desert, a semi-circle of open fire pits, movable picnic tables and benches, food-and- drink shacks set around a concrete dance floor with a raised platform for the singing cowboy and his band. That night was the kickoff of the campaign to make July 31st the Day of the Cowboy a national holiday, and the place was filled with men and women riders on horseback, dressed in parade outfits, celebrating with regular customers. One of the employees recognized us and knew why we were there, all dressed up.

"John and Kristene Hansen, come on up here!" the singing cowboy announced into the microphone. "Come on up, you two, we want to say something to you !" I escorted Kristene onto the stage and faced the cheerful crowd of about a hundred people that included kids below ten (children are welcome in bars in Arizona if accompanied by an adult) and couples in their seventies, some mounted on horses.

"Folks, meet John and Kristene. They live here in Scottsdale, and tonight they are celebrating their *twenty-fifth* wedding anniversary! Conratulations! So let's give the Hansens a big hand!" Everywhere in the flickering light of bonfires and outdoor lights was a sea of smiling faces, upraised beer bottles and glasses, cheers and applause as we waved to the crowd, holding hands. We ate and drank and danced until late and then moseyed back to our hotel room to extend our evening.

For four days we tuned the world out except for our cell phones; no news, no radio or television. We moved to a different hotel every day, sunbathing, swimming, eating, drinking, lovemaking, and sleeping for four days. It was the most time to ourselves we had had in years, and it was rejuvenating. We couldn't get enough of each other. When we got home, there were signs that the kids did have guests over, but the house was remarkably cleaned up.

Matilda was becoming less responsive, eating less and sleeping more. Her vital signs were weakening and fluid collected in her throat as she slept, triggering frequent coughing spasms. It was time for Helen Hood, Matilda's last remaining sibling, to come down from Washington to say goodbye. Aunt Helen, herself then eighty-six, a widow since 2004 (the same year Ron died) and showing early signs of dementia, arrived in a week and stayed with us for about six days. When Kristene took her to visit Matilda, the two broke into Croatian, chattering happily for an hour or so, then Matilda tired and needed rest. On subsequent visits Helen danced and sang songs in Croatian for her sister, the absence of music making for an awkward stillness in the room that made her effort seem barren. Yet for all of Helen's loving exertions, Matilda stared unseeingly into space, open-mouthed, saying nothing, and Helen gave up, said her fondest good-byes to her last sister, and left.

We entertained Helen before she went home, showing her around Scottsdale and Kristene took her to see the Grand Canyon and other places, for she had never been to Arizona before.

We were in bed when the phone rang. "Hello Mr. Hansen? This is Mike at the hospice. Please tell your wife that her mother's breathing is labored, I have had the doctor here and he says she could expire tonight."

"We'll be right over, thanks," I said. It was early evening and Kristene and I drove the short distance to be at Matilda's side, neither of us speaking, for we knew. She was comatose in the awaiting stillness of her room, a hushed expectancy hung in the air as Matilda lay supine on a narrow bed wedged between the wall and the nightstand in her small, clean room, lighted dimly by the lamp on the dresser, her breathing labored; shallow breaths through her mouth.

We knelt together at her side. "Me and John are here now, Mom," Kristene said softly, stroking her mother's hair. Matilda didn't respond.

Matilda would be passing on at any time and we knew we must pray effectively. Together we entered the Lord's throne room the way it says to do in the Bible: by giving Him praise, acknowledging Who He is and His attributes, then thanking Him for what He has done for us and what He is about to do. We thanked Christ for coming down to earth and living amongst us to show us what God the Father is like, for submitting Himself to death on the Cross, and rising from the dead and for sitting now at the right hand of God to make intercession for us. Then began our petition:

"Lord, tonight we come before You as two whom you have joined together and declared to be one flesh; we come on the basis of Christ's Blood, shed for us; we come to intercede for Matilda tonight. Lord, Matilda is Kristene's flesh and blood and she has accepted You as her Savior, and we lift her up to you now."

At this point we stopped; we didn't know where to go next, there was more to be said than this, Matilda was about to step off into eternity. More prayer was needed, but we lacked the words. "Lord," I petitioned, "show us how to pray now."

Taking Kristene's hand in mine as she held her mother's hand with her other hand, we waited in silence until the heavenly language bubbled up out of Kristene, flowing river-like, the words unknown, gentle yet powerful and effective, and my own prayer language joined hers and the two became one tongue, one prayer, alternately urgent and supplicating and praising in tone. We prayed together thus for hours, kneeling side-by-side, our bodies going into and then beyond the pain and discomfort in our knees, hips and backs and numbness in our legs and feet, until at long last I had the sensation of angels in the room with us, their wings brushing the air. We were exhausted and nearly asleep when Mike the owner checked on us. It was two in the morning.

Matilda's breathing had not changed and Mike said he would stay with her until dawn. We were exhausted and went home to rest.

Crawling into bed, we embraced and gave God thanks for taking care of Matilda, and fell asleep. Only an hour later the phone rang and Kristene answered. It was Mike: Matilda had passed on a minute ago. I believe her spirit was waiting for Kristene to leave so she could depart. Matilda was eighty nine.

CHAPTER THIRTY-ONE

Matilda Kinssies was buried next to her husband in Aberdeen, Washington. A graveside service was held for her, attended by only a handful of close relatives. Of our household, only Kristene went, at her own wish.

In October, my father and his wife Jeanne came down for a six-day visit, and we showed them around town, seeing something different every day, and a different restaurant every evening, all without leaving Scottsdale except for one trip to Phoenix. Dad absorbed everything he saw; he couldn't get over how much more house could be bought here for less money, how much there was to see and do, how young the population was and how strong the industrial and business bases were. Upon going home, Dad expressed his appreciation, saying now he could understand why I was always anxious to be home again when I was in Washington.

Kristene's lower back pain returned after Dad and Jeanne left, and she resumed visiting chiropractors for treatment. She and John had been to the same chiropractor during 2004 and 2005. John's lower back pain had resulted from high school football injuries. Now in late 2006, x-rays revealed degeneration in Kristene's lower spine, but this she concealed from me; I only saw that her pain was now more persistent, despite how often she went for treatments and realignments. At times now her walk was noticeably unsteady, and it was sometimes difficult for her to rise from a chair. Always one to take wine with dinner, Kristene began drinking wine before meals on a daily basis. We changed bed mattresses

305

several times in an effort to find one comfortable enough for her back, but with any of them we had limited success, and the lump in her left breast was still there; the same size as before, not sensitive to the touch, but still there.

Kristene assured me that she was seeing a doctor about the lump in her breast but wouldn't elaborate. I saw the bills and the canceled checks she wrote; none of the doctors or clinics names were familiar to me. She had a cupboard full of prescription and healthstore remedies in the kitchen, a plethora of capsules, pills, liquid drops and ointments, and she was reading several books on natural medicine and healing.

We had been members of the same church all this time, and attended and tithed there regularly. Each of us were involved in different ministries, had taken classes and made acquaintances but in general we felt socially isolated, unable to connect. This church has a huge membership of over ten thousand; although we knew many strong Christians there, the teaching was solid, and the senior pastor was amazingly available and responsive to any member, our comfort zone was in smaller church settings. To remedy this without leaving where we were, I pushed Kristene several times to host a Bible study in our home, or at least join one, but she resisted on the basis that I was gone so much on business that much of the responsibility would be hers, and she was burned out.

Christmastime 2006, Kristena and I resumed our tradition of decorating the front of the house and yard. In the cold we draped strings of lights along the eaves and over the bushes that bloomed pink and yellow flowers every spring. We put up a seven foot tall inflatable plastic snowman and a lighted manger scene. It wasn't as elaborate as a few of our neighbors' homes were, but it looked downright jolly and Kristene's compliments were enough for me. That year we did the smart thing considering where we live: we bought an artificial tree. John and I put it up, and he and Kristene did most of the decorating. Kristene was always the lavish decorator at Christmastime: angels and an electric choo-choo train, holly wreaths and long strands of green and white and red ribbon everywhere in the house.

On Christmas morning there were presents under the tree for everyone, as always, but at this age the kids wouldn't allow me to video tape them. Kristene busied herself in the kitchen as she had always done, making huge holiday meals, everything from scratch, yet she seemed down; not distant from me, but down. Things were not the same. We were still physically intimate, and since she wasn't open to talking about it, I assumed that she was coping with the latest round of losses in the family.

Between Christmas and New Year's I made forays deep into the desert in a modified four wheel drive rig I bought to explore areas of the desert I had always wanted to see. On one trip, my son was going to go with me but cancelled at the last minute. I was listening to my Catty Creek Band CD on my way home, and when 'Red River Valley' came on, such a heavy sorrow came over me that I began weeping uncontrollably. I was almost home when this happened; the grief was so overwhelming that I had to pull over, for I could not drive. I was grieving for Kristene, but I didn't know why. Then I paid more attention to the lyrics:

From this valley they say you are going,
We will miss your bright eyes and sweet smile,
For they say you are taking the sunshine,
That has brightened our pathways awhile.
Come and sit by my side if you love me,
Do not hasten to bid me adieu,
Just remember the Red River Valley,
And the cowboy who loved you so true.

The realization that 'Red River Valley' is a farewell song produced a cold knot of nausea in my stomach. When I pulled myself together, I drove the rest of the way home and went into the house, half expecting

307

to see her hurt or sick. But no, she was busy in the kitchen, the kids were watching TV in the family room, food was on the stove and in the oven.

"Hi Honey, how was your day in the desert? Johnny! Please set the table! Everybody wash your hands - we'll be eating soon. Honey, wash your hands and take the turkey out of the oven, would you?" For a moment I was speechless. Was I losing my mind? It must have been my imagination. I wondered if maybe it was me that something bad would happen to, or would die. I brushed the premonition aside and told no one.

With the arrival of 2007 I volunteered to retrain horses for a ranch on the Mexican border that was a base of operations for the border security movement. The horses were to be used for mounted volunteer patrols in remote areas, spotting and reporting smuggling activity to the Border Patrol, and retraining them was my best way to contribute to the border security cause. For two months I went to the ranch on weekends, bringing my own saddle. On one occasion the ranch owner himself flew me from the Scottsdale airport to the ranch in his private plane.

It was dangerous work. The horses had been allowed to regress to a nearly wild state, and had hurt everyone who tried to ride them, but within two months I brought them around to being useful mounts again. If Kristene had seen what I was doing: riding horses that bucked, reared and leaped on all fours into the air to get rid of me any way they could, risking severe injury or death for the fun of it, she would have blown a gasket. But horses are in my blood; I was having too much fun to let her interfere, so I let her think I was just 'riding horses' as in just exercising them.

I couldn't understand it, but three times on my trips home from the Spencer ranch in my truck, I broke down in deep grief over Kristene when the recording of Red River Valley came on, yet all was normal when I arrived home. This repeated grieving bothered me; something was very wrong and I asked God to help me understand it, but there was no answer. I stopped playing the CD. Kristene seemed to be feeling normal; the lump in her breast was shrinking again, she walked and got around normally and she wasn't complaining about pain in her back. Maybe all these strange doctors and their potions really worked after all.

Knowing that I am ever a cowboy at heart, Kristene put together a surprise weekend for me on my sixtieth birthday: two nights at a motel in the little desert town of Cave Creek, where we enjoyed dancing to live country music and dinner at one of the cowboy bars, trail rides on rented horses for the two of us on Saturday, and again on Sunday with the kids. It was great to get away for a couple of days, relax with her, and see the kids.

Kristene went even further than the weekend activity to honor my birthday: she had rescued all twenty nine of my horseshow ribbons from the attic of our Issaquah home without my ever knowing it, for by some miracle they did not mold when the roof leaked after the last storm. She had them steam cleaned and pressed and hired a local craftsman to make an eight foot wide by two foot tall shadow box of dark-stained wood frame with a brass plaque in which Kristene mounted all my ribbons. The box was mounted above the headboard in our master bedroom. I was a blessed man indeed.

In April I got a surprise phone call. "Hi Cousin, it's Jane: how are you?"

"Fine. It's been awhile - how are you?" I replied.

"Good. Say listen, I have a deal here you might like. One of my horse-shoeing clients has a big gelding that has constant problems with hoof-rot in this damp ground up here. She needs a new home for him in a dry climate; I told her about you living in Arizona. This would be a really good horse for you, and the price is right," Jane said.

Yeah, I thought, the price could hardly be right enough for me at this point.

"How right?" I asked Jane.

"Free, and they will trailer him to you at their expense."

I sat forward in my chair. "No kidding? I heard you right – free, including bring him here?"

"That's right, do you want him?"

"Absolutely, but I will have to ask Kristene first. If I do something this major without asking, I could be sharing a stall with the horse. I'll call you back in two days or less," I said.

It took a whole day for this to sink in. Kristene was never an animal person. I was sure she would say no, but keeping a horse was too big an obligation to do on my own without asking her first. I waited for what I felt was the right time. The next day we were alone at home and I asked Kristene to sit in the family room; she sat on the couch across from me.

"Well, uh, Honey, uh, I got a call from Jane, and she told me about this horse that one of her customers has that has to live in a dry climate because of a hoof-rot problem. Jane says this is a gentle, very fine horse, it's free and the owners will bring him here at their expense and I wanted –"

I stopped speaking when Kristene slid off the couch onto the floor and began sobbing "Thank you God, thank you Jesus, thank you, thank you!" I was too surprised to speak.

"Kristene, what's going on?" I asked.

"Honey, when I saw on your birthday how much having a horse meant to you, I asked God to bring us one – and here it is! I can hardly believe it!" she sobbed.

I am rarely at a loss for words, but this was one of those times. Instead of trying to say anything, I took Kristene in my arms and held her for a long time. I was a blessed man.

That night I told Jane we wanted the horse, and immediately the owner, Brenda Roberts, emailed photographs to us. He was fine looking – very tall and handsome, and his name was Taylor. I found a boarding facility called Pretty Penny Ranch within sixty seconds of our house and rented a stall there in anticipation of Taylor's arrival. Three weeks later in May, Brenda and her cousin arrived with our horse. Taylor was taller and a lighter shade of sorrel than he appeared to be in the photographs; his coat was the color of copper and had a metallic sheen that glistened in the sun. He had a very handsome head with what people call 'human' eyes and a blaze of white on his face. We bought grooming supplies and tack items at the local feed store and I began teaching Kristene and the kids to ride, and I rode every day. For all his size and power, Taylor was a smooth, gentle ride, he was intelligent and interactive; a perfect fit for our family, and Kristene and I called him "our holy horse," for he was from God.

At the end of the school year, our son John, then seventeen, wanted to live and work with my cousin Jane in Washington. Jane was a professional farrier, (horse-shoer) by trade, and also owned a string of several horses and had a side business of raising Red Angus cattle. I required John to live and work two weeks at Glenn Spencer's ranch on the border to see if he was capable of that kind of life. For two weeks he was up with the sun, working ranch chores all day and asleep at night in the bunkhouse with the other men. He was so successful that he was told he had a job there as long as the ranch was there, and I took him up to Washington where he extended his summer stay into the fall season. When he returned home by Christmas, John had not only gained muscle, but working knowledge about horses, dogs and cattle, use and repair of tractors and trailers and ranch life.

The new decade so far had been a trough of passages for us, a season of harvesting for the Reaper, a drastic thinning of the family ranks from which we hoped and longed for respite, a return to earlier, happier years, but it was not to be. During the summer, Kristene received word that her brother Bob had been taken to the emergency room for excruciating back pain; he had been shoveling gravel in his driveway when it overtook him. The diagnosis was stage IV cancer when the test results came back. I do not know the exact details, but it was my understanding that Bob at first declined the offers of chemotherapy and radiation, and that the doctors told him it was too late to implement those procedures when he later changed his mind. Bob went home to spend his last days, and Kristene and Richard went there individually to see him before he passed on. Bob was fifty nine; a good man he was, a devoted husband and father.

That fall season, I was called to Seattle on a case of industrial sabotage that lasted for almost three months. The first time I was away on this case I was gone three weeks, and Kristene took care of Taylor every day while I was away, even riding him bareback, and the kids either visited him or rode him every day, and thus Taylor became part of our family fabric.

As 2007 was closing, I was retained to provide security for the estranged wife of a man I knew from many years before to be emotionally and mentally unstable and potentially violent. Two days before my flight to Seattle to meet the client and go with her to eastern Washington, I became violently ill with the flu very suddenly, forcing me to postpone my trip. When I recovered, I received a call from my sister Cindy that our father had been taken by ambulance from his home in Port Ludlow to Harrison Hospital in Bremerton. My client went to her home in eastern Washington without me and was completely snowed in by a huge storm for weeks and I had to refund the retainer. Again it was the Lord's timing: had I gone to eastern Washington as planned I would have been unable to respond to my father's emergency.

Dad was ninety one, and had suffered for years from multiple health maladies until he was taken by ambulance to the hospital because he was unable to urinate. He never returned home again. I remained with him through the winter months until just days before he passed away. Before I left for Arizona I asked Dad if he knew where he would go after he passed on, as it was my understanding from him that a year earlier a local pastor led him to Christ, yet I saw that he continued to curse and take the Lord's name in vain. In response to my question, Dad cursed me and told me, in effect, to get out of his room if I was going to "talk that crap." I said goodbye and left for home that day. I didn't know it then, but that was to be the last time I would see my father.

Kristene came up to Washington to help me drive our son's Volvo back home, for John had returned home to finish high school. We took the coastal route back, along the 101. We had a pleasant trip, stopping at small towns along the way, finding great little places to eat and stay overnight. We greatly enjoyed our time together even though Kristene's back pain returned intermittently and we constantly adjusted the seat position as we drove. Two nights after we were home I had a vivid dream that I was standing in the hallway at a medical facility when a doctor and a nurse appeared, pushing a gurney that had my dad on it with a sheet draped over him. The next day I received a call from my sister Cindy that she had been notified that Dad had passed away. My father was dead at the age of ninety one, and I grieved privately for him.

Newlyweds Ray and Shirley Hansen on their wedding day in June, 1946.

CHAPTER THIRTY-TWO

The domino effect of people dying in our family continued. My father died on March 28, 2008, and his wife lost her long battle with cancer shortly afterward, passing away weeks later in May. Kristene and I went up to Seattle for my father's funeral, and when Jeanne passed away, Kristene returned without me to help Cindy take Mom, who was no longer and help her look for an assisted living facility.

My mother had been living alone in her large home for several years, and she had begun stumbling and falling more frequently and leaving stove burners on. Cindy and I had already removed the area rugs she was tripping on and took other safety precautions, but Mom was eighty-eight and showing early signs of dementia. In her lucid moments that were becoming fewer and fewer, Mom agreed that an assisted care facility might be in her best interest. After the funeral, Kristene stayed with Mom for three weeks, helping her around the house, getting it ready to sell by clearing out old clothes and clutter from her closets and giving them to charity. She researched and personally visited various assisted care homes that were close to Mom's present home and took Mom to dinner. For the first time, it was noticed by Cindy that Kristene tired easily and had to lie down to rest in one of Mom's spare bedrooms each afternoon; this was a new development, but I did not know of it until long afterward.

When Father's Day arrived, I was depressed and angry. I was helplessly watching my world collapsing around me. The ones dearest to me were dying off, and with some of them unpleasant truths had been coming to light. Since the death of my father, I learned that my relationship with him was not what I had believed it was, it was too late to try to clear up misunderstandings; death is unforgiving and final. In his later years, there was hostility in Dad's attitudes and mental outlook that seemed to exactly parallel the deterioration of his health. In the end, he became someone I did not know. My father continued to be a man at war with himself, and he left this world that way. To the asset column of my dad's life's ledger is one thing I will always admiringly remember him for: as tough as he was, Dad was quick to show compassion and help others in distress. All his life he disdained the pretensions of the prideful, the self-righteous and those who had not earned themselves their wealth or position, for his own wealth was self-earned and often greater than that of most professionals who put on snide airs. He had a heart for the underdog, the working man, and the disadvantaged that he often acted upon, helping others often and was never ashamed to associate openly with working people. These traits I inherited from him.

He not only came to our house to physically pitch in to help us during the second flood, he gave generously to us after the third flood, when we had lost everything. Both times did he help us without being asked.

And now there was Kristene. There were alarming signs that something beyond chronic back pain was wrong. She was seeing more and more pain doctors and drinking more and more red wine and vodka than ever before, and her mood swings were becoming more severe. My mother was steadily losing touch with reality, flip-flopping over whether to sell her house, mentally confused between who was alive and who had passed away and even what year it was. She was telling people everywhere that Kristene was trying to take over her house. It was, however, lost on no one that Kristene was graciously giving of her precious time and energy to help the very woman who had maligned and scorned her for so many years and continued to do so even as her mental powers dimmed.

Kristene mentioned to me several times that she enjoyed riding, but Taylor was too tall for her. So while she was in Washington, my cousin Jane gave us a gentle young mare named Red that was a more suitable size for Kristene. But when Kristene came home, the pain in her hips and pelvic bones made it impossible to mount Red, even once from a raised platform.

Signs that we were entering the beginning of the end appeared shortly after what would be our last anniversary on August 1. Neither of us saw it that way then, for we had stopped thinking very far into the future.

We celebrated our twenty-seventh anniversary late by going to the Indian Market in Santa Fe in mid-August. Kristene was barely able to walk, except very slowly, like an old woman, along level sidewalks, clinging to my arm, like my grandmother used to do in her last years, pausing to rest every few yards. The pain for her was terrible – at its worst ever, yet she smiled and complained not; determined she was to enjoy herself and make the most of our trip. For her sake and the sake of our time together I kept silent about the agony I felt watching her suffer. With the help of pain medications she had with her we went to the Santa Fe Opera, saw art displays and traveled to see the town of Taos. She explained her pain to me as 'back pain' and said nothing of what she knew was the real cause. At her request the hotel let us change rooms three times in search of a comfortable bed for her back. At the trip's end she needed a wheelchair to go through the airport. I was worried.

Our son and his closest friends were out of high school now, and preparing to enter adult life. Not knowing what was ahead for us at the time, I wrote a tribute to my son and his friends that had later prophetic implications, for they had become known to the parents as the Band of Brothers, such was their loyalty to each other.

The fall season brought more change. Kristena resumed carrying a full load at college, excelling in subjects such as accounting. She also worked part time. John worked part-time at Costco, part-time as caretaker of the horses of a wealthy family, and carried a partial load of credits at Scottsdale Community College. I had an enormous amount of new cases in Seattle that only I was qualified to do, requiring me to be away three weeks out of four, leaving John alone to take care of his mother.

Our son John heroically stood up to the plate for his mother during this time, tending to her needs in addition to his two part-time jobs and a partial load at college. John drove her to doctors' appointments, picked up her prescriptions, fixed meals for her, shopped for groceries, did the laundry, and kept the house picked up and the kitchen clean. On weekends Kristena took over for him so he could go to one of his buddies' homes to sleep uninterrupted. Every time I came home, I saw that Kristene walked with greater difficulty and struggled to get out of bed or sit in a chair for long. She had been seeing a naturopathic doctor named Cheryl DeRoin in Scottsdale since about 2006 who was selling her all kinds of herbal pain medications, none of which was effective for long.

By November John acquired a pair of crutches for his mother because she could no longer walk on her own without hanging on to the wall with one hand and taking one slow, sliding step at a time. The kids and I prepared Thanksgiving dinner and set it up in the dining room, as we had in years past. When everything was ready, Kristene came out slowly on crutches, wincing in pain with every move, no matter how slight, yet smiling lovingly, cheerfully at us, at the dinner her family prepared, wanting to make the very best of it. For the kids and me it was wrenching to see her in pain and suffering, for we knew her pain was worse than she was letting on. For her sake, we kept the conversation bright and cheerful by talking about the dinner preparation, ribbing each other, and cracking jokes. True to her loving nature, Kristene's countenance glowed as she listened to her kids bantering back and forth, absorbing the essence of her offspring as only mothers can. I was proud of them that they had the savvy to not do or say anything that would draw attention to their mother's condition and instead buoyed her up with light-hearted talk. After dessert Kristene wasted no time getting on her crutches and returning to bed. I saw her to the bedroom and helped the kids with the dishes and cleanup to allow Kristene a chance to settle in; it was early evening. I checked on her as soon as the dishes were done and the kids were putting leftovers away. She was asleep.

In the morning I made our coffee and asked Kristene to tell me specifically about her health situation.

"Doctor DeRoin has told me that the program she has me on is detoxifying my tissues, especially my lymph nodes, and that it would get worse before it gets better. I believe in her. She is the only one around who does what she does," Kristene told me.

Kristene seemed confident that her recovery was on the way even though the lump in her left breast was now larger and sensitive to the touch. I told her that I was uncomfortable with what Dr. DeRoin was telling her and I would feel better if she saw a regular doctor or at least another naturopath for a second opinion. Kristene said she had seen regular doctors in the past, and because she had seen the suffering her father and Cindy's husband Chuck went through as a result of relying on regular doctors and died painful deaths anyway, in spite of their scorched-earth, high-tech remedies that maimed and tortured; therefore she would not entrust herself to one.

Some nights Kristene groaned in pain when she shifted or moved in bed, and sometimes getting out of bed to use the bathroom was slow and painful for her. When she did sleep, I could not; I stared at the ceiling, wide awake, wondering what I should do. It bothered me that she was drinking more wine than ever, this being the advice of naturopathic doctors before Dr. DeRoin, but I was uncomfortable with this too. In the previous months she had John juicing fresh vegetables daily for her at home, and I took over doing this for her.

After the Thanksgiving weekend, I returned to finish my cases in Seattle, leaving Kristene in the care of our son and daughter and Dr. DeRoin. Before leaving home again, I decided that once the open cases were completed, I would stay home with Kristene. Christmas that year was somber. We put up the tree and placed only a few presents under it. There was a definite dread in the air that took the joy out of Christmas, for Kristene's condition had not changed since Thanksgiving. At New Year's both kids were out with friends while we stayed at home together, Kristene falling asleep early and sleeping well through the night. After the New Year, I told Kristene, "I don't see where you have turned the corner that Dr. DeRoin says you would, and it's time for us to have a meeting with her when I get back from Seattle."

I returned from Seattle for the last time two weeks later and resolved not to leave Kristene again. At a meeting with Dr. DeRoin, I was told by her that an MRI exam performed earlier under an assumed name confirmed that Kristene had bone cancer in her pelvic cradle, and this explained the pain in her hips and lower back. I was shocked and angry that I was not informed until now. Dr. DeRoin also went into some detail about why she was confident that the cancer in Kristene was reversible. I came away from the meeting wanting to believe Dr. DeRoin, but the symptoms were mounting evidence that just the opposite was true.

"Why didn't you tell me?" I asked Kristene when we got home.

"Honey, you were going through so much with your dad, I didn't want to pull you away from him," she said.

"You are more important to me than anyone else. I am hurt and angry that you left me out like this," I said.

Specifically, Dr. DeRoin told us that she had successfully treated cancer patients before, even bone cancer patients. She said the only patients she had "lost" were those who didn't follow her instructions. She told us she believed Kristene would recover and that the way the pain was manifesting itself was an encouraging indication the treatments were working. Kristene was crying in terrible pain trying to leave Dr. DeRoin's office when the meeting ended, and when I saw that Dr. DeRoin offered Kristene no assistance but instead stared coldly at her and at me, I was angry and became more skeptical of her competence and integrity.

At home, Kristene's moods fluctuated more markedly than ever. She clung to me day and night. In bed she wanted to be held by me and often awoke just to see if I was still there. On the other side, Kristene was given to bouts of unusual anger and hostility, for no apparent reason, usually directed at me in scolding tones of voice that surprised John whenever he was home to hear it. I did not react because I understood this was a combination of fear and pain manifesting itself. I noticed that Kristene had stopped drinking wine or alcohol in any form, and that, though always an avid Bible reader, she was reading her Bible more frequently now than before.

One afternoon when we were alone, I left the house on an errand but forgot the car keys. As I came back into the house, I heard Kristene, in the bedroom, thinking she was alone, pouring her heart out to God in great sobs: "Oh Lord, when will You heal me? I have waited and sought You so long! Please have mercy on me, Lord!" At this she wept mightily from the depths of her soul, and I knew then what she knew.

I went to her; she was sitting in a swivel chair in our bedroom, and I knelt down and held her in my arms, and she cried.

"I thought you left, Honey," she said as she pressed her wet cheek into my shoulder.

"I did, but came back for my keys. Darling, let's pray together right now. You know what it says about the power of agreed prayer."

"Okay, you start," she sniffed, wiping her eyes with a tissue.

"Father God in Heaven, we approach You through the blood covering of Jesus Christ, Your son and our Savior. We come before You on the basis that we have accepted Jesus's death on the cross on our behalf, and that years ago You declared us one spirit, one mind, and one flesh in your sight. In the Book of Matthew Jesus says that if two of us agree on anything on earth, it will be done for us by our Father in Heaven. Your Word also teaches us in the book of First John that if we ask anything according to Your will, You will grant it. Father, we stand in agreement before you, asking that You bring complete healing to Kristene, and we thank You for it in advance," I prayed as she held me close to her.

"Amen, Father," Kristene prayed. "And I thank You for my husband and I ask You to watch over him in all his ways, no matter what happens to me."

And then we talked for awhile.

Kristene's pain worsened as January passed into February. She required my help now in getting out of bed and onto her crutches to use the bathroom. The pain in her pelvis was so severe that she groaned or even cried every time. At night her body literally shook violently for minutes at a time as she laid supine, gripping my hand as she sobbed quietly. Neither of us ever slept the night through; sunrise always arrived with both of us exhausted. I was at a loss at what to do for her, as she refused my offer to call the medics or give her any of her pain medications, and she continued to refuse to see a regular oncologist. The helplessness I felt put me in a state of anguish I had never known; the one I loved was in terrible suffering, and there was nothing I could do. I added fasting on a weekly basis to my prayers, but I could see no change. One morning we were both awake and exhausted after a long night of a lot of pain episodes and spotty sleep.

"I am very worried about you," I said.

Kristene sat up in bed, looking at me, her countenance worried and weary, and a haunted look in her eyes.

"I don't want to go," she whispered fearfully, and of her meaning there was no confusion.

That afternoon I was with Kristene in the bedroom; she was awake, lying in bed, resting, and I was sitting in my chair next to her, reading.

"Darling, Ron was just here," she said.

"Ron? Your brother Ron?" I asked.

"Yes. He was here just now. I saw him. He stood beside me and laid hands on my head and prayed for me. Then he went away," she told me matter-of-factly.

I didn't know what to say at first; I didn't doubt Kristene had really seen Ron, but the timing was telling. It was the second time that I knew of that Ron had appeared to Kristene and spoken to her since he died in 2004. I had always known Kristene to be gifted in prophetic things and to have experienced open visions in which she had glimpses into the spirit realm before. I finally told her that if Ron was praying for her, then it must mean she would be all right. It was beyond my experience, but to me it seemed ominous.

I had a private meeting with Dr. DeRoin at her office about Kristene's situation. Dr. DeRoin's comments and responses to my questions added to my suspicions that she was not competent and did not have Kristene's best interests in mind, and I thereafter worked with Kristene to find another physician and get another opinion. On her own, Kristene found another doctor to see. At first I thought this one was a regular medical doctor who also practiced in natural medicine because his practice offered "limited chemotherapy" administered in his clinic. I took Kristene to his clinic once, only to find he was a naturopathic doctor only. I looked this man up on the Internet to find that he had been run out of two states for fraud and there were multiple warnings posted to stay away from him. That was enough.

During February, Kristene's pain worsened; she continued to receive prescriptions for pain from Dr. DeRoin that only provided temporary relief. I had more than one phone conversation with Dr. DeRoin, who said her license allowed her to prescribe morphine for Kristene but for reasons that were not clear, even though Kristene was in agonizing pain, Dr. DeRoin refused to prescribe morphine for her. In one conversation, Dr. DeRoin told me, "I think I know what she has: internal shingles."

There was no mention of the cancer in her bones we had all been discussing earlier. Was I wrong in my understanding that cancer was a painful disease in its final stages? I was too distraught and confused to think clearly.

The next morning I was having coffee in our bedroom with Kristene. She was propped up in bed, and I was seated in a swivel chair next to her. Kristene had slept unusually well the previous night, so we both felt relatively rested and alert for a change, and she had been reading her Bible earlier that morning.

"Honey, I saw Ron and Bob last night," she told me.

"Was it a dream?" I asked.

"No. I was wide awake. It was early—about two, I think. I was awake just thinking and watching you sleep when there was Ron and Bob, standing together at the foot of our bed. They stood next to me, laid both their hands on me, and prayed over me. It was longer than last time," Kristene said.

"Do you remember what they said?"

"No, I don't," she replied.

Outwardly I maintained a calm composure, but inside I was shaking. This was three times Ron appeared to Kristene after he died: the first time was a couple weeks after his passing; she saw him in Heaven, a little of which Kristene saw then; the other two times he appeared to Kristene was at her bedside after she was very sick; the third time Ron was with Bob, who had passed away a year and a half before. The only people I confided this to at the time were Bob O'Leary, my closest friend, and Kay, Ron's widow. I mentally filed Kristene's open visions away for future consideration, because too much was happening now that was demanding my attention.

On March 3, I took Kristene to a clinic in Scottsdale where she underwent a full-body scan, a procedure known as a PET Scan, the latest in medical technology. The results would be made known to us in about five days.

March 5 was a Thursday. It was a fateful day. Kristene had slept little the night before, and was tired by morning. John left for work at Costco late in the morning, and I chose to stay in with her all day. I made her vegetable juice in the juicer, and when she napped, I went to the family room at the other end of the house to pray out loud, as is my custom. During mid-afternoon I prepared a light lunch, which we ate in the bedroom together. At about 5:00 p.m., Kristene asked me to help her go to the bathroom again. She sat up in bed and touched feet to the floor as I handed her the crutches and helped her up off the bed onto the crutches. I opened wide both French doors leading into the tile-floored bathroom. She was in obvious pain and winced as she crutched her way into the bathroom, making slow progress toward the toilet. She was favoring her right side by putting more weight on her left leg as she moved; she seemed very shaky, and I kept within a foot behind her and to the left. Suddenly I heard a loud snap from Kristene, and I wondered what caused it, for Kristene shrieked in pain as she started to fall. I caught her in my arms before any part of her body could touch the floor. I half-carried her back to the bed; her left leg was dangling by the skin, and Kristene was shrieking in pain.

"Call Dr.-----!" (the naturopath with the bad record) she shouted to me.

"No, I am calling the medics. We need help," I said as I dialed 911.

"No, Honey, please don't!" But I cut her off by telling the emergency dispatcher where we were. I coached her through the pain in a manner similar to what we did in childbirths years ago as I stood with her waiting for medical help. Within minutes the medic van arrived. They immediately gave Kristene an IV of morphine, and as it took effect, she became calm and rational again. They brought in a gurney and were lifting her onto it when John came home from work, and stood in shocked silence as his mother was strapped onto the gurney.

As the medics rolled the gurney carrying Kristene down the hall to the front door, she called out instructions to John which lights were to be left on and which were to be turned off for the night. She was talking calmly with her caregivers as she was loaded into the van, and I rode with her to the hospital.

At the Scottsdale Healthcare emergency room, Kristene was placed in bed 11, and X-rays were immediately taken in another room. She was still calm when she was brought back. John arrived and sat with me next to her; he had called Kristena, and she was on her way. As we waited, a Dr. King came up to me. "May I see you for a minute, Mr. Hansen?" he asked.

I went with Dr. King to an adjacent room where Kristene's X-rays were posted on a light board. My heart nearly stopped; no medical training was necessary to understand what I was looking at, for the deterioration of bone mass was severe. Both femurs were thin; the left femur was completely broken in the middle, both ends were apart and were jagged, obviously a result of the fall, and both sides of her pelvic cradle, especially the right side, were so eroded as to look moth eaten. I stared in disbelief, unable to move at first.

"It's my guess that your wife was favoring her right side by shifting more weight onto her left side when she walked," Dr. King told me. "As you can see, the right femur is already eaten away for all intents and purposes, and the pain of this caused your wife to lean more to the left, not knowing that her left femur had deteriorated to the diameter of a pencil. The left femur is completely broken, and if you look here, most of her pelvic cradle, especially on the right, is gone already," Dr. King said.

The snap sound I had heard was Kristene's femur breaking in two. Looking at me, Dr. King said, "Mr. Hansen, this could be life threatening."

CHAPTER THIRTY-THREE

The nightmare we had been living deepened and accelerated like a powerful shark on the line, plunging unstoppably through darker and darker depths toward the ocean bottom; all we could do was hang on for dear life as Kristene's life was being peeled away like line on a fishing reel. We were all desperate. The hospital ran five diagnostic tests on Kristene before she was placed in a room to sleep. I slept in a reclining chair next to her, and the kids went home in shock, unprepared for that which was to come. Starting at just after 2:00 a.m., more tests were conducted, including blood draws and tissue samples. There were visits from various physicians the next day, offering chemotherapy and radiation therapies, and others prescribing medications for pain management and infection prevention. Kristene's entire left leg was encased in a traction boot to prevent the jagged edges of her broken femur from causing further tissue damage.

Stress continued to mount during the weeks that followed. We all sensed the ultimate outcome, but in our hope against hope we dared not give utterance even once, and perhaps because of that, an emotional numbness came over all four of us, like a hovering dark cloud in a gathering storm, certain to unload heavy rain; but when it would be, no one knew. Kristene refused chemotherapy and radiation when informed of the gravity of her situation without explaining to the doctors that she feared the potential for disfigurement that the severity of traditional treatments could cause, and that she preferred an approach that would utilize more natural, gentler measures instead, measures they were not offering.

It was then that I first learned she had been communicating with Cancer Treatment Centers of America for months about admission there, because it employed both traditional medicine and holistic treatments in its approach to defeating cancer. By not disclosing her ultimate intentions to physicians at Scottsdale Healthcare, Kristene gave them the understandable impression that she did not comprehend the gravity of her situation.

More than one physician tactfully explained to Kristene that at best, chemotherapy and radiation could only extend her life now by a few months, not one of them offered her any hope that she would recover. Even before test results were available, emergency room X-rays revealed cancer had spread throughout her body to an irreversible extent. I was with Kristene when she asked one oncologist about her estimated life expectancy; he replied that without chemo or radiation, she might live about four months, and six months or more if she accepted those treatments. Another surgeon refused to operate on her leg because the risk of further complications, such as blood clotting leading to potential stroke, was unacceptably high. Kristene was so surprisingly calm—stoic, even—that I wondered if she really grasped the crisis she faced, or if she expected a miracle from Cancer Treatment Centers of America. It was painfully clear to me that the last opportunity to defeat the cancer medically had come and gone months ago. Except for a miracle from God, it was too late.

It's when the chips are down that you learn who your friends are and who they aren't. I couldn't have known it then, but I was about to learn that this is true of even the church, that in the Body of Christ some are truly His sheep and others are goats who only purport to be His. People we least expected to hear from came forward to stand with us, and many people I thought of as genuine Christians and our close friends, turned their backs on us in our darkest hour.

I sought God's help with an earnestness that exceeded any other time in my life in Christ. To reach into the spirit realm for a miracle for Kristene, I prayed fervently, without ceasing; in my car, at home alone, and with Kristene; desperate, often on my knees or face-down on the floor for long periods of time. I needed more help to bombard Heaven on Kristene's behalf. In Matthew 18, Jesus taught that prayer is more powerful when people pray together in agreement on a matter, so I obtained prayer support from several sources: my close friend Bob O'Leary, my sister Cindy, and Pastor Jack Rozelle, now retired from pastoral and missionary work, two other close friends of mine, and the prayer line at the *700 Club*. Jack Rozelle and a couple from our days at Neighborhood Church, Ted and Marietta Terry, became mainstays of spiritual support for me during this time, calling often to see how we were and to pray with me. In addition to prayer, I fasted weekly, going on liquids only for two and three days at a time.

To get more people praying, I tried to reach the new pastor at our church, for help. We had been tithing members there for almost seven years. Now my wife was dying and fighting for her life. I was desperate and needed to know if he and the elders would come and lay hands on Kristene, and anoint her with oil and pray the prayer of faith over her as it says to do in the Book of James, so that she would be healed, as it says.

But I was told by the front office that I could not reach the new senior pastor; I was put in touch with an associate pastor, instead. I explained our crisis. I told him that my wife had stage IV cancer that had spread to her bones and I wanted a pastor and some church elders to pray over Kristene and anoint her with oil as it says to do in the Book of James. He enthusiastically agreed and said he would round up some elders and would get back to me right away to set a date. He also told me he would put us on the church prayer chain. I never heard from the associate pastor again, even though I called several times and left pleading messages for him when I mentioned my wife's crisis every time

I stopped by the church office to pay my tithe; the office personnel there merely smiled and said nothing as I handed them my check.

After personally hearing two doctors give Kristene essentially the same prognosis of her life expectancy, I urged her to reconsider chemo and radiation, but she declined. The hospital ordered a psychiatric evaluation because of her refusal of chemotherapy and radiation and her tendency to self-direct her treatment by accepting some medications and not others. I sat through the psychiatric exam with her; Kristene calmly answered all questions and conversed amiably with the psychiatrist, who concluded that Kristene was rational and able to make her own decisions. Seeing my wife in a hospital, being told by doctors that her life was in imminent danger, seemed like a bad dream; I could not believe this was happening, and I kept thinking everything would be normal when I awoke.

But it was no dream. During Kristene's first week at Scottsdale Healthcare, the results of both the PET scan performed the day before she collapsed and the results of Scottsdale Healthcare's diagnostic tests came in at about the same time. The report on the biopsy of her left breast showed estrogen + progesterone + receptor positive; Kristene was HER2 negative; she had infiltrating ductal carcinoma or IDC. It was explained to me that IDC starts in the breast ducts and later breaks through the duct walls, infiltrating the fatty breast tissue. Once it breaks through the walls, it can spread throughout the body via the lymph system and blood stream. The results of the earlier PET scan and subsequent scans performed at the hospital were consistent: cancer had spread from her left breast throughout her skeletal structure, including her spine to the base of her skull, her jaw, left arm and shoulder, ribcage, her entire pelvic cradle, especially the right side, and both femurs. Moreover, there were indications that the cancer was beginning to spread to her lungs.

As one person, the kids and I took turns spending the night with Kristene so she wouldn't be alone. Kristena and John usually stayed with her during the week, and I took over on weekends. These nights were extremely stressful, for Kristene cried often, throughout the night, either from physical pain or emotional trauma, or fear of dying. Nurses came in at all hours, breaking her sleep and mine to check her blood pressure and pulse, her IVs, and give whatever shots or pills she needed. It occurred to me that this practice made it impossible for a patient to ever get the full night's sleep needed to promote a healing environment for the body.

During the day, the kids and I took turns making and bringing Kristene home-cooked meals, foods recommended by a friend who had survived cancer in large part by starving cancer cells and feeding the healthy cells through diet. The principle theory behind the diet was that sugar feeds cancer cells; if certain foods, such as sugar or foods that the body converted into sugar, were eliminated, cancer cells would die without destroying healthy cells, as chemo and radiation are known to do. The program required that a strict diet of certain vegetables and foods was followed. Usually I prepared scrambled eggs and corn tortillas for her breakfast; on weekends Kristena and John made vegetable soups, steamed broccoli, brown rice, and vegetable juice for lunches and dinners in large batches that were refrigerated and could be heated and brought to her. On other days I bought cooked meals at a health food store and brought them to her. I bought a compact refrigerator and set it up in her room to reduce the number of trips we had to make between the clinic and the house for her meals.

Through all this, Kristene kept up an amazingly positive attitude in both word and deed. She made a point of knowing her caregivers by name and enough about them to enable as much bond to occur as the situation and relationship allowed. She was diligent in taking vitamins and exercising as her strength allowed.

It was disturbing to learn how long Kristene had been keeping me in the dark about her having cancer; or that she had been working with Cancer Treatment Centers of America for months without telling me.

I felt a mix of emotions, mostly anger and a sense of betrayal for being left out on something so life-threatening. But we were too far into the crisis now to make an issue of it with her. I could only speculate on her reasons. Possibly it was because she was in denial, possibly she was in fear; certainly she understood the gravity of her situation and wanted to protect me, I never knew the reason. Her communications were with the Chicago area location, because the Phoenix facility had just opened in December 2008 and there were no oncology surgeons on the staff there at that time. CTCA, as it is called for short, required in part, that patient applicants be capable of walking fifty steps, whether with a cane or a walker. At present Kristene could not accomplish this, so I found an oncology surgeon who would rebuild Kristene's left leg and hip so she could have mobility again. We went ahead with this surgery so she would be able to be accepted by the Cancer Treatment Center in Illinois, but the gains in mobility the operation gave her were short-lived, lasting only a few weeks.

On Saturday, March 21, the first wall of heavy grief hit me. Unstoppable mourning and weeping unlike anything I had ever experienced, took over as if someone had pushed me out of the driver's seat of my car, taking control, and drove it back and forth over me all day; its crushing effect could not be masked with a smile. I wanted to get away, and I didn't want Kristene to see how devastated I was, for that would nullify her efforts to keep a positive focus. My son saw that I was troubled, and he took over spending the day with Kristene for me; I needed to get away for at least a few hours.

I saddled Taylor and rode alone into the open desert as I had done so many times before, but this time was different, for my state of being was under seige. Taylor readily picked up on my angst, for when we reached the Pemberton Trail, he exploded down it for over two miles at full tilt, and then cut along a desert path at the old miner's shack for a hundred yards to a dried-out creek bed and back up in the same direction in the deep sand of the creek bed, trotting uphill for another two miles, eager to run. The sun and the wind in my face, the solitude of the desert, being afforded a fresh perspective of our crisis by being astride a mighty animal that elevated me another four feet above the ground cleared my head and temporarily tranquilized my heaviest encounter yet with grief, enabling me to step back, collect my thoughts, pour out my soul to God, tell Him in the plainest terms how bad the predicament appeared to me at the time.

I came back from that ride clear-headed, with understanding that I did not have before. I had experienced deep grief for the first time; it was a palpable force, unseen, but not unknown, for grief had tip-toed around me two years earlier through the music CD I had heard and had to set aside. Grief would return more forcefully in the future, but I was not alone in this; the One Who raises the dead was with me and He was in charge. Then I thought of Uncle Leo's years of sacrificial care for Kate until she passed on, and I returned to Kristene's side, confident that even in this, as in all things, God was at work for the good of us who adhere to Him.

I became more focused on working *with* God in our crisis, and I set myself to seeking Him to guide me to do what He wanted me to do, minute-by-minute. I focused totally on serving Kristene to the exclusion of all else and entrusted all outcomes to God. I became set on being dead to myself and alive to God and to Kristene, and as I did this, peace came. But it was a strange peace, one with no apparent earthly basis because Kristene's suffering was intensifying, almost by the day. It was becoming undeniably clear that God was in charge, yes, but He was taking Kristene home early. I remembered how as far back as Mercer Island Kristene repeatedly told me "I am going to go before you do." Now it was really happening. Now I understood that way back then, she knew; she must have. Even so, I went into denial, blindly I held onto hope; she was my beloved. I would have taken her suffering upon myself if it would free her from it; but this was not possible.

On Monday, March 23, I was filled with purpose and knowing as I checked Kristene out of Scottsdale Healthcare and into another hospital for surgery on her left femur and hip. Her surgery was a success, and in two days she could put full weight on her left leg and even walk a little with the help of a walker. On March 26, Kristene left Mayo Clinic and moved into Lifecare Center of Scottsdale for "skilled recovery."

On her second night at Lifecare, I was sleeping in the bed next to Kristene when at about 3:00 a.m., I heard a male voice say "Time for your 3:00 a.m. shot, Mrs. Williams. Just stay as you are and I'll be quick about it." I looked up to see a large male nurse standing over Kristene's bed.

"You have the wrong room. This isn't Mrs. Williams, this is Mrs. Hansen, and I am her husband," I told him.

"You mean they moved Mrs. Williams?" he asked in surprise.

"That's my wife there, and I'm sure not Mrs. Williams," I replied.

Embarrassed, he apologized and left. In the middle of the night Kristene almost got a shot of who-knows-what intended for someone else; it was alarming, to say the least. It took a couple of weeks to arrange it, but I moved Kristene to Scottsdale Heritage Court, where she was much more comfortable, and her communication with Cancer Treatment Centers of America and our health insurance provider continued while she participated in physical therapy.

Seeing Kristene in unrelenting decline week after week was breaking us down, exacting a heavy toll of deep stress that gnawed and accumulated, gnawed and accumulated and overwhelmed my focus on the Lord. There were brief episodes of apparent recovery that gave us hope, but these were brief and left us depressed and discouraged when they ended and her decline resumed. The trend was worsening, and nothing anyone did could stop it. We, along with Kristene, were being forever changed by it. At home, where Kristene could not see us, the signs that the stress was exacting a heavy toll on the kids and me were clear. Kristena vented her fear openly, often in angry, emotional outbursts. John held his emotions in check and gradually withdrew emotionally and mentally, and I resorted to a nightly shot of whiskey with melatonin tablets, for without these I could not sleep. Yet we worked together to aid Kristene, dreading the final outcome of it all.

I tried fasting with prayer, but each time I was so weakened that I eventually stopped; I needed my strength. I prayed more often for what seemed like long periods in the Spirit, and even though I didn't understand what I was praying, my thoughts and emotions were more stable when I did. I also prayed daily or several times a week for Kristene's healing on the phone with others and mentally focused on the idea that she would pull through. Getting real sleep was all but impossible; when I laid down at night, whether with Kristene in the hospital or alone at home, my mind and body were so tense that all I could do for hours was stare at the ceiling while my mind raced. When sleep finally came, it was from emotional and mental exhaustion, never long or deep enough to be the restorative rest that I needed.

Where was our church when we needed them? Days and weeks passed, and I wondered why the associate pastor who promised all this response, nor anyone else from the church had not called me. Kristene was receptive to a pastor and elders praying over her in accordance with the Word, and our kids knew that I had called the church, and I was sure that they, like me, were wondering why no one came to our aid. I called the office more times and left messages asking for a call back. None came.

I could at least be thankful that Kristene's pain was under control with proper pain management and medications and she was able to sleep more than she had in months. Still, she was weakening; I brought her Kristena's compact Bible from the house because her hands and arms were too weak to hold a standard-size Bible. There were times she wouldn't hold hands with me because of the pain in the bones of her hand. I bought her a travel-size CD player and CDs for learning Spanish and German; she had classes in German in high school and wanted to learn Spanish. She kept her mind active by working books of crossword puzzles and word games I brought her. She read her Bible voraciously and kept an informal journal on letter-size yellow legal notepads. I increased the time I spent with her, though she was sleeping more now. I read the Bible and other books and worked crossword puzzles while she dozed, and also use the time to quietly repair my riding shirts, 19th century Mexican style, lightweight cotton with banded round collars, large roomy sleeves and striped print pattern. With needle and thread I re-attached buttons and repaired tears from cactus and barbed wire until she awoke, happy to see me still there.

On April 18, Kristene's birthday, I brought her breakfast I made at home, flowers, a birthday card, and a cup of Starbucks coffee. We spent the day together, and the kids came by.

Kristene's entry for April 27, written in pencil commemorating her brother Ron's birthday, is noteworthy because it reflects her positive outlook:

6:30 PM, April 27, 2009

It's a special day. Happy Birthday, Ron!!! We're doing just fine here (not without you-—but fine because of you). You just made some things to seem so "that's just the way it's going to be" and they were and they still are but... ... the ever-changing world here is a bit overwhelming for some of our taste and style. God's in charge. We're taking charge where needed. I want what He has for us only. Life is fragile, and I treat it in that way. Kay is doing a fine job and has a heart that I've never quite seen in another human being before. There's so much growth.

P.S. Please let us sing that song for you. Just save me a piece of that cake!!! XOXO Your Baby Sister

Kristene's next journal entry was for the following day:

4/28/09
6:30 AM 7 oz. drink
8:00 AM Breakfast. Corn grits
10:30 AM 4 oz. drink
9 AM PT (heavy workout), 2 ½ hr. P.T.
12:00, Tortillas (chicken/cauliflower/broccoli/brown rice/ new balance cookies)

Very emotional/tired

*Pain was at a minimum. Had a lot of endurance, a lot of drive. The brace is a good fit.
*Learning to get up out of chair. Use stomach muscles to get up out of chair.

On May 1, Kristene was transferred from Scottsdale Heritage Court to Health South for physical therapy. She had a beautiful room, as she described in her notes:"

5/2/09. Saturday. SHOWER. XXX WOW XXX. 8:30 AM 3 eggs over medium. Thank you, Jesus.

John moved my things into room 311. Thank You, Lord. This is truly a gift from You, Lord, thank You.

Room 311 has its own kitchenette refrig/microwave/kitchen sink/cabinets/storage—for food, bath/sink, patio door window, a place to sit a place to be with my family and the Lord.

Oh! And don't forget—its own private shower!

For the first week at Health South, Kristene was already wearing a back brace and was able to participate in physical therapy at Health South and was showing progress. I spent almost every night with her there, leaving only in the daytime to tend to my own hygiene, prepare meals for her, and take care of household bills. In the evenings we watched movies I rented; we prayed and talked and prayed throughout our many hours together. Her bravery was amazing, for she always maintained a positive and cheerful outlook no matter how grim things looked. Never once did she permit herself self-pity or bemoan her situation.

5/7/09. Thursday. The next appointment with Dr. Beauchamp will be around 6/16/09 (look in mail for schedule).

NOTE
6:00 p.m.
Please remember! This is strictly a medical approach to my situation! My hope is way beyond this approach! My faith is buried deep within Jesus! And my life is and belongs to Him without any reservation, wavering, or sidetracking of any kind.

My love is in my family, and my family unit of John, my husband beloved and eternal forever in the next life (which only matters), my children Kristena Rose and John Raymond III.

One day we will all be together in God's home for us all.

Richard, please find your way home. It's the only way to a forever life with all of us who have gone before you. It won't be easy, but we're all waiting for you, my big brother.

On Mother's Day, May 10, 2009, the kids and I visited Kristene and brought her cards and flowers. She had a fever that day, was on oxygen, and was visited by her doctor, Dr. Vincent Cariati, who ordered tests to be done with regard to the fever. Kristene's journal entry:

> *5/10/09. Sunday. Up at 4:15 a.m.*
> *Sick all day long!!!*
> *Flem!*
> *More Flem!*
> *X-rays came back fine*
> *Slept on/off all day long.*
> *Flem*
>
> *Oxygen was ordered and came in today. I can breath so much better, and I can also feel better because oxygen is getting to my brain.*
>
> *IV antibiotic was ordered and brought in, and in a very short period of time I was feeling so much stronger. I'm staying on the program that they have given to me -I am stronger for it (which includes vitamins/the one steroid for swelling of bones in lower back-*
>
> *The pulse is constantly taken throughout the day the Drs And RNs are so attentive and thorough. The nearest Dr (or RN) will stop to check and see how I am doing.*

During the following week, Dr. Cariati informed Kristene and me that the fever was caused by an infection of her left hip incision, where the leg and hip surgery was performed earlier. .

On Friday, May 15, 2009, and Sunday, May 17, 2009, Kristene had temperature spikes. Dr. Cariati also noted that Kristene's tongue was curled to the right; this was a new development.

After about two weeks at Health South, Kristene reported to Dr. Cariati, that her legs and her face were swollen, and when an ultrasound test of her left leg tested positive for dvt, deep ventricular thrombosis, she was transferred back to Scottsdale Healthcare on May 18, 2009.

At this time Kristene's acceptance by Cancer Treatment Centers of America seemed imminent; I spent hours on the phone with Marcia Kamm, a coordinator there, and was awaiting approval from our insurance carrier. Things were looking up, if only Kristene could hold out. On Thursday, May 21, 2009, Kristene was transferred back to Heritage Court.

On Memorial Day, May 25, 2009, I arranged with Kristene's doctor and the staff at Heritage Court to take her out for a drive and lunch at a restaurant. It was to be our last date together, and I am sure now that we both knew that. Kristene's doctor approved her getting out for a day and prescribed the proper dosage of morphine for her, which was administered before I was to take her out. As I helped Kristene into the wheelchair I bought for her earlier and took her down the elevator to the car, her frailty was agonizing to see, and I mentally pushed it aside, focusing instead on making the most of our time together. I had borrowed my son's late-model Pontiac sedan because it would be easier for Kristene to get in and out of it and more comfortable for her to ride in than my truck. As I lifted Kristene out of her wheelchair into the car seat, my mind went back almost twenty-eight years to when I first carried her as a new bride across the threshold of our home in Bellevue on our wedding day, and I struggled to keep from breaking down in front of her.

I returned the wheelchair to her room, and we went for a sightseeing drive north, eventually arriving at the stables so she could see the horses; it was an outing that I commemorated for family and friends in Washington, and I attach it here:

LAST DATE

This past Memorial Day of 2009 I was allowed by the medical staff at Scottsdale Heritage Court to check my lovely Kristene out for a drive. She needed time out of the four walls of her room and to be in the sunshine and fresh air even more than that. I wheeled her outside and lifted her from her wheelchair into our son John's car and returned it to her room. It was sunny with a soft breeze - cool for Arizona, a perfect day and Kristene wanted to visit the horses. On our way to the stables I drove through one of her favorite little shopping centers outside of the main Scottsdale core. She was shocked to see that almost every small shop except the Safeway store and one Italian restaurant were all boarded up, a sign of our economic climate.

When we arrived at the stables I parked as close to the stalls as I could get. Kristene sat in the car with the window down; she wanted to see Red, her own horse, first. I brought Red around past the front of the car so Kristene could see how she has slimmed down and how shiny her coat has become. Standing at the car window it was only a few short minutes before Red remembered and recognized Kristene. Red tends to be reserved, an introvert, her affections awarded to only a chosen few. It had been months since she had seen Kristene but she warmed up to her as recognition and remembrance returned. Red stuck her muzzle into the car window and Kristene petted and stroked and talked softly to her and thus they enjoyed a brief little reunion.

I brought Taylor around next. Kristene was awed to see how fit and beautiful he is, muscles rippling, veins bulging, his copper coat having a metallic sheen in the sunlight as I walked him past the front of the car for her to see. Taylor, always the outgoing one, the extrovert, walked right up to the open window and stuck his head in to see who it was, as if to say "Hi, how the heck are ya, anyway?" Taylor remembered Kristene immediately. Kristene petted him and then he eased his head back out. A few seconds later Taylor very slowly and softly eased his head back into the car window and paused, looked directly at Kristene; it was clear he detected something was wrong with her. He removed and very gently re-inserted his head two more times, his head less than a foot from Kristene, each time he was making steady eye-to-eye contact with her for long seconds at a time; the look in his eyes clearly asking "What's wrong? Are you alright?" He could detect her illness and was trying to assess what was wrong. He nudged Kristene softly and let her stroke his head, something he doesn't like and allows no one but me to do. Kristene told me later she was amazed and comforted by Taylor's responsiveness and sensitivity and I could see that she was pleasantly surprised by his sensitivity and concern.

After I put Taylor back into his stall I drove around to the back of their stalls so Kristene could see them one more time before we left. Both Taylor and Red made eye contact with Kristene, and Taylor walked immediately up to the edge of his stall and stood as close as he could get to the car, leaning his chest up against the pipe rail fence. He re-established eye contact with Kristene and for a long minute seemed to reach into her with his eyes. We turned the car around to leave and I looked over my shoulder;

Taylor remained there at the fence and I saw that he watched us until we were out of sight. As we left I could see that the horses had had a refreshing effect on Kristene, her mood now happier and satisfied and anticipating.

We drove across the desert to an Asian restaurant where we ate in the car. For a little while it seemed like old times and we reminisced of those times, savoring our outing and each other, commenting on the food, kidding each other and joking around and for a little while we put her health crisis behind us and rejoiced in each other. We had been out on our little date over three hours when I brought Kristene back to the nursing facility; she was tiring and her pain medications were beginning to wear off. I stayed with her a couple hours later until our daughter Kristena came and spent the night with her. After such a long spell of grim hospitalization we finally had a day of pleasure in each other's company and relaxation that both of us will always remember.

Over the past weekend Kristene's sister-in-law Kay Kinssies from Bellevue visited us and spent a night with Kristene. Our neighbor and Kristene's very close friend, Letty Andrews, worked for hours to bring us a home-cooked meal that lasted me and the kids two days. Their kindness and generosity meant more to us than either of them will ever know.

Kind Regards To All Who Read This,

John

Kristene was transferred from Health South to Scottsdale Healthcare because the state of her recent infections made it impossible for her to continue physical therapy there. Scottsdale Healthcare stabilized her infections and transferred her to the Heritage Court because she refused chemo and radiation and was out of immediate danger but in need of skilled care, including pain management.

On Sunday, May 31, 2009, after at least four attempts, I still had not heard from anyone at our church, not the senior pastor or the associate pastor, nor any of our so-called friends or acquaintances there who knew of our crisis. My kids were wondering where the church was in our time of need, and I was angry and embarrassed at such arrogance. I wrote a blistering three-page letter of protest to the new senior pastor that described my grievances that I hand delivered to him at the end of the evening service and walked out.

During the first week of June, we decided it would be okay for our daughter Kristena to go on an overseas trip that had been planned for months; and we felt Kristene would be in Chicago at Cancer Treatment Center of America by the time Kristena got back.

During the first week of June I received in the mail a handwritten response from the senior pastor of our church, in which he apologized for the failure of the church to respond, and that he would have a certain member of his staff call me during the next week. I noted that nowhere in his letter was there any mention or concern for my wife's condition or the well-being of my children. I didn't understand why it would be a week for anyone to call, but nevertheless I waited, hoping to hear from the man who was to call me. As I waited it occurred to me that the new senior pastor had taken an entire week to respond to a letter so urgent, so life-threatening, that involved one of his flock that it was hand-delivered to him. And worse, his letter said it would be another week before I got a call from a staff member. It occurred to me then that if I had been one of the church 'elite Christians' in his inner circle, or a high-dollar donor to the church, he would have personally beaten a path to my wife's bedside.

Kristene resumed physical therapy at Scottsdale Heritage Court, but during the first two weeks of June, her pain increased, requiring ever-larger doses of morphine to mitigate the pain, and she was often too weak to complete physical therapy sessions. Cancer Treatment Centers called to inform Kristene that she had been accepted and the details of the travel arrangements would be emailed to us shortly. CTCA had generously provided free roundtrip airfare, meals, and lodging for Kristene and me; her first appointment was set for June 22.

On June 17 we received email confirmation from Carol Odom of CTCA of our reservations on American Airlines flight from Phoenix to Chicago's O'Hare airport on June 21, 2009, with reservations at the Radisson Hotel. I was now extremely nervous, for Kristene's condition had deteriorated markedly in the months since the last charts and X-rays were sent to CTCA. She could no longer walk with a walker, and her speech was becoming less clear, indicating the cancer was approaching her brain, a medical condition known as aphraxia, all of which caused me to fear that she would not survive the trip. But because she had waited and hoped for this for so long, and was excited and eager now, I prepared to go with her to Chicago. Her notes for that day are as follows: "*6/17/09—Oh Boy - new lease on life this week.*"

On her calendar Kristene marked Sunday, June 21, "Chicago" and Monday, June 22, was marked "CTCA" and circled. I notified the management at Heritage Court that Kristene would be checking out on the twenty-first.

On June 19, Kristene received a phone call from CTCA that I called to confirm: oncologists at CTCA where we were headed had conducted a routine last-minute review of Kristene's charts from Health South and her most recent Scottsdale Healthcare charts. It was their conclusion that cancer had eroded her spine to the point that a trip through an airport and boarding a plane and back again would be life threatening to her if she were bumped in the wrong way. Secondly, they told us that cancer had spread to the point that there was nothing they could do for her and they declined to accept her as a patient.

I sat with Kristene in her room, alone, looking at each other. She was propped up on her bed, facing me; neither of us could speak at first. I was surprised that she showed no emotion, as if this was the outcome she was expecting. After a minute she said, "Get the yellow notepad from my table over there, and take out the last page and read it."

I did. It was dated June 4, 2009, and read:

Request from Mom:
Please have an autopsy for the sake of:

My beloved Husband John Hansen
My beloved children, John R. Hansen III (and Kristena Hansen)
My beloved brother, Richard Kinssies
My beloved nieces & nephews and any blood relatives
that may Benefit from its results.

Please have my remains sent to:

Messinger Mortuaries
8555 E. Pinnacle Peak Rd.
Scottsdale, AZ
480-502-3378

When remains arrive, please have them forwarded for families decision on burial.

Thank You,

Kristene Hansen

I sat in shocked silence, staring at my wife. I wanted to speak, but there were no words coming.

Kristene broke the silence. "Honey, there's a hospice I want you to take me to. It's called Hospice of Arizona and it's near the house on Mescal Street off Scottsdale Road."

My insides began to tremor, and I hoped she couldn't see it. "How do you know about this hospice?" I asked, my voice hoarse with emotion.

"I went there last December to check it out. It's small, clean, and quiet, and the rooms are nice. Take me there. Now. Please," she told me.

Without telling a soul, Kristene had decided last year upon the place she wanted to be when she died. My legs wouldn't move at first, and I felt my face flush when I stood up, staring at my wife. She was still as beautiful as ever; even cancer couldn't take that from her. I leaned forward and held her, and we cried together, but even that much physical contact quickly became too painful for her. I stopped by the manager's office and informed her of the change. Then I drove to the hospice. I walked into the office and spoke to a friendly woman there who had kindly eyes. As if by divine appointment, she informed me that Room 406 was just becoming available, and I made the arrangements for Kristene to be taken there by ambulance the next day.

I went home, called Richard, and informed him of his sister's predicament. It had always been Kristene's wish to keep Richard out of the loop regarding her illness, for she was the protective sort. When Richard turned sixty in January, she had concealed the true reason she would not be able to be there. When I called him, I apologized for not informing him earlier and explained the reason. Richard was shocked at the news. I promised to keep him posted of any and all changes in Kristene's condition.

I then placed a call to Kristena overseas. I left a message that it was urgent that she call me. It was time for her to come home: now.

CHAPTER THIRTY-FOUR

The momentum of my beloved's decline was quickening, yet her countenance reflected a calm resolve, a serenity that was not there before. The depth of her bravery in facing the approach of death was not lost on me. She was now ready to leave this world and be with Christ, where she would have no more pain and would see her family again. Between us we shared the cold realization that this was it, the end was coming soon. A narcosis-like numbness settled upon me; a certain matter-of-factness that enabled me to push past the pain to make last decisions and take steps toward what we accepted would be the final transfer.

Early the next morning I filled out paperwork at the Heritage Court manager's office, while Kristene was seen by her physician and given more morphine before she was released for transport to Hospice of Arizona. I loaded her belongings into my Tahoe, and together we waited in her room in silence, agonizing silence, holding grief in check until the ambulance came. I followed her to the hospice and got her settled into her new room. The environment and the setting here were a major improvement over her room at Heritage Court. It was a small, one-story facility on a quiet street. It was peaceful and private, with carpeted floors in the rooms and the hallway, and everyone on the staff was warm and accommodating. We were fortunate to get room 406 for her, a large private room at the end of the hall with a full bathroom.

As soon as Kristene fell asleep, I headed for the house to pick up things she might need. I was almost there when I received a call on my cell phone from the hospice admissions desk.

"Mr. Hansen, this is Mary at Arizona Hospice. Your wife is starting to show indications of the early stages of dying. A staff medical doctor will be seeing her right away. Is there a doctor you would like us to notify also?"

I pulled into a parking lot to speak with her. This was happening too fast.

"No," I replied, "Kristene was just seen by her doctor at Heritage Court before leaving there this morning and she does not have a personal physician." I asked Mary "What do you mean by 'early stages' — how much time are we talking about?"

"In our experience here, your wife is exhibiting indications that she could pass away in days, maybe a week," she told me.

"Is she awake now?" I asked.

"She woke up briefly and then fell asleep again just now", Mary replied.

I went home and called Richard; he dropped everything and took the next flight from Seattle to Phoenix, arriving that same evening. I called Helen Scott, Kristene's cousin, and informed her of the situation; Helen booked a flight for the following Monday. I called Kay Kinssies. She offered to come down to be with Kristene, but her daughter Meaghan was in labor with her first baby. I told Kay that Kristene expressly told me it was her wish that Kay be with her daughter for the birth of her first grandchild. I called my sister Cindy and Bob O'Leary and others on our prayer support team, including Pastor Rozelle, Ted and Marietta Terry, and Julie Brunk, wife of pastor Dave Brunk at Eastside Foursquare Church. I took fresh clothes to Kristene and stayed with her in the room, fielding calls on my cell phone while she slept.

People began pouring in. Kristena arrived from Europe and stayed at the hospice with the rest of us. John called his best friends, Dillon

Jackson and Colt Kimmel, members of the old Band of Brothers. Colt was attending school and working in Flagstaff, over two hours away, yet he dropped everything to drive down to be with John and us in this hour of need.

A round-the-clock vigil began, with all of us sleeping wherever we could find a couch, bed, or chair. Kristene was in and out of consciousness. She was simultaneously glad and upset to see that Kristena had interrupted her trip to come home; she was the same way when she saw Richard and a bit chagrined with me for telling him.

"Richard is your brother, he had to know," I told her.

During the first evening at the hospice, I had time alone with Kristene. She was peaceful, settled, and totally aware of her situation. Speech seemed difficult for her, possibly because she was exhausted, possibly because of spreading cancer, or other medical reasons. She told me that she was ready to go; she was tired of fighting the pain, and all she wanted now was to be with Jesus, where she would also be with Ron and her parents. She told me she had hoped to live long enough to see our grandchildren, but now that was up to me. There wasn't a trace of anger or bitterness in her as we talked of end things and wept together. I could see that Kristene had come to terms with leaving this life, of going on to her true home in Heaven; she cried, yes, but she was resolved that this was her time to go, and there was an unusual peace about her, like I had never seen before.

"I don't know how the kids and I will live without you," I told her.

I left the room so that Kristena and John could come in individually to talk with their mother, followed by Richard and then others to say good-bye. As the night wore on, I slept on the empty bed next to Kristene, with Kristena sleeping in a chair next to me. Kristene had slipped into what was not yet a coma as Colt Kimmel and Dillon Jackson sat at her bedside through the long hours of the night, holding her hand, reading Bible verses to her, and themselves weeping for the one who had been as a second mother to them all through their school years.

On Sunday morning, the severity of the pain in Kristene's spine was worsening; morphine was no longer sufficient to mitigate her pain. An IV pump release of six milligrams per hour of dilaudid, a more powerful drug, was established and was immediately effective. One of the nurses who was especially loving and kind toward us was Debbie DeVries; she was one of the first to sign a book the hospice supplied, a book for visitors to write personal messages to Kristene. A stream of visitors, including nurses and caregivers from Heritage Court, came by to say farewell.

On Sunday evening, many of us were crowded around her bed when Kristene suddenly opened her eyes, looked around the room at all of us, pointed at us with her finger, and smiling, exclaimed, "Whoa!" and went back to sleep. The following afternoon, as I was sitting with her, Kristene opened her eyes again and began trying to speak. I made eye contact with her, leaned close, and asked her if she knew who I was. "My husband," she whispered, barely audible.

"I love you," she said softly, her hazel eyes looking at me longingly. Then she fell asleep again. Those were her last words.

Hours later, as Kristene's coma deepened, I cleared the room and sang the old traditional hymns to her from a hymnal that I must now confess that I stole from the church we attended years before when the kids were little and I was active in jail ministry. I used it to memorize the old hymns to sing to the jail inmates. My singing voice is so bad that it was always the butt of family jokes, and when I began singing to Kristene, her eyes suddenly snapped wide open, staring at me for but a brief moment, then she smiled contentedly and slipped back into her slumber. I read passages of Scripture to her for a long time, and she squeezed my hand now and then to indicate that she could hear me.

The next morning was Monday; Kristene's cousin, Helen arrived. It was crowded in Kristene's room when a woman minister from the hospice came in, prayed aloud for Kristene, read Scriptures, and anointed her with oil; when she sang a hymn in her very beautiful, angelic-sounding voice, several of us broke up, unable to stop the tears. Then she asked me as Kristene's husband if I would like to anoint my wife with oil and pray for her. I said I would and prayed out loud for her as I poured a dab of oil on my hand and placed it on her forehead. I sensed the Spirit of God anointing me as I prayed in a loud voice, my words broken and halting from emotion as I took Kristene's hand in mine and interceded before God for her.

"Lord God Almighty, I come before You in the Name of Your Son, Jesus, on behalf of my beloved Kristene, the one You gave to me as my wife. Lord, I remind You that years ago You declared to me in an open vision that Kristene and I are one flesh and one spirit in Your sight. Lord, today, Kristene is about to leave us, and she is not able now to speak for herself. On the basis that You Yourself told me that we are one, if there is any unconfessed sin, anything at all between Kristene and You, I repent of it now on her behalf, so that nothing may interfere with her entering Heaven. Lord, on the basis of the oneness You gave us I plead the Blood of Christ over my beloved Kristene. Let her be with Jesus, with Ron and her parents, and with a new body. Thank You, Lord. Amen."

As I finished, my son John, who had been standing behind me, could hold his composure no longer and bolted from the room.

About an hour later I was in the visitors' lounge when a minister from the hospice, a man about my age, tall and muscular, introduced himself to me. His name was Epi Rodriguez, and he listened attentively as I poured out the story of Kristene and me. He shared with me how years ago he too had lost his wife of twenty-seven years to cancer, and that he had two adult kids then, like me. From his own experience, he was able to speak of what was in store for me in the months ahead, and give me wise and practical counsel that forewarned and strengthened me for the trauma I would face in the immediate future.

God saved my life by sending this man to me. Without his counsel, I would not have survived the grief to come. Because of his words, I knew what to expect in the times ahead after Kristene would be gone. He knew I was apprehensive about what lay ahead for me and my kids and that I had been wrestling within myself with whether I had done all I could to save her.

"God gave Kristene to you for a time, and now he wants her back. If you think she was beautiful when she was here, she'll be even lovelier when you see her again. Your job now will be to see to it that you and your kids will be able to rejoin Kristene in Heaven," he told me.

"Your grief will be very different than what your children will experience. They have their lives ahead of them, and as close as they were to their mother, there was an expectancy that she would go ahead of them," he told me. "For you, the surviving spouse, the pain will be deeper, harder, and will never end, but it will become easier with time."

I noticed that he had a wedding ring on and asked him about that. He told me he was happily remarried and his wife now was not at all like his first wife. I asked him how he could love again if the grief was still there.

"Over time, the memories and the pain compartmentalize in your heart, and as this happens, you can move forward and love again," Epi gently replied.

I asked him about the memories of his first wife; I wanted to know how are those memories to him now that time has passed and he has a new life.

"It was seventeen years ago that she died, but in my mind, those events are like it was *yesterday*!" The tone of his voice was guttural, from the belly; his intense dark eyes looking at me through the pain of a loss that haunts him still, wistfully seeing into a past with a hurtful longing that will haunt him unto the end of his days.

Kristene's condition declined rapidly through the night. Sensing the end was near, my kids, and then me, followed by Helen and Richard, took our turn at her bedside to say whatever was on our hearts. At 6:30 the next morning, she was unresponsive and had begun what is called agonal breathing, rapid, heavy breathing through the mouth with the jaw in a fluttering motion. Only Kristena and Helen were in the room with me. I sat with her until about 8:15; there was no change in the breathing. The nurse told us she could pass away within the next four hours or so. I decided to get a change of clothes for myself from home, which was five minutes away, for I had not showered in two days. I had gotten to the driveway when my cell phone rang. It was Kristena. Tears were in her shaking voice. "Dad, she's gone."

I had only left her side five minutes ago, and she was gone already. She had waited for me to leave the room before she departed her body, so strong were the ties between us. I raced back to the hospice, running red lights and praying all the way. I parked and ran to the building. Kristena was sitting in a chair outside the hospice front door, distraught and numb at the same time, on the phone, holding a cigarette. "Its' okay, Dad, Helen is with her," she said. I ran down the hallway and into the room to Kristene's side. Helen slipped out as I came in.

She was gone. My bride, the one I had carried in my arms across the threshold into our home on our wedding day so long ago was gone; her body lay there supine, in her blue flannel nightgown, eyes half open, unseeing, lips parted slightly, her body limp and still warm. I reached down and scooped her into my arms for the last time on this earth and held her close to me, shrieking at the top of my lungs, bellowing like a wounded bull, sobbing from the inside out so that my body shook with grief and despair, yet noting that her body now felt oddly lighter and was cooling as waves of grief, devastating grief; cruel, crushing grief rolled over me. I knew I had to let go of her, but I could not — not then. I held her in both arms, pressed her cheek next to mine, and stroked her hair. I kissed her cheeks, forehead, her lips once more. She had lost none of her hair in all this suffering, nor had her skin become dry and aged. Yes, my beloved was a woman of beauty to the very end, and I knew she had waited until I left the room before she departed from her body; my presence had been holding her there. I howled like a ghoul for I don't know how long, but it was awhile. I was surely disturbing others in the building, but I cared naught — my love was gone; gone. I laid her back down on her bed and stayed with her body, holding her hand, stroking her hair, kissing her and talking sweetly to her until the mortuary man came. I went outside. I watched her being loaded into a maroon colored hearse, a sheet draped over her body. She was only fifty-seven. I was a broken man.

That first night was the darkest of my life. I shut myself in my room and grieved alone while my kids were in the family room, finishing work on a DVD dedicated to their mother's life and memory. Before their mother passed away, they worked to assemble a photographic history of their mother's life set to music on a DVD. There were six songs selected, two songs from each of us. The song I selected in particular was "Not Enough" by Emmylou Harris; all of its lyrics were prophetic for me, but two stanzas hit me the hardest:

Oh my friend, what could I do?
I just came home to bury you
The road is long, the road is rough
You're in my heart, that's not close enough

I still have your memory
One or two pictures of you and me
Life is long and life is tough
But when you love someone
Life is not long enough

It ran about twenty minutes and was played at the funeral in Scottsdale and again at the memorial service in Bellevue. There was not a dry eye at either service.

Richard stayed a bit longer to help me with funeral arrangements before going home, for he saw how unraveled I was. I was proud of him and deeply grateful to him for his care and support of us; just his presence was a source of strength for me in the darkest time I had yet known. He proved himself a true brother. Richard went home before our Scottsdale service. Helen had left quickly, before I could think to thank her for being there for us like she did. The actions of Helen and Richard affirmed what we taught our kids since they were little: the ties of blood and marriage are sacred and unbreakable, and blood is thicker than water.

A beautiful floral arrangement covered the casket at the funeral in Scottsdale, with ribbon that honored Kristene as loving wife, mother and daughter. I arrived at the mortuary ahead of everyone and entered alone the sanctuary where her casket was, whereupon I tried to open the lid to see her one last time, and when it would not open, I laid my chest upon it and my arms on the sides of the casket in an effort to hug her one more time. Choking on tears, I poured forth a mighty torrent of words of love and devotion upon her, recalling our wedding vows that she had selected so long ago, and now I uttered them again with deep despair and groaning, over and over.

"I plight thee my troth, I plight thee my troth, O my Darling! We are still one flesh, one heart, Kristene, my Love!"

I was utterly broken; unable to come to terms with it that the one I had loved for twenty-eight years was inside that casket, yet I knew it was only her body there now, for the real Kristene was alive in Heaven.

I pulled myself together in time to greet the friends and neighbors who came to honor Kristene and be with us. The kids and I were pleasantly amazed to see who came; people we hadn't thought would care, arrived, and their presence and support made the service a very moving one.

Two days after the funeral in Scottsdale, the man from the church, the one the pastor mentioned in his letter would call me, called. It was three weeks after the time the pastor's letter said he would call. When he announced who he was, I told him my wife had died two days ago, and that the pastor's letter said he would call three weeks ago. This man's only response was "I didn't know." He never said he was sorry, nor did he offer any help or condolences whatsoever; his arrogance and insensitivity to our suffering angered me greatly, and I let him know what I thought of him and the current pastoral staff at the church, calling him and them 'white-washed tombs,' 'modern-day Pharisees' that Jesus told Peter to "Feed My sheep," but instead of being His under-shepherds, they were merely religious CEO's, interested only in themselves, the type Jesus was angered by. Even then there was no apology or compassion or offer of help for us coming from this man; I paused enough to give him time to offer help but he maintained a stone-cold silence that exposed his lack of compassion or respect for the people he is supposed to serve. This man's contempt for us in our suffering caused me to boil over; I had to say something.

But if I had learned anything from Kristene, it was to not bear grudges, but to forgive. The Bible teaches that if we don't forgive others when they hurt us, God won't forgive us. Angry and hurt as I was, I knew it would be hard to let it go, but I knew I must. This is a good church, God's church, not mine. Even the best churches can stumble and fail us; only God is infallible, and for all I knew He was allowing this to happen for His own purposes. It would take time, but my anger would subside, but for now there was Kristene's burial and memorial services in Washington yet to handle, and I needed my strength for that.

We shipped Kristene's body and flew to Seattle the same day; the airline gave us three seats together, and we sat in silence. I rented a car and immediately drove to Aberdeen where I bought a gravesite in the cemetery not forty feet from where George and Matilda are buried side by side. The next day we held a graveside service of relatives only, no minister, and my son picked up Uncle Leo, then ninety-one, at his home so he could attend. Leo, who was still walking without a cane and didn't need glasses, sat with us and wept openly for Kristene.

I stood at the head of the casket that held the body of my beloved, quoting the words of the Twenty-Third Psalm, my body weak and quivering from grief and sleeplessness and spoke the words of the Twenty-Third Psalm, in a tremulous voice that didn't sound like mine, choking and halting on tears, I uttered these words:

"'The Lord is my shepherd; I shall not want. He makes me lie down in green pastures; he leads me beside quiet waters. He restores my soul.' Kristene, you were the green pasture that God gave me. Your love for me was the quiet waters where God led me, and our love restored our souls. Yours was a life well lived, and I will be with you again."

I had to stop there, for I could say no more; my grief was too much. As her casket was lowered into the ground, handfuls of earth were loosed upon the lid in the traditional way, and I stood watching, numb and disbelieving that my beloved was in there.

A day after the burial, a memorial service was held at Ron and Kay's church, Eastside Foursquare. Over a hundred people attended, which was saying a lot for a holiday weekend. Among those who made the most effort to honor Kristene's life were my mother, who was brought to the service from her assisted-living facility in a wheelchair, sincerely heartbroken and grieving profusely; the entire Cowgill family and Ron and Brenda Egge, lifetime friends who had come from far away to pay respects to Kristene and to us, and Nate and Heather, who used to work for us and were now married with a child of their own.

Richard hosted a family reunion that weekend, with lots of BBQ, beer, wine, and food, and the count of those who came was thirty-two, all of us related by blood or marriage, and not a few babies, all signs that life was moving on, and Richard was now the head of the extended family.

I flew back home the next day, allowing Kristena and John to stay with relatives for as long as they needed and come home on their own schedule. Bob O'Leary picked me up at the airport and wisely stayed with me when I entered the house, for the first thing I saw was that the floral spray that had been on her casket was dead and brown, and the sight of it felt like my heart had been stabbed.

Ever the true friend, Bob stayed with me, and for several hours we sat at the kitchen table, talking and drinking coffee, for he sensed how I dreaded my first night alone there. He was loathe to go, but knew he must, so he left, albeit reluctantly, leaving me alone, and the silence and the dead flowers were deafening. The whole house spoke of Kristene; she was everywhere in it. While she was in the hospital I had been able to adjust a little to being in our bed alone, for then she was alive and there was the remote possibility she would come home again. But now it was different. She was gone and wouldn't be back, and that made the house, the bed and the bedroom different. Death is so final. After Bob left it seemed the walls were closing in on me, telling me she was gone; reminding me of her suffering. I cried and drank whiskey until I finally fell asleep, and awoke to a grim dawn. She was not there to have coffee with me; not any more. I wept and howled and prowled the house all through the next two days. For days I could not face the walk-in closet we shared, for her things were all still there; none of them did she take with her.

She is gone now, and the time and manner of her departing was devastating to us, leaving us scarred and at a loss as to what to do; struggling, but unable to cope, yet cope we must, and marshal the strength to move on. Though there is life ahead of us, time itself will never heal this wound. Not really. We are forever changed.

Kristene, age 50 in 2002. Her Arizona driver's license photo.

Christmas 2005 in Arizona

Trail ride on rented horses. Birthday weekend,
March 2007, Cave Creek, Arizona.

Our Silver Anniversary at the Royal Palms, Phoenix

AFTERWORD

Epi Rodriguez saved my life by forewarning me about grief, for I am sure the grief I went through would have killed me had God not sent him. For six months I had next to no interest in being alive. I wasn't suicidal; I just didn't care if I saw another sunrise or not. Grief engulfed me at unexpected times, night or day, rolling in like an ocean floodtide, so that no matter where or with whom I was, I wept uncontrollably, making it necessary to somehow immediately seclude myself until it subsided. My ability to maintain a train of thought was reduced to a few seconds, and my short-term memory evaporated. I read books about the grief process but these were of little help because they were written by women and were intended for women. Men, as I have observed, are wired very differently than women, and yet there was next to nothing out there specifically for men undergoing grief. There were many nights when my grief was so severe and the physical pain so excruciating that I thought my kids would find me dead in the morning.

To what can I compare this suffering so those who do not know it can have understanding? It was like having part of my intestines and a leg removed by a surgeon without anesthetic, stitched up and sent home the same day, in great pain and no longer whole, yet having to cope with finding a new way to resume life as one now permanently impaired.

I had been through two divorces before I met Kristene, and I can tell you that as bad as they were to go through, they were picnics compared to this. In a divorce, both parties are still alive, and at least one of them wanted to make the choice to split, and eventually the other partner will accept it and move on. But in our case, neither of us wanted to part, but parting came, with cruel pain and suffering on all levels. When death causes the parting, suffering is more severe, because death is so final and unforgiving.

"Where are you Kristene? How could you be gone from me?" I shouted at the top of my lungs when I was home alone. The finality of her being gone was crushing, the silence of her voice deafening. I kept rolling over in bed at night, reaching for her, but she wasn't there. Over and over I called her cell phone just to hear her voice. I watched old family videos of our early years, drinking whiskey right from the bottle and every time I saw her on the screen and heard her melodic voice I utterly collapsed, sobbing and shouting. The pain was horrible and unending, tearing me apart. I paced the house, looking at family portraits and photos. Oh how blessed we were with each other! Why did it have to end?

With her gone I was no longer the same person I once was. In many ways being alive held little interest for me, I didn't know what to do with myself from one day to the next. Of future things I had little concern except for my kids; I was too numb, too indifferent to care much what happened, and this was the point where I was in crisis: I was beginning to die, not from illness, but from grief. Life within me was ebbing away; I was disconnected from myself, enveloped by a horrible numbness, so that even prayer was difficult. I lay in bed for hours during the day, staring at her pictures on the wall. I often slept with articles of her clothing, holding them for their scent of her, and wept bitterly. Like this I could not last long. Life that does not call to life is making the turn toward the final accounting, but in my inner man there was an understanding that my day of reckoning is not yet at hand, that God has more that He wants me to do for Him before my time is up.

It would be understandable to many if I turned against God for taking my beloved so early, but I had walked and communicated with God too much, too long for that; I had experienced answered prayers and His care and attention too many times to ever think He had cruelly snapped the rug out from under me by taking her. No, there was aught for me to do but run *to* Him instead.

I reflected on what God had done for Kristene and me; He had led us into a marriage of the rarest type, the kind that others only dream of. A surprising number of people told me during both services that they had viewed our marriage as a model for theirs; God had been using His work in us all along to benefit others without our even knowing it. So a month or two after Kristene's passing, I began *thanking* Him daily for the twenty-eight years we had together, for they were a gift, an amazing love adventure. And as I did this, peace came and healing accelerated. During a grief counseling session I was asked how I thought I would handle the issue of guilt, which the counselor said was to come next. My reply was that I had no guilt; I had always given 110% of myself to Kristene, as she did to me. That I was so consistent in loving her for all those years and have no regrets will continue to reward and sustain me for the rest of my days, and will bless the lives of many others for years to come.

I needed a new church home now, where I could re-start my life. I had learned from Kristene not to bear grudges, so I forgave our former church for letting us down so badly. Sooner than I thought it would happen, I wound up being led to return to my spiritual roots; the roots my maternal grandmother chose against for unknown reasons nearly a hundred years ago, full-circle back to the essence of old-time tent meetings, of canvas and sawdust, and heartfelt, on-the-knees worship, repentance and rejoicing to honor and praise God. It was upon the suggestion of my son that I visited Scottsdale First Assembly (recently renamed as North Scottsdale Christian), where Pastor David Friend and his son, Ed met with me for coffee more than once, and they were very helpful and supportive of me in those early months after Kristene passed away.

"The best counsel I can give you now is to make no major changes in your life for at least a year. Your life has been turned upside down. Allow some time to let the dust settle. Don't remarry, sell your house or move, buy anything major or get into binding commitments for a year or more. Just rest and take life one day at a time," Pastor Friend advised me over our first coffee together.

Pastor Friend had given me sound advice. I wasn't ready even to remove anything from Kristene's closet; being surrounded by her things was a comfort to me at that point, a way of staying connected with her, and I think Pastor knew this. I had found in David Friend a pastor like Jack Rozell had been to me, a man utterly true to his calling as pastor, a rock-solid, no-frills preacher with a sense of humor. I related well to him because we are the same age, and like me, he was in the secular world long before becoming a Christian. Dave is an Army infantry Vietnam combat veteran, and was a very successful banker, real estate developer and custom home builder before he answered the Lord's call to pastor that meant a severe drop in income. To my surprise Kristene's hospice nurse, Debbie DeVries and her husband Terry were members there; they have a ministry in grief counseling, and I received life-saving counsel from the two of them.

I quickly joined that church and became active in it, forming new friendships that were cornerstone to my new life. I stopped drinking, for as I had been advised by a nurse friend, I found that alcohol deepened my depression, and rendered recovery from grief next to impossible. I kept myself physically fit by riding my horses and joining a local gym. I continued to be active in my church and started a weekly men's Bible study in my home. I joined the Maricopa County Mounted Sheriff's Posse, which does mounted search and rescue work in the desert. I focused on helping others who were in trouble and worse off than me in prayer as well as in material ways.

I wasn't much company to my kids for the first year, for we were all going through the loss of Kristene in different ways, but I did what I could to help them reach their goals. Over time, the grieving became less intense and less frequent, and as the process of my life with Kristene becoming compartmentalized within me progressed, I came to accept that no matter how much life improves for me, it will always be hard for me to believe that she is gone, and the words of Epi Rodriguez ring true: I will never get over the loss of her.

During the early winter of the following year, the theme of our town's annual mounted parade was to recognize breast cancer. The kids and I rode horses in the parade with a group of friends, all of us wearing pink silk scarves, and pink signs pinned to the backs of our shirts that read "In loving memory of Kristene Hansen." It was cold and raining that day, weather that matched how we all felt.

In His mercy, God prepared each of us for Kristene's early passing years before it happened. Why it happened I still do not know. To me the question of why is a moot point; it is of no benefit to dwell upon the reason now. God is sovereign and doesn't owe an explanation to anyone. If I were to ask the Lord why after I reach Heaven, it would be just as moot then as it is now. Even if I knew the reason, it wouldn't bring Kristene back. I must seek Him by pressing forward, for God means life on earth to be lived with purpose; whatever I do now, for good or bad, counts for eternity.

I returned to Kristene's grave on the first anniversary of her passing, having rented a car at the airport and driven straight down to the Aberdeen cemetery. It was late afternoon when I came into town, bought flowers at a small florist shop and headed up the hill into the cemetery. It was typically gray and cool and threatening rain, as I quickly found her grave and the upright gray marble headstone that read "Kristene Kinssies Hansen, Beloved Wife, Mother and Daughter." Someone had been placing fresh flowers at her headstone, some were the plastic kind; who they could be from I didn't know. Fresh flowers in hand, I collapsed into deep mourning as I knelt and hugged her headstone with both arms, rocking back and forth, calling out to her and to Jesus. I must have gone into a strange reverie, for the next I knew, it was completely dark; no one was about. The gate was closed; it was past eight and I had been grieving there for more than four hours. Now I was locked in. I drove around on different dirt paths until I found a way out.

I checked into a cheap motel near the waterfront wherein I grieved for Kristene through the night, as if she had just passed away. I returned to the cemetery with another vase of flowers in the morning. I laid upon Kristene's grave talking to her (on the off-chance that she could hear me) and to God until early afternoon, updating her on the kids and me, and everything else that came to mind. I picked up my personal hero, Uncle Leo, and took him to lunch. He was ninety-two and still a man of certitude, walking without a cane, able to drive, needing glasses only to read. The topic came around to his beloved Kate as we sat there, and I saw his kindly blue eyes take on a faraway gaze as they beheld loving memories that still haunt and cause him suffering even after all these years (it never really ends) and wistfulness and longing narrowed his lids to a squint as I knew he saw Kate again for but a moment, a glimpse, and from the change of his countenance it was clear to me that the love between Leo and Kate, like ours, defied the grave.

I took Leo home and drove to Westport and visited again Kristene's first home. I haunted the dock and the places we had visited as restored newlyweds with Ron and Sally Mebust; weeping profusely but silently as I reminisced, savored, relived those wonderful times. I ate at one of the dockside restaurants the four of us ate at back then, hiding my tears with glasses as I sat at the counter. Back then I would have never dreamed I would be the one yearning for those days to be again.

O how blessed I was then! How greatly did God bless me through her, and how little did I appreciate it until she departed this world! And *now* what do I do? Of this I knew naught.

I returned home to Arizona. The kids were still living at home with me, and Kristena continued to step into her mother's shoes as the female head of the household, my new right hand, led of God (without knowing it, perhaps), working in many ways to hold the family together during a long season of despondency and dysfunction. The pain and the grief eased gradually, yet for me I understood the words of Epi Rodriguez: grief will be with me unto the end of my days, but I am getting better. It became my experience that the cruelest aspect of grief was that the very bonds we forged when we were together, that held us together, are now the very ones that cut into me the deepest and hurt the most, so that moving on often seems beyond my ability.

Christmas was less bleak for us than the previous year, for it was brightened by Kristena graduating from college with top honors and a full-time, salaried position in a major firm. Her mother would have been so proud. In photographs for her graduation announcement, Kristena wore her mother's green silk dress, the same one she wore on our first date after we were engaged. Kristena had taken it and wore it in honor of her mother. In that dress was Kristena photographed with Taylor, the horse who came to us as a result of her mother's prayers.

About this time I experienced a burning desire to write the story of our marriage, to share with others what we did to achieve marital success. When I prayed about it, the Lord impressed upon me to title the book after the vision of the waterwheel. I had completely forgotten about it, that open vision; it was so many years ago. As I began writing, I began to realize the countless ways the Lord blessed us – so many I would be forever writing were I to include them all. The Lord made me aware that He had more purpose in mind than just the two of us when

He blessed us and held us together over those years: God wants our story told so others will turn to Him and be blessed as we were.

My understanding of God the Father has been completely changed as a result of my years with Kristene. Before my rebirth I was influenced by the parochial schoolmasters of my eighth and ninth grades to perceive God as an angry judge, Who shackled His people with mulish grimness and was ready to swat any of His followers who dared to enjoy anything of earthly life. After my rebirth I came to understand Him only as a sort of impersonal but benevolent fog in the sky that only Jesus could have feelings for, because Jesus came to earth from Heaven. Even though the Bible commands us to 'Love God with all our strength,' for most earthly men, loving what we perceive as an impersonal fog is difficult at best. Something in the message was missing.

But after twenty-eight years of seeing His hand in the marriage adventure I had with Kristene, I see God the Father as a real Person, the Ultimate Father, Who is young in the sense that He is ageless, ever virile and strong, always on the move, creating, redeeming, leading, guiding, nurturing, slow to anger and abounding in love, forgiving our sins and healing our diseases through the sacrifice of His Son on our behalf, seeking and redeeming the lost, always doing the unexpected. Through the example He gave us by the life of His Son on earth, He is not impassively sitting on a throne somewhere far away.

The truth of the matter is that He is never far from us, but always near; He is vitally interested in us with a loving father's interest. He is a proactive God, Who wages war against evil and thwarts the plans of the wicked, while granting mercy and bestowing peace and blessing on His servants right in front of their enemies; never is He boring. When we come to Him for real, He strengthens us and remolds us for greater things by putting us through strenuous tests, in the same sense that a bodybuilder tears down his muscles so they will grow back stronger. God is so favorably disposed to us having earthly pleasure that He gave humanity not only the joy of marriage, but romance and sexual pleasure to enhance it. He authored the love Kristene and I knew, fitted us together, and the depth of the love He gave me for Kristene was so beyond ordinary human capacity that I am at a loss for words to describe it. The love God gave us for each other literally recreated and redefined us. When I approach Him in prayer now it is in confidence not in myself but in Him as a Person I want to know better, to follow, and be like.

I returned to Kristene's grave on the second anniversary of her passing. I had come to some other conclusions during the past year: the first is the realization that I am not the first man to lose his wife to death early in life, nor will I be the last. The second is that one key to the success of our marriage was in our learning to meet each other's deepest needs: I had learned to love Kristene at the deepest level, and she learned to respect and honor me above herself. Love does not come naturally for men; respect is equally difficult for women, which is why the Bible teaches us to do this. In our case we had done this without being conscious of it; God was at work behind the scenes all along without our knowing it.

But now that I have taken a long look back, I see the wisdom of God and the intentions of God when He made men and women so needful of each other and yet so opposite in our wiring that the close unions we want with each other cannot work well over the long haul in life unless we employ a certain principle, a key. So what is the key? Kristene and I were unconsciously practicing it all along and reaping its rewards. The key is *putting others ahead of yourself.* Being self-oriented blocks God's work in us and makes our relationships an uphill struggle. To be able to do this begins with personal repentance. As I saw in Kristene's life, the environment of our love enabled her to love those who had hurt her as if she had never been hurt at all, and those who hurt her most are in Heaven now because of the power of her love and forgiveness. So yes, God in His wisdom wired men and women so differently that we turn to Him, to His ways so that our marriages, families and relationships flourish and flow according to their original design.

My mind went back to the time of our last trip together, to Santa Fe. That Kristene secretly knew then she was dying of cancer will haunt me unto the end my days. It was for us, and to be with me just once more, that she willingly endured terrible physical pain; pain that as severe as it was, could not compare to the mental and emotional anguish she suffered as she sacrificed what little of her well-being was left to have one last outing with me. When I consider that she *knew* it would be her one last trip with me, I realize now how much greater was her love for me than I could have ever grasped back then. Realizing this broke me again. No doubt God was pleased when He made Kristene, for she embodied womanhood as He intended it to be.

Losing Kristene so early in life, after we had been together for so many years took a heavy toll on me, and wrought profound changes in me in every way. Seeing her lifeless body and holding it in my arms while it was still warm, led me to thinking deeply on matters of life and death. This thinking came after the severest shock had passed, of course, and the first change I became aware of was that I no longer fear my own death. Because God has gifted me in prophetic things, I expect I will foreknow my time when it draws near, and I anticipate that when I go, there may be a brief gateway of physical pain to pass through, after which leaving my earthly body will be as simple as slipping out of a loose-fitting jacket. When that happens I will have a new body, I will see Christ face-to-face, and I will see Kristene again, and my friends and relatives as well.

Over the course of the second year since her passing I tried dating several different women, but it was futile and is another story in itself; I was really just trying to fill the huge hole in me that was created by Kristene's passing, so I stopped.

Dating was a waste of time. If I am to ever love again, I will let God lead me into it. When I set dating aside I became aware that however much time I have left, the time is short, when the scope of eternity is taken into account, and what I do with it will count for all eternity. As brutal as grief has been for me (it nearly killed me), I needn't worry about Kristene at all, because she is in Heaven forever (though I still cannot help but continue to grieve the loss of her), where she is safe, with a new body, free of pain, sickness and sorrow. She will be there when I arrive, whenever that will be. In the meantime I must busy myself with hearing my Father's instructions to me concerning His kingdom, and carry them out fully. That is what I am about today. As I understand my mission as of this writing, it is that I am to write down how focusing on the Lord preserved and strengthened my life as He brought me through a time of devastation, so that it will bring about the strengthening of other men who have or will go through the grief process, and face picking up the broken pieces and building a new life from the ashes of great loss.

It was with these new understandings and much healing that I returned to her grave the second time.

As usual the weather was cool, cloudy and raining off and on as I brought a vase of red roses to her. I was surprised at the intensity of the grief I felt then; I hadn't healed as much as I thought. I was getting past the worst of the grief, but not my love for her, that would never end, it now was a love that stood in defiance of death and the grave. It had been a year since I had been there, and the flowers I placed there last time were now withered in their vases, but someone put new flowers there, the plastic flowers from the year before were there, and there were new fresh and plastic flowers there too.

I spread a piece of plastic over the grass atop her grave, for it was wet, and I laid there talking to her again as if she was there (for who knows, there is always the possibility she could hear me in Heaven); I noticed the grief was still hard, but it was not as hard as last year. I could see that I am getting better; the compartmentalizing Epi Rodriguez spoke of is happening. I drove to Westport to eat at the same places we always went to, and spent the night at a motel near the docks; it comforted me this time to be there, and relive the time we were there with Ron and Sally.

I awoke early, before the pre-dawn light, when people were tramping down to the docks to board charter boats being readied for a day of deep sea fishing as we had done here twenty seven years ago. I saw myself becoming something of a ghost, haunting the places we used to go to, in a quest to reconnect with a past that was her. My mind was clear, and being where I was made me able to see long into the past, and there I lay, reliving, savoring and reflecting on those early years.

It came to me then: what if I had not? What if I had not surrendered my will to God and asked Him to bring me the woman He wanted for me? I would never have met Kristene! And what if we had not decided to make God our foundation from the very start? We would not have known marriage as God intends it to be: a shared adventure. What if I had not persevered in trusting God when she left me and it all looked so hopeless? What if she had not prayed for me so consistently all those years? Of a truth, we would not have had the extraordinary marriage we did, nor would we have known the lasting love and the fullness of life we did, or the great kids God gave us. Kristene left a lasting legacy of love and forgiveness to many, and we had had a romantic adventure that revealed a side of God that few ever even think about. God gave us such a marriage that inspired others to do the same. It was worth it, yes, well worth it, even with the pain, the suffering and the difficulty in moving forward; so worth it that I would do it again.

I breakfasted at a café we had been to with Ron and Sally before heading out of town. As I entered the turnoff to Seattle it suddenly came to mind to visit Uncle Leo. I turned around and headed for Hoquiam.

A shovel, wheelbarrow and a fifty-pound bag of potting soil were in the midst of his diggings in the soil of the front flowerbeds as I turned into his driveway, signs that Leo was still active and strong, still the faithful steward of everything God had entrusted to him. This had included his care of Kate, and now that she was gone, he pressed on, waiting patiently and obediently for the call. He was in no hurry for this, yet he was ready to face the final accounting. A devout man, Leo has sorely missed his beloved Kate these dozen years or so now. He has used his remaining time in keeping with his character – living wisely, modestly, unselfishly considering others better than himself, as Christ taught us to do.

Leo is an amazing man: before Kate he had never been married, had never had children, had never loved anyone other than Kate, who had been married before and had a child with someone else, and then suffered a stroke only a short time after Leo married her. The care he gave her was much more than one-hundred percent of himself as a husband, and it was out of unending, unconditional love for her that he did it. Alone now at ninety-three, he is still strong, capable of doing his own heavy work. Leo is a quiet hero, a man of the rarest sort today.

He greeted me warmly at the door, garden soil from yard work was on his hands and khaki pants, and he still had no need of a cane or glasses, except to read, and he was still as clear-minded and articulate as men more than half his age. We sat in his living room and talked for awhile, sharing family and personal news. Sitting with him refreshed me, for Leo was mentally sharp, thoughtful and well-spoken, he was always interested in how my kids were, and loved to hear my stories about life in Arizona.

Just as I was about to leave, out of the blue I remembered to ask: "Say, Uncle Leo, I have been coming to Kristene's grave for two years now, and every time I do, there are always new flowers there, some are plastic," I said.

"Yeah, John, that would be me, honoring Kristene. Began putting the plastic ones there because they'll last longer; it's getting harder for me to get out, and I don't know how much longer I'll be here," Leo said, looking at me with a solemn nod, his hands on his knees.

When Leo told me that, my mind flashed back upon the open vision God gave the marriage counselor so many years ago, of the "waterwheel that was steadily turning over, blade by blade, rotated by the water."

She is gone now, yet the waterwheel that had been turning all those years, blade by blade, will keep on turning, without end, until the end. And at last I understood its meaning.

And God will wipe away every tear from their eyes; there shall be no more death, nor sorrow, nor crying. There shall be no more pain, for the former things have passed away.

Then He Who sat on the throne said "Behold, I make all things new." And He said to me, "Write, for these words are trustworthy and true."

Revelation 21:4,5

CPSIA information can be obtained at www.ICGtesting.com
Printed in the USA
BVOW080116210912

301001BV00001B/15/P